**MANDAP**
AND OTHER PLAYS

## Mandap
*A view from the hill*

## In Transit – A Double Bill
*A double bill by the undaunted*

## In Memoriam – A Double Bill
*A double bill laid by the stick*

## In Absentia
*The body in question*

## Second Shift Muster
*Conversations with moving parts*

Vitasta
LET KNOWLEDGE SPREAD

BANGALORE
LITTLE
THEATRE

# COMMENTS ON THE PUBLICATIONS

"*Glocal is the word that comes immediately to mind when I think of BLT's long history and ambitions. One can be local in one's view, without being insular, and one can be global, pulling voices from elsewhere into the context one inhabits, without becoming deracinated. BLT's house is strong because it has been built in the here and now; it is doubly strong because its windows have been open to the oxygen from elsewhere and from other times.*

*Ecosystem is another word I would use to pinpoint BLT's aspirations. It has understood that its strength is derived from the strength of the field in which it works. Whatever BLT knows, it has shared, and this sharing has taken many forms – from the training it has imparted to budding actors and directors to the support it has provided to fledgling theatre groups. The same commitment has propelled BLT's initiative to publish multiple volumes of plays that have been spawned by its admirable play development programme. There is a hunger for strong dramatic texts in India, where theatre production has grown far more rapidly than playwriting. In that context, these volumes will be seen as yet another precious gift that BLT has given to the theatre community.*

**Anmol Vellani**
Theatre Director and past Director of India Foundation for the Arts

*I am delighted that you are presenting all these plays that are at one and the same time enjoyable, revealing and memorable!*

**Roddam Narasimha**
Science Historian and Professor,
Jawaharlal Nehru Centre for Advanced Scientific Research

*This initiative would allow theatre practitioners from other parts of the world to access this work and look at the possibilities of staging these plays in multiple languages and in multiple cultural contexts.*

**Vidyanidhi Vanarase**
Founder-Dirtector, International Association for Performing Arts and Research

*We have eagerly awaited the publication of these volumes. They have finally arrived. They will reach performers and audiences right across national borders and far beyond.*

**Sai Paranjpye**
Theatre personality and award winning film director

*An international leader in our field, especially its serious investment in new play development, including the publication series that can benefit all of us theater makers across the world.*

**Bill Rauch**
Artistic Director, Perelman Performing Arts Center at the World Trade Center, New York City

*These are a valued resource .... they celebrate authors past and present and their translators as well, making the local, global.*

**Richard Crane**
Playwright-Director,
Co-founder of Brighton Theatre

*The new publication series produced by the Bangalore Little Theatre are an important and most welcome addition to world theater knowledge. Bravo!*

**Arthur Giron**
Founding Member of Ensemble Studio Theatre, New York, formerly Head, Graduate Playwriting Program, Carnegie Mellon University

*Bangalore Little Theatre has reached veteran status in Indian theatre with their powerful theatrical interventions in the community, spanning 60 years...these volumes enrich our understanding of the capacity of theatre to create spaces for potent ideas, that demand our engagement.*

**Yvette Hardie**
President: ASSITEJ (International Association for Theatre for Children and Young People)

*This work is not only important for India, it also makes plays from Indian writing known across the world. It is a very important and necessary project.*

**Ursula Werdenberg**
Dramaturg-Playwright,
Secretary General of The International Playwrights' Forum

*My warmest congratulations. This is a significant milestone and a wonderful achievement that gives readers an opportunity to think about our pasts and our presents through a history of ideas.*

**Anuradha Kapur**
Past Director, National School of Drama

*Your contribution to the goals of the International Playwrights' Forum, to the artistic treasures of your country, as well as for universal culture in general is indescribable indeed.*

**Gad Kaynar (Kissinger)**
Professor, International Theatre Institute
The Yolanda and David Katz Faculty of the Arts, Tel Aviv University

ये नाम केचिदिह नः प्रथयन्त्यवज्ञां
जानन्ति ते किमपि तान्प्रति नैष यत्नः ।
उत्पत्स्यते तु मम कोऽपि समानधर्मा
कालो ह्ययं निरवधिर्विपुला च पृथ्वी ॥

*Those who deride or ignore my work –*
*let them know: my efforts are not for them.*
*There will come along someone who shares my spirit:*
*the world is vast, and time endless.*

– ***Bhavabhuti***

*Bangalore Little Theatre is privileged to receive a substantial grant from **Kusum** and **Mohandas Pai** towards education and institutional development programmes, which include the publication of these plays.*

Published by,
**Renu Kaul Verma**
Vitasta Publishing Pvt Ltd
2/15, Ansari Road, Daryaganj
New Delhi 110002
info@vitastapublishing.com

**ISBN** 978-93-90961-11-5

MRP ₹450
First Edition 2022



Editors: Kanagam King, Papri Sen Sri Raman
Layout: Goutam Hegde, Deepak Mote
Illustrations: Supriya Kannan
Printer: Vikas Computer and Printers

# CONTENTS


*i.* *Foreword to the Series*

*iii.* *Special Message*

*v.* *Publisher's Note*

*vii.* *Salutations*

*viii.* *Preface to the Volume*

*xiii.* *Stage Directions*

**1. MANDAP**

**57. IN TRANSIT**

**133. IN MEMORIAM**

**197. IN ABSENTIA**

**243. SECOND SHIFT MUSTER**

*273. Bangalore Little Theatre*

*276. The Series Editor*

# FOREWORD TO THE SERIES

Bangalore Little Theatre is an enormous exercise in imagination. It remains an aspiration for theatre performers and a source of inspiration for practitioners. The passion, perseverance, toil and grace is the hallmark of this intimate Institution, which has embarked on many pathbreaking initiatives, programmes and productions. If the History of Ideas programme was unique, the translation and adaptation of Indian classics in English is a huge service. In the programme Vijay Padaki has presented a pertinent model, wherein the play scripts transcend the cultural specificity and period in time to speak in a universal language that addresses our contemporary concerns. Although we read the text in English, we experience the content in the original. A truly remarkable feat.

BLT has had a strong play development programme for a long time. It is most appropriate that the plays are being published now. Several volumes of plays can be expected in print very soon. This is a huge contribution to the institution of theatre in India. We can be sure they will be received with enthusiasm world-wide.

**Feroz Abbas Khan**
*Theatre director and award winning film maker*

# SPECIAL MESSAGE

For nearly 60 years, Bangalore Little Theatre has been instrumental in promoting theatre arts in Bengaluru and across the country. The ambitious project of publishing their most successful plays in a multi-volume anthology marks a great point in their story – another marker of the tremendous success they have attained.

In translating to English and adapting the plays for the modern stage, Mr Vijay Padaki (BLT) is conserving the best of Indian theatre. Each play is especially relevant to contemporary situations, from environmental concerns to resurgent regional identities, to introspecting the carnage of wars and finally the complexities of court politics.

I am certain that such a project provides us the perfect opportunity to understand, perhaps for the first time in recent years, the sheer wealth of Indian theatre spanning different cultural and linguistic traditions in the subcontinent. In producing such plays, and putting them together in this volume, BLT has undertaken a public service, one which every Indian living in the 21st century can profit from, for a long time to come.

With this, I wish BLT the very best for this and their many future endeavours.

**Shashi Tharoor**
*Member of Parliament for Thiruvananthapuram*

# PUBLISHER'S NOTE

Now we bring to you the fifth volume of plays from Bangalore Little Theatre. The plays in this series have one thread in common. They touch a chord and arouse in you a feeling of discomfort, a feeling of uneasiness. They make you face truths that you often prefer to ignore, even choose to ignore.

As the series editor Mr Padaki says, 'All the plays have a tragic quality about them.' Each of these plays brings to the fore the harsh realities prevailing in society. From rape to child prostitution, from sexual harassment in work place to transphobia, from unlawful encroachments to inhuman evictions – these plays cover a wide range of social injustices. There is necessarily no do-gooder in the plays but there is a 'conscientious' character, a character with a conscience, a do-the-right-thing character in every play.

The idea of 'servitude' also runs through all the plays. It does not seem to change with time. The feeling of power that comes with ownership too does not change much with time – be it ownership of land, a haveli or two apartments; even ownership of people like Chinku in *Unspoken*.

The volume begins with *Mandap*, which depicts a typical casteist society where the lower castes are subject to inhuman behaviour. This is followed by the 'trilogy of five plays' based on city life which was originally titled *Tales from the City*. As the author says, 'these plays may be seen as the sociology of the city, especially the underbelly, uncovering the usually unseen occupations that remain integral to the economy of the city.' In all these plays, we see the social workers hard at work but how effective are they really, we are left wondering at the end of each play.

It is only in the last play *Second Shift Muster*, that we see a glimpse of a brighter side of society, showcasing skill, but even that is overshadowed by mechanisation. The language of discourse changes with time, but whether the business of life changes, continues to be unknown yet. While we wait for Volume 6, the process of living itself is rapidly changing, all due to a virus. Set notions can no longer live in plays; the only thing we can tell our readers is, change is in the offing.

# SALUTATIONS

Volumes 1-3 of the publication project were pushed through in very little time to meet the deadline of 17 December 2019, kicking off the Diamond Jubilee year of BLT. It was on that date in 1960 that BLT had its first public performance. From the original plan of a token release of one volume we went on to release three volumes! The people who went out of the way to make this happen were Papri Sen Sri Raman, Kanagam King and their team at Vitasta Publishing. BLT commissioned the publication of six volumes of plays to Vitasta. It has been a great pleasure working with the Vitasta team, ever meticulous in editorial inputs and ever patient with the BLT team. It has been a great learning experience working with Papri and her team.

It is well known that the huge collection of play scripts in BLT had remained unpublished for years. We are thankful to the Managing Committee of BLT to take on the publication task with determination in 2019 – and for pushing us into its execution. There has been an even more powerful hand behind the publications project, invisible but relentless in drive over several years. Rupande Padaki, known to all of us as Rupa, was in many ways responsible for the publications to be taken up. She succeeded at last.

**Deepak Mote • Vijay Padaki**

# PREFACE TO THE VOLUME

Bangalore Little Theatre (BLT) was restructured in 2008. A public charitable trust was created with a non-profit status. *Theatre development* activities, which were pursued in an on-and-off manner till then, were now placed in a newly created Academy of Theatre Arts.

The planning process identified several well-planned and long-term programme 'thrusts'. They may also be seen as 'verticals' in the mission. The verticals are served by some cross-cutting activities, with their own plans and commitments – some of long standing within BLT and some adopted afresh in the ATA plan.

For example,

- *Methodology Development*, training methods, including trainer-training and training directors.
- *Play Development*, in which BLT has had a long track record.
- *Partnership Development*, reinforcing the organisation's commitment to collaboration.
- *Competence Development*, promoting talent in the theatre for new writing, new directors, new artists – both on stage and off stage.

New play development is thus a major commitment in the long-term plans of BLT. More recently, BLT created an entirely new programme called NEW VOICES. It includes the creation of a Writers Forum and the creation of opportunities for play scripts to be performed. The programme thrust is extended to colleges and universities, organising theatre festivals of only new and original plays.

In the early years of play development, a great deal of the new writing came from my desk. Ah, but very few of them were turned into theatre productions by BLT! As a highly-democratised set-up, the group had clear criteria for the selection of plays for performance, and the process was driven by the twin principles of governance – participative decisions and transparency.

I wrote for the enjoyment of writing, not for inflicting the scripts on BLT, and with no desire to be seen as a playwright. At the end of each writing project, I shared the script with a few friends whose opinion I valued, and that was it. I went on to the next writing project. Seeing the play scripts published was never the objective.

In 2019, I stepped down from all management responsibilities in BLT, continuing simply as a Trustee. The Managing Committee of BLT decided to felicitate me for the long years of service to the organisation. First, they put together a Festival of my plays, spread over the months of

May-September 2019. If that was not enough to increase my hat size by two inches, they overwhelmed me next with the project to publish all my plays. A team within the Committee took charge, worked out the arrangement with Vitasta Publishers, and here we are! We have play scripts in a whole publication series from Bangalore Little Theatre.

I succeeded in persuading the publications team to position the series as Plays from *Bangalore Little Theatre*. It is, after all, the character of BLT that has promoted new writing for the stage, and created the conditions for me to write. Play development has been led by me over many years in BLT. I sincerely hope the NEW VOICES programme will carry forward this nurturance.

In this preface, it would be appropriate to reproduce one section of the preface to Volume 1, published in December 2019.

> Bangalore Little Theatre (BLT) was created in 1960. In its very first three years, English language theatre moved out of the Cantonment to reach all of Bangalore. BLT very decisively sought an alternative theatre experience in a post-colonial social context. Reaching out to those active in the Kannada theatre in the city, they created a truly inclusive theatre society. BLT was influenced greatly by the Little Theatre movement of the 'fifties in the UK, decentralising theatre activity from London, disseminating high-quality theatre widely through training, outreach, and community involvement.
>
> Within a year of inception, BLT arrived at a character and identity for itself: to maintain pride in its strictly amateur status, but to conduct its affairs in a thoroughly professional manner. The group gave itself a constitution and, through that, a participatory style of functioning. The group was seen as belonging to a membership, and therefore, to be managed by a transparently elected management committee. The founding members were the first to give way to younger members to take the group forward.
>
> Of special significance was the group's positioning as *Community Theatre*, relating to the Indian socio-economic reality. In sum, within a short space of five years BLT was:
>
> - an *Indian* theatre group with a global outlook.
> - assimilating the best of British theatre traditions in a new Indian environment.
> - relating to Kannada and all other regional language theatre groups – actively assisting them.
>
> Related to the last point is one other indisputably important feature of BLT. It is the only English language theatre group in

Bangalore (perhaps one of very few anywhere in India) with strong links to the local-regional theatre, building bridges across language divides. Many of the stalwarts on the Kannada stage and screen have been either life members of BLT or have been prominently involved in some capacity or the other. Indeed, BLT has been a substantial support to Kannada theatre groups in their start-up stages.

*****

The plays included in this volume are different from the first four volumes in one important respect. They are not thematically compiled. These plays were written in the period 1986 to 2002 and represent explorations in combining form with content. We know, of course, that form without content is mere indulgence. (It is so in all of the arts.) I can say with some confidence that in my writing, it has always been the content that drove the form. Is there something about the content that holds the five plays together? Perhaps, yes – and perhaps without my being aware of it until now. Looking back, putting the plays together for this publication, I see a humanistic undercurrent in the plays, *an affirmation of the human spirit*, the innate ability to question the given, so often remaining suppressed, and the ability to find alternatives.

It is known that a lot of my writing has been influenced by field experiences in my professional engagements. The content of the play has often (not always) begun as a case study, intriguing in itself, but demanding an alternative perspective. The alternative perspectives have provided the raw material for the play scripts. There should be no need to explain this further. The plays should explain themselves.

Before *Credit Titles* I wrote mainly for the enjoyment of writing. *The Hindu* award did the damage of getting me to see myself as a playwright. The original script of *Credit Titles* required an 'Author's Note'. An excerpt from that might be worth reproducing here:

> The danger in winning a prize for a play script is, of course, the precipitation of the belief that one is a playwright. Of course, I am not. I enjoy writing plays, as I enjoy working with wood, but that does not make me a playwright. Or a carpenter. The truth is I enjoy working on lots of different things. That only makes me a lot of a dabbler. The truth I have to accept is that there is a lot more to a craft than displaying a toolkit. It is most deceptive when there is also a recognisable body of takers. Why, even as a schoolboy, I had an indulgent audience. Even takers for the misshapen stools and bookends that I turned out regularly. My accountant gives me

> one more good reason not to call myself a playwright: *The Hindu* award is then deemed an income. …I am referring to what was rather special for me in *Credit Titles*: the enjoyment was almost entirely in the act of writing itself, and who cares what happens to the script afterwards! With no producer or audience in mind, with little thought to how the finished product might be received, with nothing to prove to anybody, it was easier to be accepted by the characters in the play, to get their permission to sit in a corner and watch them at play, to submit to their play.

Many thanks to Asha Mathew, Minti Jain and Murtuza Khetty for the help in editing the manuscripts for this Volume.

**Vijay Padaki**
*Series Editor*

# STAGE DIRECTIONS

with the actor facing the audience

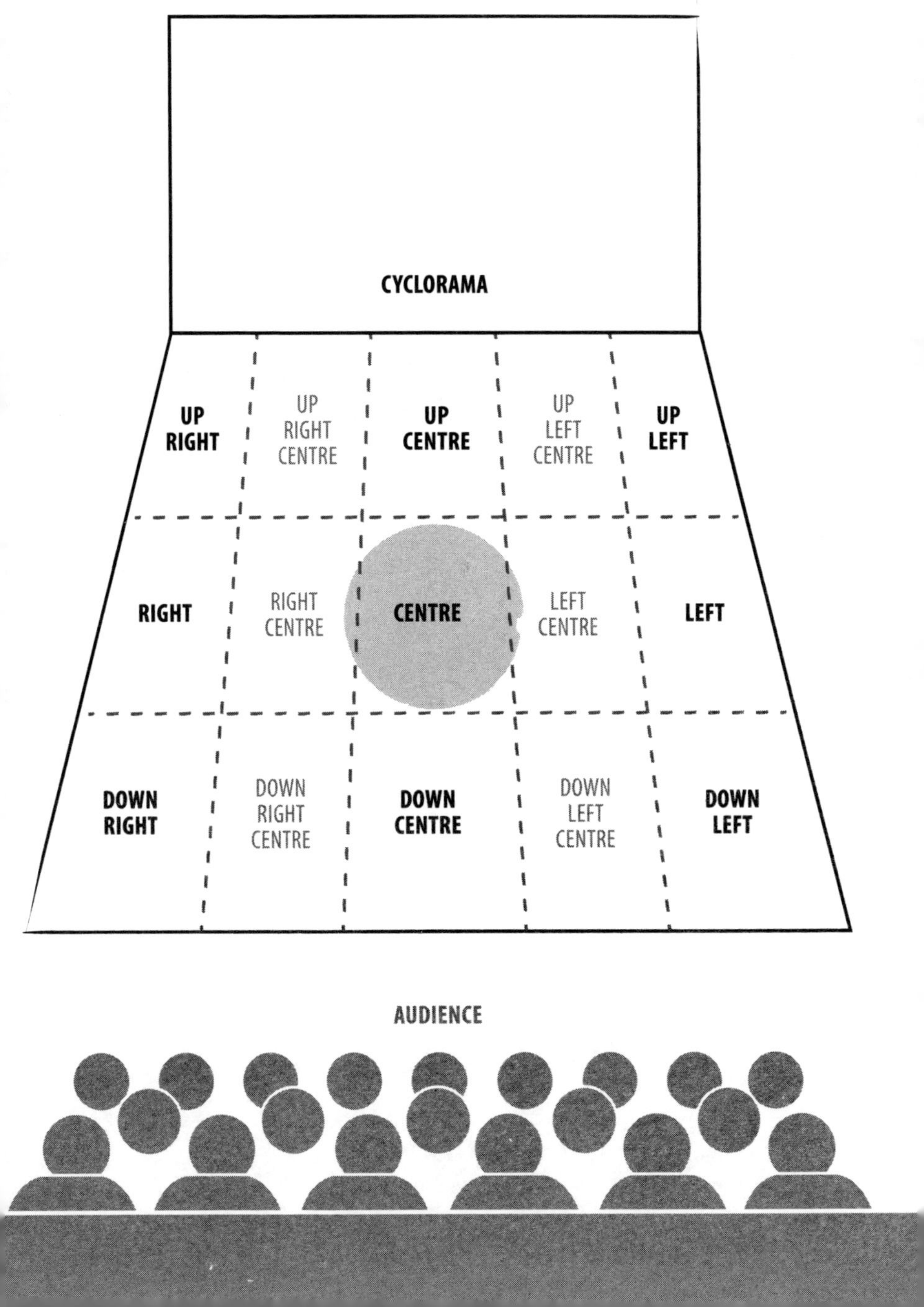

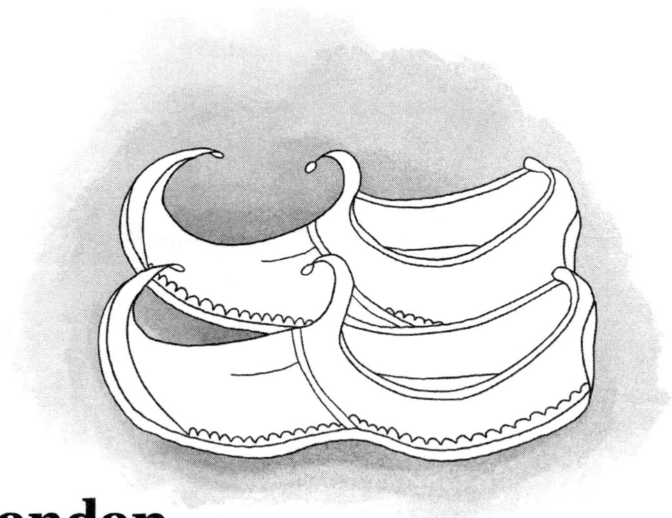

# Mandap

*A view from the hill*
***Vijay Padaki***

FOR
**HABIB TANVIR**

## CHARACTERS IN THE PLAY

GROOM'S FATHER .......... *Landlord of the estate*
BRIDEGROOM .......... *His son*
GROOM'S MOTHER .......... *The landlord's wife*
BRIDE .......... *Newcomer to the estate*
SERVANT .......... *As the title suggests*
MAID .......... *The servant's wife, assigned to the bride*
RATAN .......... *Young lad, keeper of the estate pigeon-house*
A WOMAN .......... *In the local entertainment profession*
A COMMUNITY ELDER AND A SMALL GROUP OF ELDERS
A SMALL GROUP OF HIJRAS AND THEIR LEADER
A SMALL GROUP OF THE GROOM'S FRIENDS
A SMALL GROUP OF THE BRIDE'S FRIENDS

Several parts can (and should) be played by the same actors as an ensemble. For instance:

- the same small group playing the elders and those at the funeral;
- the group playing the hijras and the groom's friends;
- the group playing the bride's friends and the mourning group at the end.

*Hijra* is a derogatory word, not in usage in contemporary literature. It is an omnibus term to refer to people whose sexual status may be anywhere in a wide range – eunuch, transvestite, transgender or hermaphrodite. In traditional Indian culture they are known to move together in small groups, often seen at weddings. They are usually paid off to avoid embarrassment.

# INTRODUCTION

## Background

The play *Mandap* was to be a major production by Habib Tanvir at Naya Theatre. He had read the play, discussed it with the author and his group, and had decided on the nature of the translation that he would personally undertake in Hindustani.

As part of my involvement in a large educational programme in Madhya Pradesh and Chhattisgarh, I went to Bhopal frequently and spent considerable time with Habibji. It included a brainstorming session with the group on the form and design of the play and the production approach. It was clear that the play was well within Naya Theatre's interest. It was planned to be taken up soon after a retrospective of Naya Theatre plays that was being put together at that time. Notes on the production commenced.

Soon after, there were two successive tragedies in Habibji's life, and the production had to be shelved. It remained an unfinished project.

Bangalore Little Theatre paid a tribute to Tanvir with a staged reading of *Mandap* in June 2009. Later, in August 2014, there was a rehearsed reading of the play when Tanvir's daughter, Nageen Tanvir, brought Naya Theatre to Bangalore on the invitation of BLT. There have been several rehearsed play readings of the play in Bangalore and in the USA.

## The play

The play is set in the estate of a landlord in a small town somewhere in the rural north of India. With due adaptation, the play can also be set in other parts of India. With some changes in the idiom, it can be located in any other part of India. The challenge is to play it in the English language. The time is now.

The play is based on factual material from field experiences. It attempts to reconstruct the conditions on stage. The unfolding story is necessarily fictional. The phenomenon of privileged rape based on caste superiority continues to be common in the northern belt of rural India where the play is set. Land ownership gives the upper caste enormous power. It remains unquestioned. The abuse of the power remains unspoken. The caste is not mentioned in the play script. However, the power equation is retained and not sanitised. The phenomenon is not uncommon in other parts of India.

## Performing the play

- The play is constructed as a string of twelve scenes. A continuous flow rather than interruptions for scene-act changes is recommended.

- The identities of the characters in the play are established early enough. There is no need to give them names. Only one character, the keeper of the pigeon-house, is given a name.
- There are three acting areas required, separable by lighting
  – the mandap area, raised, perhaps upstage left;
  – the sitting room area, perhaps stage right;
  – the flexi-space that serves many smaller scenes, perhaps stage centre to left, down-left.
- There is a great deal of action and business written into the script. There are scenes without a word spoken. It must be obvious that these are as important as the spoken word. For instance, the entire prologue is in action only. These passages need both care and ingenuity in rehearsals. It also means a stage design that is uncluttered, permitting a lot of action.
- With a good trotting pace maintained, the running time should be within two hours.
- A straight run without an intermission might well be considered. If regarded unavoidable, the intermission should be at the end of Scene 6.
- The prologue presents a series of 'moving snapshots' that can, with intelligent performance, blur the distinction between the characters as seen now and their ancestry, the unstated leitmotif in the play. Towards the end of the prologue they move gradually into the present.
- It might not be out of place to caution players against two possible dangers in performing this script: (a) trying too hard to appear rural, and (b) looking for role models in Hindi movies. This is especially important in playing the hijras. Both of these dispositions are likely to cross the line between character and caricature.
- It is not advisable to overanalyse the basic fabric of the play in terms of motive, plot, and personal tragedy. A view from the hill of the community whole might help.

## Language Notes

*Mandap:* Covered resting place, canopy, gazebo. Usually associated with some special event or function.

*Odhni:* Length of cloth worn by women to cover the head, upper half of body.

*Kanyapariksha:* Literally examination (pariksha) of maiden (kanya) for virginity.

*Hijra:* A generic term to refer to the eunuch, transvestite, transgender or hermaphrodite. In traditional Indian culture they are known to move together in small groups, often seen at weddings. They are usually paid off to avoid embarrassment.

*Paan:* Betel leaf (chewed).

*Kaanta-chammach:* Fork-spoon (cutlery).

*Bahu:* Daughter-in-law.
*Kabootarkhana:* Kabootar (pigeon) + khana (house).
*Akhada:* Wrestling pit, gym for wrestlers.
*Behen:* Sister. Behenji – woman/girl addressed with respect.
*Dahi:* Curd, yogurt.
*Arhar dal:* A common pulse/lentil used in many foods.
*Teetar:* Partridge.
*Bakwas:* Nonsense talk, jabber.
*Karthik:* Name of month in Indian (lunar) calendar.
*Shamiana:* Large decorative canvas cover for special occasions.
*Muhurat:* Inauguration, auspicious start.
*Dhanda:* Occupation, trade.
*Budtameezi:* Ill mannered, irresponsible, impertinent behaviour.
*Thana:* Station – police station.
*Baraat:* Wedding procession.
*Chhuchhunder:* Field mouse.
*Kothi:* Literally large bungalow. Connotation of old style brothel where the girls entertained with music and dance.
*Paltan:* Platoon.
*Rangoli:* Traditional designs drawn on the floor, usually with rice flour and other (coloured) powders.
*Durga Mata:* Durga (name of goddess) + mata (mother).
*Chalo:* Let's go.
*Haveli:* Manor, family home, usually large, for joint family.
*'Him':* The husband – as a married woman is not supposed to take the husband's name.
*Haan ki na:* Yes or no.
*Pehle aap:* After you, you first.
*Mogra:* Jasmine.
*Shikar:* Hunt.
*Nazar:* Literally the look or gaze. Refers to 'evil eye', envious view of others.
*Maidan:* Open space, field.
*Chabootra:* A large birdhouse, usually for pigeons. Space for feeding birds.
*Shist:* Style, carriage.
*Chhote Nawab:* Young nawab.
*Izzat:* Respect, standing.
*Dum dum diga diga:* Popular song of the seventies – like Obla-di.
*Puja:* Ritual worship.
*Shira:* A sweet snack.
*Badam:* Almond.
*Zamindar:* Landlord (Zamindari: serfdom).
*Haq:* Right, prerogative.
*Dabba:* Box, container. Tiffin box here.

*Jooti:* Slip-on footwear.
*Bhajan:* Religious group song.
*Haldi-kumkum:* Literally turmeric and vermillion – two coloured powders used in many traditional rituals. Distributed at pujas.
*Mushroo:* Traditional silk-satin weave.

## FIRST PERFORMED

As a staged reading at Attakkalari, 27 June 2009

*Narrators* .............................. PRIYA RAO AND RAVI SRINIVASAN
*Elder* .............................................................. RAVI SRINIVASAN
*Groom* .............................................................. NAVEEN KUMAR
*Groom's Mother* .................................... SUNITHA RAJAGOPALAN
*Bride* .............................................................. ALIYEH RIZVI
*Maid* .............................................................. PADMAVATI RAO
*Servant* .............................................................. ANAND RAMPRASAD
*Groom's Father* .............................................................. VIJAY PADAKI
*Ratan* .............................................................. PRITHAM KUMAR
*Hijra Leader* .............................................................. FIRAZ PEER
*Coordinated by* .............................................................. PRIYA RAO

**REMEMBERING HABIB TANVIR**
Habib Ahmed Khan 1923 – 2009

## SCENE 1

## PROLOGUE

*The mandap. The play opens with the lights picking up the mandap. The sound of a sugary, sentimental, Hindi film song from the '70s approaches. The servant enters with a 2-in-1 transistor player, sets it down, and starts work, decorating the mandap. After a while, the song on the 2-in-1 changes to a more raucous tune.*

*Crossfade*

*The lights pick up a small group of young men seated downstage, towards the end of a binge. They are on a high, but not staggering drunk. In the middle is a woman who is transparently attractive. We do not see her face, covered in chiffon, but who cares. She is collecting glasses from the men on to a tray, while the group is teasing the groom in a not-so-subtle manner on his supposed masculinity and impending doom. Finally the groom takes out a bundle of 100-rupee notes. The evening's fun is on him. He caresses the woman's face with a finger and places one of the notes between her lips. She accepts it. The others clap. The groom then places a note in his own lips. She approaches and takes it away with her own lips. More cheer. The next note is placed on his thigh. Repeat. There are some more notes...*

*The performing group must decide whether to mime this scene (preferred) or improvise speech. In either case, the sounds we hear must be subdued, secondary to the visual impact.*

*The music changes.*

*Crossfade*

*The mandap. There has been progress in the decoration. The servant is standing on a folding chair, tucking a string of flowers in place. The father enters, inspecting the arrangements. The servant climbs down, turns off the 2-in-1, and stands obsequiously before him. The groom's father offers suggestions on the decorations, motions additional instructions, makes enquiries on jobs. The servant is sufficiently experienced to know that the best response to all of his master's initiatives is to simply go along. The father then picks up another folding chair from a stack, settles himself, and opens the morning paper. The servant begins to put other chairs from the stack in a row next to the father's.*

*The same discretion to be used by the players – full mime (preferred) or unobtrusive speech.*

*Crossfade*

*A group of young women huddled around the bride. She is being prepared. It is a canopy of odhnis of different colours through which we catch an occasional glimpse of the bride's face, half-expectant, half-embarrassed. There is much giggling and teasing. Yet again there is some urgent whispering in an even tighter huddle, the periodic burst of laughter. It is girl talk, but we do not hear actual conversation.*

*Crossfade*

*The mandap again. The servant is putting some finishing touches to the decorations. The maid (his wife) appears, carrying an aluminium kettle and glass tumblers. She keeps them on one of the chairs and begins to help the servant. He moves away to another part of the mandap. She finds a way to join him there. He excuses himself, comes down to the chair, sits, and pours himself some tea from the kettle. The maid joins him there. He gives her his glass, avoids her gaze. She takes a sip or two and puts it away. They sit still, staring ahead. Suddenly she begins to sob, buries herself in his chest, and weeps loudly. He consoles her as best as he can.*

*Crossfade*

*A kanyapariksha. The group of young women sit in a semicircle, quiet and solemn now. The bride is led in by the groom's mother to the centre. She begins to undress. As she proceeds, the semicircle rises, holding up a curtain that at least partly conceals the two women. After a while, the young women sit again, revealing an empty space. If this is difficult on some stages, we can show the mother towering over a kneeling bride. She blesses the girl approvingly and strides out.*

*Crossfade*

*A small group of hijras. They are dressing up, putting finishing touches, adjusting saris, make-up, flowers, taking great care over details, and helping each other in the process. The leader among them, paid the slight extra attention by the others, nods approvingly to them one by one as they appear to be done. With a series of claps they move towards the mandap.*

*Crossfade*

*The servant and the maid recover their composure with the sound of approaching claps. The hijras appear. They stand still. The servant approaches them to negotiate. They break into suggestive smiles. The maid goes up to them with her kettle and glasses. They stop clapping and regard her curiously. She inspects them as in a guard room drill, stops, offers them tea. The hijras snigger and break into claps again. The maid withdraws.*

*The father appears, stands in a corner. The servant goes up to him, receives a few 500-rupee notes, and returns to the hijras with the money. They are not satisfied, and announce their disappointment with a few sharp claps. The servant goes back to the father, gets two more notes, returns to the hijras, slips all the notes into the hands of the leader who, in turn, blesses the party and the mandap and leads the group off. The servant and maid exit in the opposite direction. The father sits on the first chair.*

*The lights change on the scene with the sound of serial firecrackers followed by loud marriage band music.*

*From one side comes a procession of community ELDERs. They are all at least as old as the father, perhaps older. They look solemn. They take their seats one by one next to the father.*

*Abrupt end to music.*

*The bride enters, escorted by the mother. She is now seen as very young, hardly out of her teens. She has her head bent, covered with her odhni. We can imagine that she is as pretty as a morning blossom. She is led to the first ELDER, seated at one end. The mother withdraws. The bride bends to touch his feet. He raises her gently. She then sits on the ELDER's lap. He blesses her, not without some fondling, and passes her on to the second ELDER. The sequence is repeated till she reaches the father on the first chair. As she bows to touch his feet, the ELDERs leave. The father raises the bride, raises her chin, parts the odhni the slightest bit to look into her eyes, and leads her off slowly.*

*Crossfade. The first ELDER is seated with a paan tray before him. The groom is making a paan for him, looking at him anxiously now and then. The ELDER remains still. He receives the paan, puts it into his mouth, savours it well, spits out the excess elegantly into a shiny brass spittoon, and finally speaks, still looking only straight ahead.*

**ELDER**

Wait till it is well after half past twelve. Tonight the period between half past twelve and half past one is the most auspicious for new unions. Do you understand?

**GROOM** *(Mumbling)*

Yes... yes, I understand.

**ELDER**

Tonight as well as the next two nights this week... up to the sixteenth of this month. The best time is between half past twelve and half past one. Will you remember that?

**GROOM**

Huh? Yes, yes, I'll remember.

**ELDER**

What you do until half past twelve is unimportant. You have to kill time... play with her... play with her as much as you like, but don't go any further...

**GROOM**

I'll wait... here, in this room.

**ELDER**

There's no need for that... foolish boy. You can go up there whenever they let you both in. Only don't be in any hurry... don't show any hurry... play. Wait till the time is right. Making her wait will also be good for you... you will see.

**GROOM**

I don't know her, so...

**ELDER**

A mandap serves a journey, and in that service becomes part of the journey itself. The acts you perform in your marriage are re-enactments of the acts of your ancestors, and thereby make you more wholly the ancestry itself. Do you follow?

**GROOM**

Yes, I think I do.

**ELDER**

You cannot have an ancestry in parts. It must be the whole.

*Crossfade*

*The group of young women are now at work in the mandap area making it into a bridal chamber. They move in dance-like steps, they joke among themselves. They slip an attractively wrapped gift between two pillows, spray perfume around the mattresses, mime wedding night scenes from the movies, and generally enjoy a feigned naughtiness among themselves before skipping out of the scene, held bright and colourful for a few beats.*

*Crossfade*

*The bride is with the groom's mother. She is weeping. The groom's mother wipes her tears with the edge of her own sari and talks to her. She is trying to be warm, but her firmness is equally evident.*

**GROOM'S MOTHER**

You know what our families are known for... bravery... our family, your family, all our families. Bravery in everything we do... not just bravery on the battlefield, not only in those days when we were called to take up arms, but a bravery in all things done... in our everyday lives... in looking after our lands, in running a business... in bringing up our children. There is so much we have as tradition, such solid foundations. You are a lucky girl... such a lucky girl, with all the stars in heaven on your side.

You will make my son so happy... you will, won't you? Heaven knows, not all of us have stars like yours... but we all have bravery on our side. It's a new life that you begin today. Think of yourself as a new person, starting a new life, starting on a completely new journey. It only takes one step to get started. A new life, and you are a new person. I remember my own start on that journey, god knows how many years ago. I went there to meet him, your young man's father. I must have been fourteen then, no more than fifteen...

*(The bride's crying is now more intense. She breaks away from the mother and cries to herself in a heap.)*

There, there, now. That won't do at all. Come, come here to me. Let me help you tidy up. Tomorrow in the morning you'll hide your face from me again, but in a very, very different way. Take it easy now, easy, we'll go up in another ten or fifteen minutes...

*(Slow fade out over the last lines. In the dark the burst of firecrackers again.)*

## SCENE 2

*Fade in film music on the 2-in-1. Fade in mandap area. It is curtained, looking just a bit like a giant four-poster with the mosquito net down. Fade in downstage area. The 2-in-1 is kept in a corner while the maid is mopping the floor. As she finishes, the servant, now bare-chested, lays out a set of floor mats and stainless steel plates and tumblers.*

**MAID**

How many more meals on the floor do you think?

**SERVANT**

All of today, maybe till lunch tomorrow. All the big guns will have moved out by lunch. The dining table can come back after that, I suppose.

**MAID**

And then?

**SERVANT**

And then the chairs with the table, the place mats, the kaanta-chammach, the crockery, what else?

**MAID**

What else?

**SERVANT**

What else is there?

**MAID**

What else?

**SERVANT** *(Avoiding)*

Oh yes, an extra place at the table for our new bahu.

**MAID**

Clever! You know very well what else.

*(There is no response. The servant busies himself, arranging three covered dishes and a jug of water on wooden boards on the floor. He takes his place in a corner. The maid joins him. They are both seated, silent, waiting.)*

How much longer do you think?

*They rise quickly. The Elder and the father enter, inspect the places set, and occupy two places. The mother enters next, finds her place, and sits. There are now two vacant places, one on the men's side and one on the women's, with a gap between the two sections. The tableau of five waits.... The curtain in the mandap parts, the groom steps out, walks down to the dining area, pauses briefly, and walks out. The group watches, but does not react. Finally, the father lifts the lids off the dishes, inspects the contents. He signals the group's readiness. The servant moves forward and serves from the dishes, the maid follows, serving the water.*

*Crossfade*

*The mandap now has all the curtains parted, revealing the bride seated at the edge, lost in thought. The group of girls enters, first on tiptoe, then running up to her, flitting about her, throwing furtive glances at things in and around the mandap, and finally leading her out, gently and lovingly.*

*Crossfade*

*The downstage area. There are now only two places on the floor. The servant sits in his corner, head buried in his knees, asleep. The groom enters, takes his place, and waits. He then inspects the dishes, rather like the father, but silently, and serves himself. The maid leads the bride in, guides her to her place, and then moves to nudge the servant. He wakes up to see the bride standing quietly at her place and the groom feeding himself without looking up. He moves to do something about this, but the maid draws him away and they exit. After a while the bride moves to serve the groom a second helping.*

*Crossfade*

*The mandap is getting to be stark and bare. The servant is putting away all the decorations. Other workers are carrying away the mattresses, sheets, chairs. Soon the servant is left alone. He has a string of jaded flowers in his hand. He inspects the bare mandap one last time, sits at the edge, his gaze lost in the flowers in his hand. He rises slowly, wipes a tear from his eyes, and exits quickly.*

*Crossfade*

*There is only one place on the floor. The mother is seated, eating. The maid is waiting on her.*

**MOTHER**

Pigeons! That's the way it works, pigeons. Have you seen that boy Ratan working on them? The best kabootarkhana in this part of the country. So many prizes we have won – endurance flights, long distance, so many things. But when you first put a pair of them together in a cage to breed, oh... oh... oh, what a scene! They fight, they sulk, they claw at each other, ignore each other, then suddenly attack each other again. Real rough and tumble, just like the wrestlers in our akhada. It lasts a week, maybe ten days. Then all of a sudden, wah! They are so different, so devoted to each other, they can't do without each other. You know that sort of behaviour, lovey-dovey it's called. What else! The male, he is always walking about with his chest sticking out, like a subedar-major or something. And the female, presenting her backside to him all the time, laying eggs for him the rest of her life.

*(She stops, concentrates on the meal.)*

**MAID**

Behenji, aren't you having your dahi today?

**MOTHER**
If I haven't touched it, what does it mean?

**MAID**
Yes, behenji.

**MOTHER**
Keep it in the machine. I might have it with dinner.

**MAID**
Yes, behenji.

**MOTHER**
Dahi at least once a day. Necessary to cool the system. At least once a day.

**MAID**
Of course, behenji.

**MOTHER**
Raw arhar dal is what Ratan feeds those pigeons. Heat producing arhar. Why doesn't he soak it in dahi and then give it to them?

## SCENE 3

*The mandap is now a deserted watchtower on a hillock on the outskirts of the town. The hijra leader is standing with his back to us, casually munching peanuts. When he hears approaching voices, he turns and waits.*

**GROOM'S FATHER** *(Off)*
A whole morning out in the fields, and what do we have to show? One skinny rabbit and half a teetar. Buss! *(The father enters with the groom, the servant, and Ratan in tow. He is carrying an ancient single-barrel shotgun. The cartridge belt across his chest is mostly empty. The servant has a game basket slung over his shoulder. There are other hand props as needed.)*

**FATHER**
What is this country coming to? Abey Ratanlal, son of a prickless country dog, where is that flock of wood pigeons you promised? At the old watch tower, you said. Well, where are they?

**RATAN**
They should have been here, huzoor. They are always here at this time, huzoor. Maybe they have just...

**LEADER**
Maybe you should not be making so much noise when you go out hunting.

**FATHER**
Who is this stick of camel dung? What is this... this... ?

**LEADER**

The more noise you make on the hunt, the less you will have to brag about later. *(The servant is whispering in the father's ear)*

**FATHER**

This one? This is the one? But here... ?

**LEADER**

The view of the town from here is really grand. On this side, you can see right up to the new colonies near the highway... and on that side, the old township around the temple.

**GROOM**

What brings you here? This is not the place for...

**LEADER**

Not the place for?

**GROOM**

No matter. We have come here to rest for a while. We don't want to be disturbed. So, just move on. Go to any other place you like, for whatever you were doing.

**LEADER**

For what I was doing, there is no place better than this, but since you object to my presence...

**RATAN**

What were you up to anyway?

**LEADER**

Making a road plan for tomorrow.

**FATHER**

What is this bakwas?

**LEADER**

Sahib, huzoor, you must accept that the wedding of the young master here was not the last one in this season. The month of Karthik has one more week to close, and at least three good days in the week. Tomorrow, you see...

**FATHER**

There are two important weddings in town tomorrow.

**LEADER**

Three important weddings. You are forgetting the owner of the new jaggery mill. Can you see the shamiana coming up there? Three of your important weddings, but as for us, a total of eleven muhurats between seven in the morning and noontime. There, you can spot all of them from here. Two there, one next to the post office, another just across the school playground...

**SERVANT**
All right, all right, we understand you were not – what do you say – you were not here for any...

**LEADER**
Doing anything criminal.

**SERVANT**
You were only carrying out...

**FATHER**
All part of the job. When you have a dhanda like that...

**LEADER**
Sahib, huzoor, every creature to its own dhanda. Scanning the earth is god's dhanda, scanning the country is the prime minister's dhanda, you have your dhanda scanning the labour market, and we have ours...

**FATHER**
Enough budtameezi. Enough of your...

**LEADER**
Our most important responsibility, huzoor, is to take out the evil spirits from an auspicious gathering. You might even secretly wish that we came, and that the job was done with.

**FATHER**
Shut up! Or I'll stuff your mouth with pig shit.

**LEADER**
There you go, raising your voice again, huzoor. You'll drive all the game away. Did they not tell you that, huzoor, when they first showed you how to hold your gun? *(By now the groom and Ratan have placed themselves between him and the father.)*

**FATHER**
I'll grind what's left of his brains under my boot. I'll...
*(He raises his gun threateningly)*

**RATAN AND GROOM** *(Together)*
>> No, huzoor...
>> It's all right, I'll take care of this...
>> Please, please...
Etc. *(The groom takes the gun away and steps aside.)*

**LEADER**
And never to point your gun at anybody, never, unless you mean to use it. They must have told you that, huzoor. Never play with your food, never pick your nose, and never keep your gun sticking out.

**FATHER** *(To the groom)*
You! Tell this sack of night soil, standing there, that in less than an hour from now there will be a call from the police thana.

**LEADER**

The police thana?

**FATHER** *(Still addressing only the groom)*

The Inspector is known to us, related to us, through your wife's first cousin.

**LEADER**

And his first sister's cousin is with us.

**FATHER**

Enough talk! We will see what needs to be done when we get back.

*(There is a ring around the hijra leader, close enough for a rough-up, yet held back. They can't quite look the leader in the eye who, in contrast, is unaffected by the ludicrous situation.)*

**LEADER**

Meanwhile, I have to see to preparations for this afternoon's reception. The grain merchant in Mahadevwadi is expecting the baraat at about four o'clock. How can they proceed without us? May I have your permission to withdraw, huzoor, gentlemen of the court... ?

*(The leader exits. They watch him leave.)*

**FATHER**

Look at you all! Men, are you? Look at this one, standing with a gun. Stick that between your legs like the tail of a pie dog, you good-for-nothing son of your good-for-nothing mother! Are you a man or a chhuchhunder? Go look at yourself in the mirror. Look at that dried up chilli dangling in front of you. Go show it to all the girls in the kothi and see if they can do something about it! Bunch of impotent chhuchhunder, I have around me. A she-goat farts in their faces and they go home staggering. Get out! Out, all of you!! This country is doomed – I have to go out hunting with a chhuchhunder paltan...

(*Fade out through the last lines)*

## SCENE 4

*Another corner of the stage now reveals a sitting room area. It has the stock outfitting of a reasonably well-off home transiting to urban norms. On a low centre table is a cane tray of freshly cut flowers waiting to be arranged. The bride and the maid are sitting on the floor before a large calendar picture of goddess Durga. On the reverse is a complicated diagram, half rangoli, half tantric, that contains, among other things, some 'houses' that will be referred to and all the letters of the alphabet. The bride is holding a string tied to her wedding ring.*

**BRIDE**

Where did you get this durga-mata?

**MAID**

He gave it to me himself.

**BRIDE**

The sadhu?

**MAID**

He was not just a sadhu. Not like the ones you see near the river. He was very different, a great man with great powers.

**BRIDE**

Let us hurry. I'm supposed to finish with the flowers before he returns. If he sees me playing with my wedding ring...

**MAID**

Don't worry. They won't be back for another hour. Now... sit back... keep your hand out with the ring hung just above the centre of this chart. That's right, keep your palm straight... Now close your eyes and relax... The string is standing still, absolutely still. Just concentrate on the ring now. Do you feel it moving? Keep your palm steady... There, it is moving now. Open your eyes slowly and see how it is moving...

**BRIDE**

Oh, it's moving by itself! I swear, it is moving by itself, I haven't done anything!

**MAID**

Of course, it is moving by itself. Let us see, which way it is moving... Ah, do you see the two houses at the two ends of its swing?

**BRIDE**

Yes, this one here, and that one there, both drawn in pink.

**MAID**

There are only two ways in which the ring can move. Either it moves in a circle, or it swings, like it's happening with you. When it circles, it suggests a strong male planet influencing your life. The swing suggests a strong female planet. Now... within this swing, we must find out which forces are playing in your life. These two houses... you see how clearly it is moving between these two houses? These two houses represent the two persons who have the greatest influence on your life. One is an old woman... too old to be your mother... your grandmother on your mother's side perhaps?

**BRIDE**

That's right, that's right. She was the closest person to me all my life. *(Suddenly)* But she is no more...

**MAID**

Ah, but that does not matter at all. We are not moving in the world of matter. We are moving in the world of spirit. Your grandmother is still there, a very important source of strength in your life. And on the other side...

**BRIDE**

If only I could see her, talk to her again. There is so much to talk, so much I want to ask her. Sorry, sorry, you were saying...

**MAID**

And on the other side...

**BRIDE**

On the other side – who's on the other side?

**MAID**

On the other side, in perfect balance with your grandmother's influence, is a young man.

**BRIDE**

Who? Of course, you know who!

**MAID**

It does not say who clearly. It only says a young man, who keeps a certain distance but still influences you strongly.

**BRIDE**

Let him remain in the distance! I want to talk to my grandmother.

**MAID**

Now?

**BRIDE**

Yes, now. Will it take very long?

**MAID**

No, but it depends on the strength of the spirit.

**BRIDE**

Let's try.

**MAID**

All right. You can take off the string now. *(Bride does so)*

Now, you sit before the chart as before, but hold the ring standing on the centre point, pressed between the middle fingers of both hands... like this... that's right.

**BRIDE**

Is it at the centre?

**MAID**

It is. Now, close your eyes. Relax. Just concentrate on the ring. And picture your grandmother in front of your eyes.

**BRIDE**

I can see her in front of my eyes.

**MAID**

No need to talk. Just think of her... Now, if you feel a pull against your fingers, don't fight it...

**BRIDE**

It's moving. It's moving again!

*(Her hands with the ring between the two fingers start swinging – first in short strokes, gradually in longer and longer swings.)*

**MAID**

She is reaching you. She is trying to talk to you... Let us see if you have made contact. Think of a question to ask her...

*(There is a rapid reduction of the swings. The ring rests at the centre, but immediately starts moving again, this time in all directions over the alphabet. After a burst of moves, it rests again.)*

**MAID**

What a strange message... It says, 'Try behind the cushion on the easy chair.'

**BRIDE** *(Opening her eyes, rushing to one of the chairs)*

It's here! I found them.

**MAID**

What did you... ?

**BRIDE**

My pearl earrings. I asked her where on earth they might be. I've been so worried the last two days. They were right here!

**MAID**

Your grandmother must be keeping a watch over you!

**BRIDE**

Oh, I'm so happy! Chalo, chalo, now. There isn't much time. You'll have to help me with these flowers. I will talk to her again later. I must.

*(The maid folds and puts away the chart. They start work on the flowers.)*

**MAID**

You came into this house fully prepared. Good for you!

**BRIDE**

My father has a nice big haveli in Sonegaon, you know.

**MAID**

Yes, I have heard.

**BRIDE**

What have you heard? Tell me what you've heard.

**MAID**

Well, I've heard that your father lives in Sonegaon, that he has a nice big haveli in Sonegaon, that he is a very rich man, that he is also a very kind, honest, god-fearing, courageous, and clever man.

**BRIDE**

Rubbish! You're making things up.

**MAID**
No, I'm not.

**BRIDE**
Then you're mixing things up. It must be somebody else you've heard all these things about.

**MAID**
Is it? Well, maybe it is then. Maybe... maybe it is about our young master here... yes, of course!

**BRIDE**
Go on! You can't tease me like that.

**MAID**
I can't?

**BRIDE**
No, you can't.

**MAID**
I haven't even started really. Should I try?

**BRIDE** *(Short pause)*
What have you heard about him?

**MAID**
About who?

**BRIDE**
Him.

**MAID**
Him, him, him! Now, who could you possibly be thinking about?

**BRIDE**
The one you are itching to talk about – your young master in this household!

**MAID**
Oh, him! What's there to talk about him? Hundreds like him – kind, honest, courageous, clever...

**BRIDE**
Hmmm.

**MAID**
Well, isn't he?

**BRIDE**
Isn't he what?

**MAID**
All those things? And more? (Pause) Let's take it one by one. First, kind – haan ki na? All right, pass. Let's take honest – haan ki na?

**BRIDE**
Let's take courageous!

**MAID**
Oh, all right.

**BRIDE**
Is he courageous? What have you heard?

**MAID**
What have I heard?

**BRIDE**
Tell me what you've heard about his courageous deeds.

**MAID**
You mean about his manliness... ?

**BRIDE**
Well, that, if you want to look at it that way.

**MAID**
If you wish.

**BRIDE**
Only if you wish.

**MAID**
If you insist.

**BRIDE**
Uff – you'll drive a nest of hornets mad.

**MAID**
Pehle aap. You begin. You tell me if you think he is courageous.

**BRIDE** *(Pause)*
I think he is.

**MAID**
You think he is?

**BRIDE**
I think he is.

**MAID**
You want to tell me more... ?

**BRIDE**
You want to hear more?

**MAID**
To tell you the truth, yes!

**BRIDE**
Hmmm.

**MAID**
Go on. You can trust me to keep my lips sealed.

**BRIDE**
Well... one night last week, we had the window open to let in some breeze, and with the breeze came the sweetest smell of mogra from somewhere outside. It was already past midnight. I asked him if he would get me some.

**MAID**
After midnight? Oh mama!

**BRIDE**
He got them! He went into town and got me some mogra.

**MAID**
He went downstairs after midnight?

**BRIDE**
No. He said taking the stairs down might wake up his father. So, you know what? He climbed down from the window and disappeared into the night. I dozed off then. He was back after an hour. He climbed in through the window, took out handfuls of mogra from his kurta pockets, and dropped them all around my pillow.

**MAID**
He had his kurta on.

**BRIDE**
And just the other day, when his friends came on their motorbikes and asked him to join them, I overheard them laughing and talking about a shikar. It was getting dark, and I was really worried.

**BRIDE** *(Continuing)*
But I could see that he was not the least bit scared.

**MAID**
And off they went, into the night, not the least bit worried about their lives.

**BRIDE**
I couldn't conceal my worry. I picked up the courage to speak to his father.

**MAID**
You dared to speak to him directly?

**BRIDE**
I had to do it. I couldn't bear the worry.

**MAID**
And he...

**BRIDE**
He laughed it off. He said every now and then there are reports of a sighting, some fresh game prowling somewhere. But why hunt them down,

I asked. And he explained to me then that god created game to be hunted, and god created man to hunt the game.

**MAID** *(Now no more playful)*

The young master is a man. He is a courageous man.

**BRIDE**

Don't you think so? *(Pause)* Don't you think he is courageous?

**MAID**

You could say he is courageous.

**BRIDE**

Why do you say it that way? Of course he is courageous. Of course he is a man.

**MAID**

My people are too humble to know about such things first hand.

**BRIDE**

You are jealous, aren't you?

**MAID** *(Stung, but controlled)*

Jealous? How can that be? We must be grateful to our gods for what he has provided us through our births. You with your gods and I with ours. Just look at your family surname – your father's family, your father-in-law's family. How can you have a husband who is anything less than the most brave, the most manly.

**BRIDE**

I am sorry. I spoke in haste. I was childish.

**MAID**

And for the good deeds my grandparents did, god sent me to this household to serve the sweetest young bride in the land as her personal maid.

**BRIDE**

You flatter me. I should be pleased, but I am not. You sound different somehow. *(Pause. The maid smiles again, takes the last of the flowers, fixes it on the bride, gazes into her face, takes away the 'nazar' on her knuckles and exits quickly. She stops, returns to the bride.)*

**MAID**

The young master is here. Careful what you say to him about our little chat! *(The maid starts to leave. The groom enters before she can leave. She stands with her head bowed. The groom regards the scene, walks in, sits.)*

**GROOM**

Ask her to leave. *(The bride motions to the maid. She exits.)*

**BRIDE**

Is something wrong?

**GROOM**
I want to kill him...

**BRIDE**
You want to...

**GROOM**
I want to kill my father!

**BRIDE** *(Horrified, rushes to him)*
What?!

**GROOM**
I want to kill him! I want to tear him into five thousand pieces and toss them all to the vultures in the maidan. I want to remove every trace of him from this house! I want to kill him! Kill him!! *(He is sobbing convulsively. She cradles him instinctively, stroking him, consoling him.)*

**BRIDE**
There, there, now. You are all right. Everything is all right... I'm here with you... I'm with my man... my brave man... you need a little rest...

## SCENE 5

*The mandap is now the chabootra on the estate. Ratan is training his endurance pigeons, already in flight. He has a pole in his hands with a red rag at the top with which he is guiding the pigeons.*

**RATAN**
Hoorrrr! Hoorrrrr! Hoorrrrrah! Hoi hoi hoi hoi hoi hoorrrrrah! Good going, good show, one more minute for today and you can land! Keep that up, my beauties, keep that up, keep that up, keep that up... hoorrrah! Hoi hoi hoi hoi hoi hoorrrrr! Ahhh... very nice, very nice... I'm so proud of you, my beauties. You make me so proud. Anybody from fifty miles around can look up at the sky and say, 'There! Those are Ratan's pigeons. Ratan's beauties! Top class – best of the best!' All right, all right, you can land now. *(Lowering the pole)* Very good. You've been very good today. There, there, there. Go on, drink up. Easy, easy. Don't drink too fast, not too fast, easy. All right, no more flights today. You can rest now. You've given a first class show. First some rest, then your feed. *(The servant has led the bride up to the chabootra. They watch Ratan as he takes a shallow dish and tosses grain on one side of the chabootra for his prize birds.)*

There – your special treat. Come and take it when you are ready. No hurry. The champions feed! The best for the best!

**SERVANT**
RATAN!

**RATAN**

*(Noticing them, putting the dish away hastily, and bowing in respect to the bride)* You, princess, here? Please, please come. One minute, let me find a mat. These droppings all over the place...

**BRIDE**

It's all right, I'm not here on a picnic. I'll be leaving soon.

**RATAN**

But this is the first time you are coming to the chabootra. I wish, I had known. I don't have anything to offer. *(Goes to fetch water)*

**BRIDE**

It doesn't have to be the last time. I will come again, I can assure you.

**SERVANT**

Our princess has come to see you about the fantail.

**RATAN** *(Offering her a glass of water)*

Here – that's all I can offer you just now. It is so hot. Why did you take the trouble? I could have come down to the haveli any time you called.

**BRIDE**

I believe you have a gift for me.

**SERVANT**

You remember the instructions from...

**RATAN**

Yes, yes, of course. Wait, I'll get it for you. *(He ducks out)*

**SERVANT**

He is a master trainer.

**BRIDE**

I know.

**SERVANT**

He loves his birds more than anything else in his life.

**BRIDE**

And they love him too.

**SERVANT**

People come from miles around to talk to him, to deal with him, also to learn.

**BRIDE**

Have you seen what he has for me?

**RATAN** *(Returning with a white dove in a cage)*

Here, picked specially by me for the princess.

**SERVANT**

It is a fantail.

**BRIDE**
Ohhh! It's so beautiful. Is it a he or a she?

**RATAN**
It is a male.

**BRIDE**
Are you sure? How do you tell?

**RATAN**
Well... this one is male, that is sure.

**SERVANT**
Of course, he is. Look at his head. Do you see the crown? See how proudly he carries himself!

**RATAN**
You should see him when he is showing off before a female. You will see his fantail spread fully then. Royal – like strutting in his own durbar.

**BRIDE**
Just like a peacock.

**RATAN**
Peacocks are ugly! They have no class, only loud colours, and loud behaviour.

**SERVANT**
This fantail is really the best you can get, my princess. He comes from a champion line.

**BRIDE**
Can he fly long distances? Can he fly to my mother's house?

**RATAN**
Unfortunately, no, my princess. Fantails are not performance birds, they are show birds. They win prizes for their good looks and the way they carry themselves.

**BRIDE**
And those that fly?

**SERVANT**
Can you see that group crouched in the shade there? Grey, black, brown, speckled – not much on looks, but great performers in the sky.

**BRIDE**
Which one is your favourite?

**RATAN**
I love them all equally, my princess.

**SERVANT**
As a father loves all his children. Each son with a talent, each daughter with a virtue.

**BRIDE**

What talents are most important for your pigeons?

**RATAN**

Well... First, the stamina.

**SERVANT**

They must fly very long hours, my princess. They can't win prizes hopping from one rooftop to another rooftop.

**RATAN**

Whether it is in circles over the tournament maidan, or racing home from the city, eighty miles away, they need lots of stamina to fly non-stop.

**BRIDE**

What else?

**RATAN**

And bravery.

**BRIDE**

Bravery? What kind of bravery?

**RATAN**

Pigeons are humble birds, my princess. Humble, but clever and devoted to their task. The sky is full of dangerous rogues who don't work so hard themselves, but take advantage of the innocent ones who do.

**SERVANT**

And the most dangerous of those rogues is the pigeon hawk.

**RATAN**

Ai hai, the pigeon hawk. He can appear anytime, without any notice. He shoots down as if from nowhere, like a bolt from the sun, goes straight for the pigeon's heart, scooping out all he can even in flight. The next moment the hollow shell of the poor bird crashes on the ground.

**BRIDE** *(Moved)*

Have you... lost many children?

**RATAN**

A few.

**BRIDE**

You felt sad? You felt a loss? *(Ratan is silent)*

They are so brave.

**SERVANT**

They are, my princess. They don't give up. No pigeon has said, 'Enough, I'm not flying from tomorrow.' One pigeon is killed, three more go up the next day. They fly higher, longer, they don't give up.

**BRIDE** *(Changing)*

It's so nice here – so quiet, such a nice view.

**RATAN**

It is also very hot, my princess. You should be...

**BRIDE**

Nonsense, the heat is not so bad at all. There is enough shade here, and there is also the breeze.

**SERVANT**

Still, the afternoon sun can be...

**BRIDE**

You know, I have never been to a chabootra before?

**RATAN**

You honour me with your visit, my princess.

**BRIDE**

When is the next flight? Can I stay and watch?

**RATAN**

This group has just finished for the day, my princess, but my homing pair should be returning from Kishangarh in about fifteen-twenty minutes. They should be in by half past four at the latest.

**BRIDE**

I'll wait. Is that all right?

**SERVANT**

They will be expecting you to serve tea by five, my princess. We could come another time.

**BRIDE**

I'll tell you what – you go ahead and keep everything ready. I am sure I'll be back well in time for the ceremony of pouring it out into those four cups.

**SERVANT**

But the heat here...

**BRIDE**

Just do what I tell you. I'll be there soon. Go! *(The servant leaves. He is met by the maid below. They exchange notes, then decide to wait there and watch.)*

**BRIDE**

He is very handsome, isn't he?

**RATAN**

Handsome, my princess?

**BRIDE**

The fantail you have presented me.

**RATAN**

Ah, him – yes, yes, he is a true nawab. He has shist.

**BRIDE**

Can I hold him? Can I take him in my hands?

**RATAN**

You can, but I'll advise you not to.

**BRIDE**

Why not?

**RATAN**

You see, this handsome fantail is still the chhote nawab. He is still wild and free. That is why we have him in a cage.

**BRIDE**

We can't keep him in there all the time! I want him strutting about my courtyard.

**RATAN**

And what will keep him rooted to your courtyard, my princess?

**BRIDE**

What? I don't know.

**RATAN**

His own princess! *(The bride giggles)*

I have already selected his bride for him. Lovely young thing, she is from a chabootra of great izzat in Hoshiarpur. We have only to fix the muhurat!

**BRIDE**

I'd like him out of that cage as quickly as possible.

**RATAN**

Very simple. First, we clip his wings.

**BRIDE**

Oh...

**RATAN**

It is painless – like snipping your fingernails. He can strut about as much as he likes, but he can't fly away.

**BRIDE**

And his bride?

**RATAN**

Aha! She, too, will have her wings clipped in exactly the same way.

**BRIDE**

For exactly the same reason...

**RATAN**

Now, with the ceremonies over on the boy's side and the girl's side, we put them together in their... *(Checks himself)*

**BRIDE**

Go ahead, they are birds after all. *(Ratan is embarrassed.)*

We close the doors to the room and wait to see what happens. They fight, they sulk, they attack each other, hurt each other, but in the end... dum dum diga diga! That's the way it ends, right? *(Pause)*

**RATAN**

I hope my princess is not laughing at me.

*(The bride is sincerely sorry, but does not know how to show it. She rises, hesitates, finds the dish with the feed, scatters some of it for a group of pigeons, puts the dish back, and returns to Ratan.)*

**BRIDE**

He is really a handsome fellow, the chhote nawab.

**RATAN**

Once the first pair of eggs arrives, the wings are allowed to grow fully.

**BRIDE**

And they fly freely again?

**RATAN**

Freely, fully, but wild no more. Always on course, they will always return to their own nest. *(Pause)*

**BRIDE**

Can I come up here again?

**RATAN**

Whenever it pleases you, my princess. There is hardly any...

**BRIDE**

I would like to come again. *(Pause, then abruptly)*

I'll come and watch the first flight tomorrow. What time will that be?

**RATAN**

Very early. About seven. But I can wait for you if you...

**BRIDE**

Seven! I'll be here at seven. *(She starts to leave)*

**RATAN**

That's very early in the morning... I can easily...

**BRIDE** *(Off)*

I'll be here seven sharp. Don't start without me. I'll watch them take off. *(Ratan looks after her. He picks up the cage to put it away and speaks mischievously to the bird inside.)*

**RATAN**

You have it all made for yourself, no? *(Fade out mandap area. Spot on the maid and servant. They look at each other.)*

**MAID**

It might work.

**SERVANT**
It might not too.

**MAID**
Only the weak-hearted call a half-full glass half empty. *(Fade out)*

## SCENE 6

*The sitting room area. The father, mother, and groom are seated. The bride is kneeling by the low table pouring tea. It is an elaborate ceremony. There is something special about each person's cup of tea which the bride is maintaining meticulously. Each waits with the cup and saucer in hand for the last to join, which is the bride herself. She picks up her tea and gracefully slides on to her own seat. Pause. They begin to sip their tea in silence. The father finishes, puts his cup and saucer down, pauses, exits. The mother is the next to leave, followed by the groom, leaving the bride all alone, still with her tea. Presently, the sound of music on the 2-in-1 approaches. The servant enters, notices the bride, quickly turns off the music, collects the tea things and leaves. Pause. The bride turns the music on again. After a while, the servant reappears and looks at the machine sheepishly. She smiles her approval. He collects it and exits with the music on. Silence. She is alone.*

*Fade out*

***Intermission here if desired***

## SCENE 7

***Link scene***

*The mandap is now a shrine on a hill. There is a stone tablet that represents a goddess. The maid and the servant approach the shrine. He is carrying a basket, she a handful of flowers. She offers the flowers to the tablet. They prostrate themselves, rise, step back a few paces and stand in silent prayer. She signals to him. He takes out a hen from the basket and gives it to her. She offers it reverentially to the tablet and then holds it on the floor. The servant takes out a chopper and positions himself, hand raised, to strike. If the stage has the luxury of a cyclorama, the performers may consider at least partially silhouetting this scene.*

*Blackout*

*In the dark we hear the thud of the chopper striking. The same raucous tune of the kothi as at the start of the play.*

*Crossfade*

*The groom is with his friends around the woman. He is noticeably quiet. Another of the group is the host this time, and takes the lead in joking and teasing the woman. After a while, the groom slips out. The others notice him leaving but continue with the fun. The music changes to the film song on the 2-in-1, held low.*

*Crossfade*

*The sitting area, dimly lit. The servant is sitting on his haunches next to a chair. The bride is pacing, going through a letter she has just written. She sits, puts finishing touches to the letter, puts it into an envelope, closes it, and moves to the servant. The servant rises, takes the letter and the 2-in-1, and leaves. The bride sits. Silence. Fade in sound of puja bells.*

*Crossfade*

*The mother is seated on the floor in the middle of her puja. She appears distraught, her rituals somewhat excessive. She prostrates herself, rises, stands motionless in prayer, sobs to herself, collects her puja things, and exits.*

*Crossfade*

*The sitting area. The bride is seated alone, stringing a garland of flowers. The groom enters, takes a seat by himself. She watches for a while, then puts the flowers down, goes behind the seat, and begins to gently massage his forehead and temples. He relaxes, submits to her care.*

*Crossfade*

## SCENE 8

*The chabootra. The servant and the maid are looking for Ratan. She has a cloth-wrapped bundle in her hand.*

**SERVANT AND MAID** *(Together)*

>> Ratan!

>> Ratan, where are you?

>> Ratan Bhaiya!

>> Ratan, we must see you...

Etc. *(Ratan appears. He is surprised.)*

**RATAN**

Oh, you. I thought...

**MAID**

Yes? You thought it was somebody else?

**RATAN**

Well, no.

**SERVANT**

You were expecting the little princess maybe?

**RATAN**
Not at all. What do you mean... ?

**SERVANT**
Not at all! What do you mean!

**MAID**
She did say...

**RATAN**
She said what? What did she say?

**MAID**
Look at him blushing like a fourteen-year-old!

**SERVANT**
Arrey bachchu, what can the princess possibly say to us that she hasn't already said to you?

**RATAN**
Will you never stop bullying me? Please don't go on this way.

**SERVANT**
Listen to the boy!

**RATAN**
You're always treating me like... I don't know...

**MAID**
You don't think we treat you seriously enough?

**RATAN**
I don't know. You are so strange at times. I feel very uneasy inside.

**SERVANT**
Poor boy, he is upset.

**RATAN**
There you go again!

**MAID**
We must remember to check ourselves in future. Anyway, the special item at tea today is this shira, laced with badam. *(Taking out a brass container from the cloth)*
She'd like you to have some.

**RATAN**
She sent this for me... ?

**SERVANT**
You think it's for your pigeons?

**MAID**
Just for you. And don't forget the badam. You know what badams are supposed to do to young men!

**SERVANT**
That will do, that will do. If you tease him anymore he will burst pimples all over his face.

**RATAN**
I don't know what to say. Such kindness... I have never received anything like this from...

**SERVANT**
Times change. Even in this country, abandoned by the gods, there can be some change, now and then, believe it or not.

**RATAN**
But I was only doing my job. I just went to the bird market in the shandy and brought her what I was asked to bring.

**SERVANT**
It is not the old zamindari that your father and grandfather served. Times have changed. These people are human. They have human hearts, human feelings. Yes, they lose control of their tongues now and then, but...

**RATAN**
To be hot blooded is nothing wrong. It is their privilege. It is their haqq.

**MAID**
That's right. Who are we to question the privileges of birth? We must be grateful to our own gods that with changing times we have kind masters.

**SERVANT**
And mistresses.

**MAID**
And kind mistresses.

**RATAN**
What will I do with so much shira? You'll share it with me, won't you?

**SERVANT**
And what will we do with all the leftovers in the kitchen? No, just go now and share it with your mother. Tell her where it came from. It will make her happy.

**MAID**
Yes, go home and enjoy the shira with your mother.

**RATAN**
I'll be right back.

**MAID**
No, don't be in a hurry. Take your time. You can even return the dabba to the house directly. You'll have a chance to thank her yourself then.

**RATAN**

I'll do that... but she's coming here in the morning... No, it's better to return the dabba now... it's past four already... She said she'd be here by seven in the morning... All right, I'll go now.

*(Ratan exits hurriedly. Long pause. A change in mood.)*

**SERVANT**

Are you sure you want it this way?

**MAID** *(Softly, firmly)*

Haan.

**SERVANT**

The little princess... ?

**MAID**

It has to be her.

**SERVANT**

She is so young, so innocent.

**MAID**

So was I, so young, innocent, ignorant of the ways of this world – their world. I was simple minded, even foolish, but I was innocent!

**SERVANT**

We've been through this so many times...

*(Lights change. The mandap now appears the modest hutment of a young couple – the maid and the servant.*

*The playing of this scene through the part-dialogue-part-narration is best left to the ingenuity of the actors.)*

**MAID**

I was inside, cooking the evening meal.

**SERVANT** *(At Down-right corner by now)*

I was in the fields, happy that the landlord had taken me for ten whole days even in the lean season.

**MAID**

There was a song in my heart, a tune on my lips.

**SERVANT**

I was packing up, looking forward to your home-cooked meal.

**MAID**

I heard footsteps. The tune on my lips ran faster.

*(A young man enters, pauses before the mandap, takes off his jootis, enters, and draws the curtain.)*

**SERVANT**

I could guess the tune she was humming in the house, in our home.

*(There is a long wail from the maid.)*

**SERVANT** *(Approaching)*

It was a different tune that day. It sounded sad...

*(He sees the curtain drawn and pauses. There is another wail, sad, resigned. The servant rushes to the entrance, stops in his tracks when he sees the pair of jootis, struggles with himself, finally gives in to generations of conditioning, withdraws to a corner, sits on his haunches, and waits. Presently the curtain parts, the young man steps out, slips on his jootis, and strides away. The servant looks away.)*

**SERVANT**

It was a privilege, unquestioned – a haqq. The jootis left outside were a sign that... *(He breaks down and cries. The maid emerges and sits at the edge of the mandap. Lights change to the present.)*

**MAID**

There was nothing you could do. It was all written into our birth.

**SERVANT** *(Rising, moving to her)*

There was nothing either of us could do. It is not given to us to express our anger. We are not allowed to strike back.

**MAID**

We could not strike back then. His family was large and strong.

**SERVANT**

And armed.

**MAID**

The only honourable thing we could do was to run away.

**SERVANT**

The only honourable thing...

**MAID**

But we can strike back now. We could not get at him and his family, but we can get at others just like them – the same class, the same arrogant caste, the same filthy stock.

**SERVANT**

I thought your target was the old master.

**MAID**

I thought so too at one time. In the beginning, I thought we should do something to chop up his loins, so to speak, and hang them up in the mutton market. But he is too much of a fool, and it would be too easy a victory. The old cow is not worth an attack either. And who knows, the seven gods in her puja room may actually jump up and come to her aid.

**SERVANT**

What about the young master?

**MAID**

Not even the young master. Getting him will be too much like a slap for a slap, an eye for an eye. No, not the young master, not the old man, not the old cow, but the little princess! And through her downfall we will witness the downfall of the whole family...

**SERVANT**

It is not going to be easy.

**MAID**

Nothing worthwhile is ever easy. Have you watched the men blasting the hillside at the quarry? If you light a stick of dynamite on the rocks and run, you will get nothing but a loud bang. If you really want to shake up the boulders, you have to first dig a deep hole, plant the stick tightly inside, and then watch the fun with a cool head.

**SERVANT**

You want to get at the whole family?

**MAID**

Through them, their whole rotten race.

**SERVANT**

They say the older son is coming home in a week or two.

**MAID**

The one who went to work in the city?

**SERVANT**

That's the one.

**MAID**

Hai bhagwan! You know what that means for the princess?

**SERVANT**

Of course. He had to give up his share of the land by leaving for the city.

**MAID**

In return... *(A pause)*

**SERVANT**

That's right. He has the right to bhabiji's favours when he visits the estate.

**MAID**

Right! Favours! He can force himself on her and she has to accept it.

**SERVANT**

Khandani izzat!

**MAID**

The whole rotten race!

## SCENE 9

*The sitting area again. The maid and the bride are on the floor with the chart. A séance is on.*

**BRIDE**

And on this side of my life is a young man who is clever, kind, and courageous.

**MAID**

That's right.

**BRIDE**

I am in his power completely? Or is he in my power completely? Or is it a little bit of this and a little bit of that?

**MAID**

Princess, I have to tell you, this person here is not who you think it is.

**BRIDE**

Not who I think? Who do you think I think it is?

**MAID**

It is not our young master. (Pause) It is not him.

**BRIDE**

Then who... ?

**MAID**

I can't say. I don't know.

**BRIDE**

You must know. It must be him. Who else?

**MAID**

The husband's house is this one, in red. The house to which your star is hitched is this one in pink.

**BRIDE**

You are making fun of me again.

**MAID**

A bolt of lightning can turn me into ash this instant.

**BRIDE**

You are telling me...

**MAID**

As if I am telling you something to simply be wicked.

**BRIDE**

There is another person somewhere? Another young, kind, clever...

**MAID**

Something you already know? Deep inside yourself? *(Pause)*

**BRIDE**

You are right. It is another person. My husband, the man I married, is there in the red house. But that is not the real man. It is what he thinks he is – what he pretends to be. The real person is the one here in pink. This is what he really is. Red and pink are quite close to each other really.

**MAID**

But also different.

**BRIDE**

But also close.

**MAID**

Princess, you must know that our young master... *(she checks herself)*

**BRIDE**

Yes?

**MAID**

Nothing. I just thought...

**BRIDE**

Is there something you know that I don't know? Hmmm... There is always room for some bazaar gossip. But then, there could be some things I know that you don't know!

**MAID** *(Trying another tack)*

If one person can be in two houses, is it not possible for two persons to be in one house?

**BRIDE** *(Quickly)*

I am completely devoted to my husband.

**MAID**

I have not said anything about...

**BRIDE**

And a bolt of lightning can turn me into ash if that is not so! *(Pause)*

**MAID**

There is great truth in what you said.

**BRIDE**

In what?

**MAID**

The difference you saw between the man and the person. I mean no offence, but is it not possible that you are devoted to the person and not to the man?

**BRIDE** *(Giggling)*

You mean the man in my heart is actually two persons? A person with two bodies?

**MAID**
Not in that sense...

**BRIDE**
And I can't tell which is which when one of them comes into the house in the evening? *(She laughs)* Imagine being married to one but having two!

**MAID** *(Waiting for her to stop laughing)*
It could happen to anybody. It could happen to you – one princess in the blue house here and another in the purple one – close, but different.

**BRIDE**
You mean I wouldn't know myself...

**MAID** *(Matter of fact)*
Ratan was saying just yesterday...

**BRIDE**
Ratan? You saw him yesterday?

**MAID**
Why, yes. We see him every other day.

**BRIDE**
Why isn't he there when... ? You saw him yesterday? What was it he was saying?

**MAID**
Why isn't he there when?

**BRIDE**
Never mind. What did he say to you yesterday?

**MAID**
You've been there to see him?

**BRIDE**
Yes.

**MAID**
All by yourself?

**BRIDE**
Yes, but he's not been there.

**MAID**
Do they know... about your going up there to see him?

**BRIDE**
No, but it's not as if I'm going...

**MAID**
So it's a little secret.

**BRIDE**
What?

**MAID**

It's something just between the two of us!

**BRIDE**

Of course, that is understood. You would know anyway.

**MAID**

I have known.

**BRIDE**

Oh?

**MAID**

And I can tell you why Ratan was not there. Why he is not there when you have gone up to see him.

**BRIDE**

Why?

**MAID**

Because when you are going up to the chabootra you can't see him from below, but he can see you coming up.

**BRIDE**

Are you saying... ? But how silly! Why should he avoid me like that?

**MAID**

As he was saying just yesterday...

**BRIDE**

I could give him a couple of slaps on those baby-skinned cheeks of his... What was he saying?

**MAID**

He is really a very nice boy, princess. Kind, gentle, a very nice boy. Every young girl in these parts dreams of plucking him off his chabootra and planting him in her own room. I daresay a lot of the older women also have the same dream.

**BRIDE**

I should have thought of it – he is avoiding me!

**MAID**

He was saying...

**BRIDE**

He told you how much he hates me? How he despises people from the haveli coming up to him with their whimsical requests, their spoilt manners?

**MAID**

He was saying how much he loves you... He is devoted to you. He has not known anybody in all his young life who has appealed to something deep inside him. You have done that to him. He thinks you are the freshness of the morning dew on this estate. He thinks you are a goddess.

**BRIDE**
He said all that...

**MAID**
And much more.

**BRIDE**
To you? And he turns his back to me?

**MAID**
Because he is afraid of you.

**BRIDE**
Listen to that! He is afraid of me!

**MAID**
His own words. He is afraid of you, he says, because he sees two persons in you. He hears two persons. He feels two persons in his presence when he is with you.

**BRIDE**
And so he goes into hiding! Bravery is not one of his qualities, surely.

**MAID**
It takes courage to avoid seeing you. *(Pause)*

**BRIDE**
The truth of the matter is I don't know what to do. Maybe it is me that doesn't have the courage.

**MAID**
Courage, princess?

**BRIDE**
To summon him here.

**MAID**
You make it sound as if...

**BRIDE**
Of course, I can summon him here. He is a servant, on the estate staff. All I have to do is ask to see him.

**MAID**
Of course – he is nothing but a servant.

**BRIDE**
I don't know what to do!

**MAID**
Perhaps I could...

**BRIDE**
I must talk to grandmother!

**MAID**
Now?

**BRIDE**

Yes, now. I must ask her how to get a mule to grace one's courtyard with his presence.

**MAID**

A stallion in disguise.

**BRIDE**

A mule who thinks he is a stallion in disguise.

*(She is all set for another session. She closes her eyes and concentrates on the ring. It starts to move. Slow fade out.)*

## SCENE 10

*The same area. The bride is in the same position but without the maid and the chart paraphernalia. The bride has her eyes closed and is miming the movement of the ring on the chart, smiling and humming to herself. The mother enters.*

**MOTHER**

Ah, you are in.

**BRIDE** *(Snapping out, rising)*

Oh, I didn't know... Please forgive me...

**MOTHER**

What were you doing all by yourself? I thought I heard your voice and peeped in.

**BRIDE**

Just now? Oh, nothing, I was just...

**MOTHER**

You looked as if you were practicing a bhajan or something like that.

**BRIDE**

It was something like that.

**MOTHER**

For the festival the day after?

**BRIDE**

Day after? Yes, for that, too. Also for my own practice.

**MOTHER**

I wanted to ask you...

**BRIDE**

Yes?

**MOTHER**

Did you write a letter to your people last week?

**BRIDE**
Did I? I don't remember.

**MOTHER**
I happened to see it. I called that idiot servant of ours when I saw him going out. I wanted some candles for the house, so I called him. And he had a letter of yours.

**BRIDE**
Last week? Oh, yes, I did write to my mother last week.

**MOTHER**
Haven't I told you not to write to your people without letting me know?

**BRIDE**
Yes, you have. I'm sorry, I forgot.

**MOTHER**
All I want to do is include some haldi-kumkum in the cover from our puja here. You can remember that much, can't you?

**BRIDE**
Yes. I'll remember.

**MOTHER**
Nobody is saying you shouldn't write, you understand.

**BRIDE**
I was only saying that there is still so much to see, so much happening here, so many people to get to know – I get carried away.

**MOTHER**
Yes, it is a large estate.

**BRIDE**
I was wondering, could I ask my mother to come and spend some time here.

**MOTHER**
Your mother?

**BRIDE**
I want to share all this excitement with her. Just a short stay, please. She'll be no trouble at all.

**MOTHER**
Not just now. When the time comes. When you give us news that can justify her visiting us.

**BRIDE**
Oh, but...

**MOTHER**
And leave such invitations to us. Don't you go writing directly with such suggestions.

**BRIDE**
I can swear to you that I have never mentioned a visit in any of my letters to her.

**MOTHER**
There are customs to be followed.

**BRIDE**
I understand.

**MOTHER**
Another thing. Why don't you show your face in the kitchen more often? Nobody expects you to do the cooking yourself. Thank god we still have somebody to do that. But it's important to be simply present there now and then. It is part of the haveli discipline.

**BRIDE**
But I do spend quite a bit of...

**MOTHER**
Not when it is important. You are not there before the morning cooking starts and before the evening cooking.

**BRIDE**
I'm in the house. It is just that...

**MOTHER**
It's just that you are not seen more often in the places you should be seen. I'm not saying anything about where you are at those times or any other time.

**BRIDE**
I will be careful.

**MOTHER**
Nobody is saying you shouldn't go out, you understand. You should thank god we are not so old fashioned in this house.

**BRIDE**
But I am quite happy staying here and working and looking after things.

**MOTHER**
Just some control, some limits. That's all I'm saying.

**BRIDE**
I am sorry if I have been careless.

**MOTHER**
You will remember?

**BRIDE**
I will remember.

**MOTHER**
You promise?

**BRIDE**
I promise. I swear by my mother that...

**MOTHER**
No need for all that. Your promise will do.

**BRIDE**
You can be sure... *(The maid enters hurriedly)*

**MAID**
It is all set... *(She stops)*

**MOTHER**
What is this intrusion?

**MAID**
I beg to be...

**MOTHER**
What is that in your hand?

**MAID**
This?

**MOTHER**
What is all set?

**MAID**
Oh, her oil massage. Today is the day. And this is just a letter.

**MOTHER**
What? Another letter? Did we not just agree that... ? Here, give that to me.

**MAID**
Begging your pardon, but this is not a letter from the princess to anybody. It is from me – from me to my little brother in the city. She just gave me a cover to post it in.

**MOTHER**
Oh, I see. It looked like hers, so I thought... All right, you go on with your work.

*(To bride)* And remember the things we've talked about.

*(To maid)* Another thing. Have you lost the simple decency of knocking on the door? Bursting in like an escaped lunatic!

**MAID**
A hundred apologies. *(The mother exits. The maid continues to speak after her.)*

It will not happen again. It was a lapse, I didn't know what I was doing, it will not happen again. I will not utter another falsehood, ever. I will not claim a letter as mine when it is actually from the princess.

**BRIDE** *(Grateful and gleeful)*

That was wicked!

**MAID** *(Continuing)*

I will stay clear of all wickedness.

**BRIDE**

But sweet. It was sweet the way you stepped in. Clever too.

**MAID**

I will not fix an oil massage and hot water bath for her when she should actually be rapped on her pretty little bottom for her mischief.

**BRIDE**

All right, all right, you've made your point. Uff! How you go on!

**MAID**

The heavens must understand that I am doing all this only because I have been commanded to do so by the owner of the pretty little bottom.

**BRIDE**

The heavens must understand that I am doing this only because that truant upstart must be taught a lesson.

**MAID**

You must act quickly.

**BRIDE**

What happened? Tell me what happened?

**MAID**

What else could happen? I showed him your letter.

**BRIDE**

You gave it to him?

**MAID**

I gave it to him. He looked at it. He gave it back to me. He can't read.

**BRIDE**

He can't?

**MAID**

Neither can I. I can only write. I write letters to my little brother in the city.

**BRIDE**

I'm sorry, I was not making fun.

**MAID**

So he asked me to read it out to him. I did.

**BRIDE**
You did?

**MAID**
I put on a good show. I read, 'My grandmother orders you to appear before her. Time – sunset, this evening. Place – her granddaughter's courtyard. Confirm attendance through bearer.'

**BRIDE**
Did he get the joke? Did you explain?

**MAID**
No, he did not get the joke. No, I did not get it either.

**BRIDE**
Oh...

**MAID**
He can't write. So he sent a token of his confirmation instead.

**BRIDE**
Yes?

**MAID**
This fine specimen of a wing tip.
*(She produces a long, slender, white feather.)* It is from the fantail.

**BRIDE**
Sweet! At least he listened to you.

**MAID**
He had two conditions.

**BRIDE**
Conditions? Who is he to make conditions?

**MAID**
One. He will not enter the house. The meeting with your grandmother cannot be in the courtyard. He is willing to meet her on the steps to the outhouse. Two. He will not meet your grandmother alone. He insists that I must be there.

**BRIDE**
This is the confirmation my trusted maid brings me!

**MAID**
There must be a way for you to be there, and yet not be there.

**BRIDE**
I have to first find a way for you to be there and yet not be there!

**MAID**
The same thing.

**BRIDE**

Here, give me your odhni! I'll just go out there now, and sit down with my head covered. He will never know. And when he is near enough, I will give him the tongue lashing of his life. *(She tries on the exchanged cloth)*

How does this look?

**MAID**

Who is this creature before me with the head of a crow and the body of a golden oriole?

**BRIDE**

And the tail of a scorpion! Come on, I must hurry!

**MAID**

Why shouldn't it work? Go ahead! Give it a try. *(The bride starts to leave.)*

Wait! Don't give yourself away too quickly. Let him talk. You may even be able to make him come in – to meet your grandmother in the courtyard. Go now!

*(The maid watches the bride exit. She wears the exchanged odhni, slowly, delicately. The servant enters quietly, goes up to her.)*

**SERVANT**

Do you think it will work?

**MAID**

Why shouldn't it work?

**SERVANT**

He is stubborn.

**MAID**

She is crafty. She may even succeed in bringing him in.

**SERVANT**

Shall I go ahead with the trap?

**MAID**

Not yet. There is no hurry.

**SERVANT**

You may miss the chance.

**MAID**

He will come again. Don't you worry. Let them have their little fight this time.

**SERVANT**

He will come again?

**MAID**

And then again and again. Just let them be by themselves this time.

*(The servant exits. She continues playing with the odhni.)*

## SCENE 11

*The same area. The maid is in the same position, but has slipped into a slow, sensuous, dance step using the odhni to effect. She finishes coyly on the floor. Unseen by her, the father has entered and is watching her from a corner. He is dressed for an outing, carrying an ornate stick. He claps three times, slowly, in appreciation.*

**MAID** *(Trying to rise)*

Huzoor!

**FATHER** *(Sharply)*

No! Stay right there.

*(He takes his time walking up to her, circling her, taking a seat, and thinking of his next moves. The maid's helplessness in explaining the situation only emboldens him further.)*

Very pretty! Where did you pick up such a fine length of cloth? I thought only your little mistress had pieces like that. Quite a contrast, is there not, between the upper half and the lower half? *(He plays with the edge of her skirt with his cane.)*

The top is really just the tip perhaps? Hmmm? Are there other things, kept hidden somewhere? Hmmm? Come on, there is no need to feel so bad – nothing to be ashamed of. Who doesn't want a few good things in life? And you are not committing any great crime, you are not hatching a devilish plot or anything.

Now... you could do with a new skirt perhaps – one that is a better match for that fine odhni. And a satin mushroo choli that shows off the fine shape that rests above the skirt. A pair of silver anklets below... a matching choker around that slender neck... Under the dirt, there is quite a beautiful creature there, I think. Hmmm? Yes, just a few touches here and there and you could pass off for a princess. Here, let me help you up. *(He extends his hand. She takes it hesitantly and rises.)*

Come and sit here. It is all right, you can. I say so. Or are you accustomed to doing things only on an order? It would be sensible to make only a token start today. We can build on it in good time later. Do you agree?

*(What happens next is best left to the ingenuity of the players, determined partly by the set and props used. The essential features of the scene, to be taken through to the end of the play, would be as follows:*

*The Father forces himself on the Maid.*

*The Maid submits, but not without some resistance.*

*She clings to the odhni, which is visible over the Father, while she herself is not.*

*There is little or no dialogue now onwards as the scene gallops to its climax.*

*There is a parallel scene at the Mandap as described below.*

*Crossfade*

*The mandap as the old watchtower. Early morning. The hijra leader is talking to his group. He is telling them the story that unfolds below in an under-lit parallel scene. The narration and the action keeping pace suitably.)*

**LEADER**

The whole world knows what happened next. The young husband entered the room just then. Blinded by rage, he rushed forward to rescue the girl pinned under the father. Like an old lion putting an impertinent little cub in his place, the father swatted the boy to one side. But this cub was full grown now. He attacked. Of course there was a scuffle. A token fight. In no time at all, the boy had the upper hand. In no time at all, the boy had the roar of the victor on his lips and the blood of the vanquished on his hands. The maid, in a state of shock, was a speechless witness to all that had happened – and all that was to follow.

The young master, crazed with anger, moments ago, was now dazed with the sudden realisation of the smell of death. He rushed out. The choked cry for help from the maid seemed to follow him out of the room.

The cry succeeded in bringing the servant into the room. Horrified with what he saw and unable to get anything more from the maid, he drew close to the undignified heap on the floor that was once his imperious master.

The strained disbelief did not hold. It was surely him. And he was surely dead. How taut the pair of eyes were in death! How limp the neck!

By then the old man's spirit must have wafted through all the corridors of the haveli raising the expected alarm. From one side came the old mistress, the one who they say knows all but says nothing. From the other side came the young mistress, the one they call the little princess, and with her, the keeper of the estate kabootarkhana, who was at that time summoned to the house, they say, for some errands.

Poor old woman. She was sobbing quite unconvincingly that he must not be dead. With the servant practically astride the corpse of her departed, she could only reach one conclusion. It was the servant! The verdict ringing in her mind reached the kabootarwallah in a flash. He moved like the pigeon hawk he had watched and dreaded and hated, but held in awe all his life. A combination of birth and training is what does it, they say. In half a wink of the eye, he was at the servant's throat, nineteen years of the gentle exterior scraped bare in one stroke, the mere look in his mistress' eyes.

The young master returned, his head clearer now, but hung in shame. Did they all cry? Did they wail, beat their breasts? Nobody knows. What is known is that the young man would have no cover up. It was not the servant who did it, he said. It was not Ratan's fault, he said.

*(Slow fade out of lower scene through this.)*

**LEADER** *(Continuing)*

The entire responsibility was his, he insisted. They must have tried to make him see another truth, another reason. But he insisted. His voice prevailed over the others. What more is there to say? Two men died in the haveli in that evening. Two others were taken away the same night to be investigated for who they were, what they did, and what should be done with them. There are three women left there now. If only people would take a little trouble to sweep their courtyard once in a while. *(Pause)* Time to move on. Another three weddings in town tomorrow...

*They troop off*
*Blackout*

## SCENE 12

*The lights appear in the lower area to reveal the maid, the bride, and the mother in a huddle. Their faces are not seen. They are joined by the group of girls. A larger huddle, a canopy of odhnis again, but in mourning.*

*Presently the lights come up on the mandap again. It is now a funeral site. There is already a collection of firewood for the pyre. One lone attendant, the ELDER, is slowly, methodically, placing additional pieces of wood in place. Other appurtenances of an imminent funeral are seen.*

*The young girls leave the group slowly. The three women remain. Slow fade out of the mandap area. Tightened lighting on the huddle of three women.*

*Slow fade out*
***Close of play***

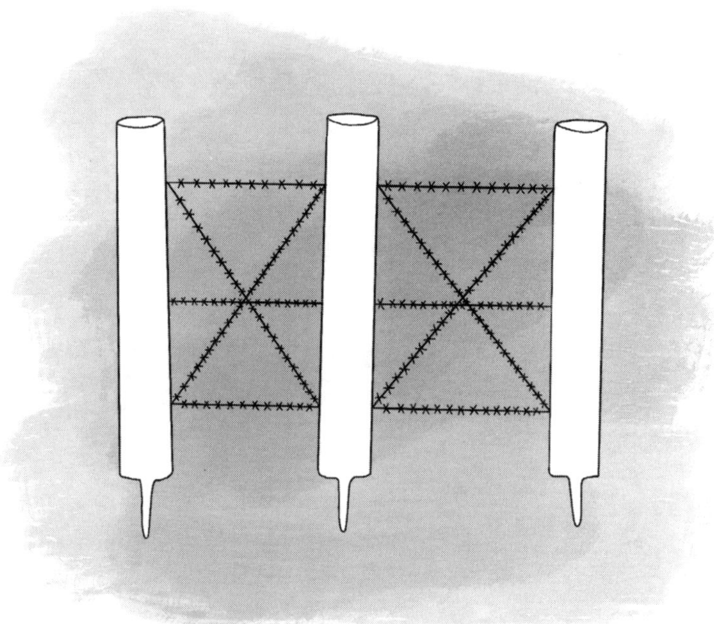

# In Transit

## Unspoken & Untitled

*A double bill by the undaunted*
***Vijay Padaki***

FOR

**S PARASURAMAN**

## INTRODUCTION

What started as ideas for a trilogy, expanded into a set of five plays. All of them are presented in this volume, although not a trilogy anymore. What do we call it then? *A Trilogy of Five Plays?* Or *Buy Three, Take Two Free?* The first two plays are grouped together as a double bill and called In Transit. The two plays are within an hour each in duration. The remaining three plays, too, are of roughly the same duration. While this volume recommends *In Transit* as a double bill, a performing group may choose any two for a double bill. The plays can also be performed as single bills if there is limited time.

The 'trilogy of five plays' may be seen as the sociology of the city, especially the underbelly, uncovering the usually unseen occupations that remain integral to the economy of the city. The set was originally titled *Tales from the City*. All the tales have an inescapable tragic quality about them. Denial of the tragedy itself appeared to be a characteristic of the city.

In the late 'nineties and early 'noughties', my work took me into the realm of Corporate Social Performance. This required moving away from the sentiment of social responsibility to emphasising the assessment of actual performance in contributing to social development goals. *Social Audit* emerged as the buzzword.

The globalisation process had set in. Western markets were ready to outsource the production activities for many goods to the developing countries with far lower manufacturing costs. However, there was a social audit requirement in the outsourcing contracts. Specialist intermediary agencies would ensure compliance of the suppliers to the social audit yardsticks set up by the Western buyers – labour conditions, environment protection, raw materials used, and so on. Child labour was a key concern among Western buyers. Major international brands had to satisfy their customers (in the Western markets) that the goods being purchased were 'safe'. Of course a few big brands continued with unacceptable practices at the source by fudging the social audits. Some of these were exposed. The practice was continued by others.

Our team in Bangalore was invited to prepare the position paper on Corporate Social Performance for Indian business and industry. It was followed by invitations for developing appropriate methods and tools for Social Audit. It was in this period that we saw the harsh reality of compromises to be able to retain the Western buyers. One particularly tragic case was the complete ban on child labour in the vibrant garment industry of Bangladesh. Almost overnight the country had child prostitution with the displaced girls. This, indeed, forms the backdrop to the first play *Unspoken*.

Over the next few years we saw how much of the 'liberated economy' of developing countries had compromises in so many different ways, with the concept of 'development' itself being largely forgotten.

The characters in the two plays of In Transit are a mix from the city and rural or small town settings. If performed as a double bill, the same actors can play the parts in both plays.

# UNSPOKEN

A commonly explored (and much exploited) subject on stage is prostitution. It is often romanticised as the world's oldest profession. We have even learned to laugh at the business of prostitution with finely scripted comedies. Alas, for every one *Irma la Douce*, there are a million untold tales of horrific exploitation, craftily maintained by well-organized human trafficking networks that are, in effect, run as business empires. The stakes are high, the business models ruthless.

The content of the play is fictional, but is derived from the field experiences of development agencies and case studies of real situations and events. The exact location of the villages in which the recruitment takes place is not mentioned, nor should it be necessary. For the purpose of focus, the city in question is shown as Madras (Chennai), but the play can be located in any other city with suitable changes in the script.

Human trafficking, with particular reference to trafficking for prostitution, can easily be recognised as a widespread South Asian phenomenon. The unholy 'golden' triangle comprising Bangladesh, Nepal, and India is well studied and documented. (So is a 'triangle' further East with villages in the north of Thailand as the suppliers.) While it is important to have facts, figures, data, and analyses to come to grips with the subject, it can too easily remain in the realm of academic kicks. Even a 'case study' can often provide a voyeuristic satisfaction, rather than an empathetic bind to the living tragedy. Coming to think about it, a play script may also end up with the same shortcoming.

Perhaps one way to cross over from academics to the real world is to get a glimpse of the violence that remains central to the system. The play would be incomplete without the violence. Yet, it is the writer's earnest advice to the performing group to capture the menacing quality of the ever-present, deeply pervasive violence, rather than be over-concerned about playing a 'violence scene' with great dramatic effect.

The play explores the tragedy of Chinku, a real person in a real trap in a real trafficking system, although with a fictitious name in the play. It must be evident to any performing group that Chinku is part of a brothel system that is part of a syndicate system that is part of a trafficking system that is part of a demand-supply system that is part of.... Where does one stop? Where does one begin?

There are four main action areas in the play:

- The front of a humble home in a village – perhaps Down-right;
- A contact point under a street lamp with a pavement – perhaps Up-centre;
- A meeting point in the city – perhaps Down-left;
- A neutral space for multiple uses – perhaps Centre and Down-centre.

The meeting point in the city should be fine with just a small table and four chairs or two chairs and a small bench. It is, in fact, the ubiquitous *kirana* shop with a chai service in front.

The performing group can decide what combination of sets and props to deploy for the locations and scenes in the play.

The village in the 'North' is not named. The performing group can locate the village as it chooses. Costumes for the women must be designed suitably.

## Language Notes

*Jibba:* South Indian name for kurta.
*Mashi:* Maternal aunt – used as suffix.
*Bada:* Big, big time.
*Ambassador:* Brand name of a car, old model, roomy.
*Khadi:* Fabric from home spun yarn – associated with politicians.
*Puja:* Ritual worship – eg in consecration or invocation.
*Bindi:* Vermillion or sticker worn on the forehead by women.
*Malli-poo:* Jasmine flowers.
*Ghazal:* North Indian musical form sung in light classical style.
*Mollagatanni:* Literally pepper water – Anglicised as Mulligatawny soup.
*Mastan:* Dream guy, hero, stud.

## CHARACTERS IN THE PLAY

JAGGA ........................................ *A pimp with a prostitution syndicate. Always dressed in a jibba and lungi, with a length of cloth around his neck that serves multiple purposes – a neck wrap, a waistband, a head dress. It is a red jibba while on duty. Minds his business, does his job.*

RAGS .................................... *A college student on a journey of discovery. He is not called by his real name by anybody at any time through the play.*

MAMA ........................................... *A middle-aged woman in a village, homemaker, devoted mother of two daughters, Chinku and Nimi, working single-mindedly for a good life for them.*

NIMI .......................................... *In her teens, growing up in the village, learning all the things good girls in the village must learn.*

PIPU .................................... *Nimi's fast friend and constant companion.*

JI-MASHI .............................. *Mama's older sister, a widow, worldly-wise, feet on the ground, but with her heart in the village and an abiding faith in humankind.*

CHAKRA ......................................... *A jobber, sourcing crafts from the villages and finding employment for girls in the city. He wears city clothes, a denim jacket, a checked shirt, sneakers, and a baseball cap.*

CHINKU ...................................................... *Once a worker in a garment factory, she is now trapped in a prostitution and trafficking business. She is beautiful and in great demand, but has lost her speech.*

WOMAN ......................... *Proprietress of a kirana tea shop that serves as a contact point and transit house for the trafficking. She is heavily built, street smart, vocal, and knows her business.*

MAN ............................................... *A go-between serving the head of a prostitution-trafficking syndicate and keeping tab on the brothels. He is powerfully built and wears a safari suit and dark glasses.*

INSPECTOR ........................ *A police inspector who has ended up serving a syndicate in a given beat in the city. He wears a motorcycle helmet. Flabby.*

CANDIDATE .................................. *A young woman being considered for placement by the syndicate.*

TWO MEN .......................................................... *Hired goons.*

VOICES ......................... *Four men and two women over the house system.*

Note: Two men actors can play the parts of Man, Inspector, and the two hired goons. At a pinch, the woman actor playing Pipu may also play the Candidate, but never facing the audience while playing the Candidate.

## SCENE 1

*Night. In the dark we hear the sound of a speeding train in the distance.*

*If the performance space has a cyclorama, there are city lights in the distance, fading out. The sound of the train lap dissolves to the soulful rendering of a folk tune on a single-stringed instrument.*

*Fade out.*

*The lone street light comes on Up-centre. The street is empty.*

*We hear voices of two men over the house system. Voice 2 is Rags.*

**VOICE 1**

Go past the chai shop. About fifty meters down the road there's a turning to the right. It is a dark lane. You will see a lone street lamp further down.

**VOICE 2**

Any other landmark?

**VOICE 1**

The street lamp is the landmark – has been since god knows when. He'll be there under the lamp post – in a red shirt.

*(Jagga, the pimp, enters and positions himself at the lamp post, cigarette in hand. He is in a red shirt or jibba, with a length of cloth around his neck that serves multiple purposes.)*

**VOICE 2**

What colour pants?

**VOICE 1**

Can't say, not important. Could be lungi, could be pants. The red jibba, that's the only thing. It can be a red shirt.

**VOICE 2**

His name?

**VOICE 1**

Don't make the mistake of asking him. He will think you are from the police. End of show. It can turn nasty if he doesn't like your face.

*(Rags enters and does what the voices are saying.)*

**VOICE 2**

Do I go up to him, or will he come to me?

**VOICE 1**

It's your first time. He will want you to go up to him. Don't look at him. Walk past him and stop. He will cough. Just nod your head once and leave the rest to him.

**VOICE 2**

You think I can do this?

**VOICE 1**

Of course you can. Go there and find out what you are made of! I will wait for you in the car here.

**VOICE 2**

Where will he take me?

**VOICE 1**

Go there and find out. One more thing. Don't ever walk next to him. You must always remain a few meters behind.

*(Jagga and Rags meet under the lamp post. Jagga puts out his cigarette and stores the leftover in an empty matchbox. He leads Rags away into the dark.)*

## SCENE 2

*Day time. The village home Down-right. The sound of a van offstage, drawing to a halt, horn tooting. Cheerful voices of girls, excited, the van horn tooting in response. MAMA comes out of the house and looks about.*

**MAMA**

What's all the screaming about? You'd think the travelling cinema was here. Or is it those wandering magicians with the dancing bears?

*(Raising her voice)* Oi! What's going on there?

*(Ji-mashi, Mama's older sister, comes out of the house and joins her.)*

**JI-MASHI**

There's only one kind of visitor that gets that reception.

**MAMA**

You mean... ?

**JI-MASHI**

It must be the agent from the city!

**MAMA**

Oh my, oh my! And here I am in these rags. I must get some tea going. Do we have something to eat in there? Some biscuits at least? Just look at my hair! *(She rushes in.)*

**JI-MASHI**

Look at her! She's more excited than the girls!

*(Calling after her)* You think the agent is here to see you?!

*(Two young girls enter excitedly, leading Chakra. The girls are, Mama's daughter, Nimi, and her best friend, Pipu. Nimi shouts to the other girls offstage.)*

**NIMI** *(To friends off)*

We'll see you at the school house! That's where he said the meeting will be!

**PIPU**

Go tell your parents! Don't be late!

**NIMI**

Bring all the bags and scarves you have made. Get them all!

**PIPU**

Don't forget the embroidery. They like the embroidery!

**JI-MASHI**

Well, well, well, if it isn't our good friend, Chakra, from the city! Welcome, welcome! You come alone?

**CHAKRA**

Alone this time, yes. We have spread out. Twelve villages to cover in two days.

**JI-MASHI**

Business doing well, I suppose. Chinku has been sending money regularly – one packet, full of notes, every month. How is she?

**CHAKRA**

She is fine. She is fine. Yes, business is good. Lots of demand.

**JI-MASHI**

They are setting up new factories every day I hear. When will we get to see her? It has been – what – three years since she left the village.

**CHAKRA**

She will come. She will come. *(Mama has come out by now. She has tidied herself up and is carrying a carpet.)*

**MAMA**

Why are you standing there like that? Like buyers in the cattle fair! Here, sit down and stretch your legs a bit. I have put the kettle on. It will take a few minutes. You were talking about Chinku? We want to see her!

**JI-MASHI**

I suppose they want more girls for the new factories. How many this time?

**CHAKRA**

New factories, yes. But you see...

**MAMA**

That can come later. Tell me about Chinku first. How is she doing? Where is she now? What work have they given her in the new factory? When will we get to see her?

**NIMI**

You should have brought her with you! *(A pause. Chakra looks at the two girls and then at Ji-mashi.)*

**CHAKRA** *(To the girls)*
I have to discuss some money matters with them. Why don't you go ahead to the schoolhouse? I will see you all there.

**JI-MASHI**
Yes, get along now. Gather all the girls. We'll be there soon.
*(The girls leave, not without some disappointment. A long pause.)*

**JI-MASHI**
Is something wrong?

**CHAKRA**
Chinku... She is not at the factory any more.

**MAMA**
Not at that factory, but another one. Also making shirts and pants?

**CHAKRA**
No other factory, no garments, no shirts and pants anymore.

**MAMA**
What do you mean... ? She can't be without a job. You promised us when you took her away...

**JI-MASHI**
Hush... Calm down now. Chinku is fine, I am sure. Let him explain. *(To Chakra)* Go on Chakra.

**CHAKRA**
It was not just Chinku. All the girls in the factory had to be turned out.

**MAMA**
Turned out? What does that mean? Turned out for what? Did they do something bad? Chinku is a good girl, you know.

**CHAKRA**
They had to go. It was no fault of theirs. They had to go because they were not old enough. That's what they were told.

**MAMA**
Not old enough?

**CHAKRA**
A white man came, one day, to the factory. He brought a government officer with him, an inspector, or something like that. They asked the factory office to show them all kinds of books and registers. They were not satisfied. The girls were not old enough, they said.

**JI-MASHI**
But there must be hundreds of factories in the city – thousands of girls there...

**CHAKRA**
All in the same trouble. Deep shit trouble.

**MAMA**

Not old enough! My Chinku, not old enough! What do they mean by that? What do the white men know about girls being old enough or not?!

**JI-MASHI**

What happened then?

**CHAKRA**

The government man said the factory had to close. The white man said he would not buy the garments until the factory had older girls. The factory owner turned out the girls to save the business, closed the factory for thirty days, and started again with a lorry-load of new girls.

**JI-MASHI**

All those girls turned out... Where are they now?

**CHAKRA**

They are still in the city, most of them. They have other jobs. Doing fine. The white men showed them a way out.

**MAMA**

I know that. My Chinku is still sending me money every month.

**JI-MASHI**

They have other jobs... And you are still taking girls to the city...

**CHAKRA**

There are other jobs. They love girls from your village.

## SCENE 3

*Night. The lone street light Up-centre. Jagga is standing under the light. Rags enters and goes up to Jagga, who greets him with a nod. He leads Rags across the stage to Down-left, dimly lit, takes a seat, and then nods to Rags to also sit. He offers a cigarette to Rags, who declines. He then takes out a lighter and the leftover from the empty matchbox, and lights up.*

**JAGGA**

Imported. The man left in a hurry, left the packet behind. Idiot. *(Pause)*

Costly bloody cigarette. Can't get it easily here. *(Pause)*

Same girl? Third time in a week... She's good, na? Tight above, tight below. Huh. She can take and she can give. She's good, what do you say? *(Pause)*

All right, you don't have to tell me. I'm not really interested. *(Pause)*

You're not getting into some love-shove business are you? Huh.

Still in college, na? Getting buggered in the hostel, I am sure. You'll grow up. *(Pause)*

She is doing a good job, na?

It's her job. She must give everybody going there a good time.

The one going in before you, the one going in after you. *(Pause)*
All right, you have to pay more today.
Ohh, the saheb is surprised. What did you think, you get a discount or something? Monthly pass? Listen to me. You are taking more time each time.
Don't think I have not noticed. I don't mind you taking two shots, but you have to pay more. You pay for the quality, saheb. *(Jagga rises and leads Rags to a dimly-lit tight spot Down-centre, where a girl is seated on a carpet with two cushions. Stage space permitting there can be a divan or narrow single bed seen behind the carpet. Jagga speaks as he enters.)*

**JAGGA**
Rise when you have a visitor. Do you have to be told each time?
*(She does)* Ohh, she has her embroidered skirt on today, what do you say?
Here, your special visitor. Huh. Take good care of him.
*(He taps his wrist watch)* I will be keeping time. *(Jagga exits. A long pause. Rags and the girl rush into an embrace. She starts to undress. Rags stops her.)*

**RAGS**
No! Wait... No, no need to... Let's just sit down and talk... *(She sits. Rags sits next to her and takes her hand. She watches Rags in fascination, never speaking.)*

**RAGS**
We must talk. All right? What can I say to you to make you talk? I want to do so much for you, I really want to. I don't even know your name.
They call you Queenie. That can't be your name. It sounds horrible.
I can't call you Queenie. Maybe Rani. Do you like that? Rani?
Can I call you Rani? Will you be my Rani? You are beautiful, Rani.
You have beautiful hands, such a lovely, beautiful face. I can see a beautiful person behind that face. How did this happen to you?
You are not from here. Where did you come from? Where is your home?
How can I help you? I wish you'd speak to me.
Oh god, oh god, oh god! How did I get into this? How can I help this girl?

## SCENE 4

*Early morning. Chai shop Down-left. It is closed. Jagga enters, knocks on the side of the shop, and takes his place at the table.*

*A large Woman enters with a kettle and a glass tumbler, half filled with tea. She keeps them on the table and waits. Jagga takes his time savouring a sip or two.*

**WOMAN**
Well? *(No response)*

You are late by over a week now. Where do I hide her? How do I feed her? Why should I be doing this?

**JAGGA**

I need some more time.

**WOMAN**

You said that the last time. Every day she is kept idle, she is a loss for you, a loss for me. A burden.

**JAGGA**

As if I don't know that.

**WOMAN**

As if you don't know what?! You know the people who delivered her here? They are after me. They want the full payment by tomorrow. Or else!

**JAGGA**

Look, I can't take this girl till we sell off the one we have.

**WOMAN**

Then why don't you? It's four months now. Time for her to go. All your customers must have had enough of her by now.

**JAGGA**

It's not easy

**WOMAN**

What's the problem? No buyers, huh? Something the matter with her?

**JAGGA**

No, no problem with her. Actually the problem is that she is in great demand. Everybody wants her. Sometimes they have to wait in a line.

**WOMAN**

Well, she has to go. Everybody has to go when their time is up.

**JAGGA**

No, it's too early to get rid of her.

**WOMAN**

And how long should I hang on to this one? You've seen her. She is top class. From the same villages in the North. Great body. They will go crazy over her.

**JAGGA**

Give me some time!

**WOMAN**

I can't wait forever. The people from across the Ring Road are already making a big offer for her.

**JAGGA**

You can't treat me like this!

**WOMAN**
I can't?

**JAGGA**
We've been doing business for over ten years. Have I ever let you down?

**WOMAN**
What do I have against you? Nothing. Tell that boss man of yours that his time is running out.

**JAGGA**
He knows.

**WOMAN**
Meet him today. Go to his air-conditioned cabin above the Tours and Travels office and tell him. He can't keep the whole supply line blocked.

**JAGGA**
Why can't your boss man talk to my boss man?

**WOMAN**
Not funny. Bad joke. You want the mongoose to talk to the cobra! Next you'll want the bosses of the boss men to talk to each other. Two ministers discussing our traffic jam over samosa and chai. It's your job to talk to your boss. Tell him his pimp is getting into trouble.

**JAGGA**
Don't call me a pimp!

**WOMAN**
Ha! What should I call you then? You think you are some suit-boot type or what? You want to be called a Sales Manager?

**JAGGA**
I just do my job – an honest job. The boss trusts me. You always trusted me. Nothing's changed.

**WOMAN**
Just make the payment and take her away.

**JAGGA**
I will have the money for this one soon.

**WOMAN**
How soon?

**JAGGA**
As soon as we sell off the other.

**WOMAN**
All right. One more chance. But you will have to give me another advance.

**JAGGA**
I think I can manage that.

**WOMAN**
Show me the money.

## SCENE 5

*Night. The street lamp Up-centre. A Police Inspector in his motorcycle helmet walks up to the lamp post and waits. Jagga arrives and goes up to the Inspector. He takes out a large bulging envelope and gives it to the Inspector, who pockets it casually, unhurriedly. He walks away, leaving Jagga there.*

*The Inspector crosses over to the shop Down-left, where the Man is seated. The Inspector takes out the envelope, hands it over to the Man, and exits.*

*The Man rises to leave. A window in the shop front opens. A hand is extended with another bulging envelope. The Man takes the envelope. The window closes. The Man exits.*

## SCENE 6

*Day time. Mama, Ji-mashi, and Chakra in front of the village home. Chakra has his head down. A long pause. Mama rises to rush into the house. Ji-mashi holds her back.*

**JI-MASHI**
Wait! Sit down! Running away never helps.
*(Mama returns and sits. Ji-mashi comforts her.)*

**MAMA**
My Chinku!

**JI-MASHI**
When did you see her last?

**CHAKRA**
I have not seen her myself, I am not allowed.

**MAMA**
Have you spoken to her? On the phone? *(A pause. Chakra looks away.)* When did you last speak to her?

**CHAKRA**
I have not spoken to her. She... She will not speak to me.

**MAMA**
She will speak to you if she knows it is you.

**CHAKRA**
She does not speak to anybody.

**JI-MASHI**
She...

**CHAKRA**
She has stopped speaking. She is silent, she speaks to nobody. But I know she is well. She is in a good shop, small, but good name. Good customers, educated people, not street rowdies.

**JI-MASHI**
At least she is not beaten and treated like an animal.

**CHAKRA**
No, no, she is fine. They look after her well.

**MAMA**
She is fine! One day she makes clothes for the whole world. Next day she takes off her clothes for the whole world!

**JI-MASHI**
Mama! It is not the end of the world!

**MAMA**
The girls from this village – what are they famous for? Tell me! The whole world knows their cleverness in embroidery, their laces, their skirts, their head scarves, their waist bands. Our beautiful girls! What are they going to be famous for now?

**JI-MASHI**
Their beauty. We should be proud of that.

**MAMA**
You are saying this?! How can you know what our Chinku is going through?

**JI-MASHI**
I should know.

*(Chakra tries to excuse himself. Ji-mashi motions to him to stay back.)*

No need! There is nothing to hide. As if you don't know already. *(Pause)* This is really for Mama. Listen carefully, sister. You know the world outside our village only from what you hear about it. You have not been there yourself. People like to call it a jungle. That is true, it is a jungle, a dangerous place. But some people find food and shelter in the jungle and survive. They learn to prosper with a new challenge thrown at them every day. There are others, weak in the knees, who only find wild animals in every path they take. They suffer. They are bitter all the time, not ever knowing that they have only themselves to blame for their suffering. *(Pause)*

I should know. I ran away from the village. I was missing for eleven years, remember? It was before the factories came up. I ran away from a village that had turned into a cruel jungle – the drunken husband, the beating every night, working my bones eighteen hours a day to clear his debts with the arrack shop. He died finally, crashing his bicycle against a bullock cart, his head split open outside, his liver bursting inside him. Even his blood smelt of arrack they said. It took two whole days to do something with his body, they said.

I returned after he died. Nobody asked where I had been or what I had done for eleven whole years. *(Mama begins to weep uncontrollably. Ji-mashi comforts her, holding her close. Chakra watches helplessly.)*

Sister, dear, dear sister... I promise, I will never leave you all again. I didn't do enough for you earlier. I will make up for it now. We must not lose heart. Chinku will be all right, take my word for it. She is a clever girl. She is a good girl. *(There are cries from the girls off stage.)*

>> Chakra! We are ready!

>> There are eighteen girls at the school house!

>> They have brought their best pieces of embroidery!

Etc. *(Mama rises and rushes into the house. Ji-Mashi and Chakra remain, looking at each other.)*

## SCENE 7

*Night. Spot Down-centre on Chinku and Rags. He appears agitated, rising and sitting frequently. Chinku remains seated. She is fully with Rags, nodding, smiling, but does not speak.*

**RAGS**

I think I will come another three to four times. Just to give him more confidence. He is looking a bit friendly already. He doesn't wait on the stool outside that lorry shed. He goes to the chai shop for half an hour and then comes to see me off. Another three to four times before we move. Maybe five.

You will remember the details? All the steps? Let's go through it once today.

First, the time. It has to be in the morning, and after an evening when I have not come here. He will not make the connection then. It has to be after nine in the morning. Between nine and nine-fifteen. That's when the office going traffic is high. Also, he will not be up by then. The others are used to seeing you step outside to get the milk and vegetables, so everything looks as usual.

Carry as much cash as you like, but no bag or bundle. Nothing in your hands.

You will watch from the bus stop. When you see the others leave to do the washing, you will get on to the bus that goes to Egmore station. The ten o'clock express to Trichy will be on the platform. Don't get into the ladies compartment. It will be easy to find you. Take the general compartment.

Get off at Rock Fort Junction. Once outside, look for a tea shop on the right. I will be there. I will have a taxi ready.

I think the best thing to do is to go South. Not back to your village. Not just now. They will think you have fled North and rush to Central Station. We will wait in Trichy for two or three months till they have given up. I have good friends in Trichy, they will make all the arrangements. Then I will take you to Bangalore to a good hospital.

We will go through this again next time. We have time to work on it some more.

Now... If only I could get you to speak... If only I knew your name...

**CHINKU** *(Struggling)*

Rra... Rraa...

**RAGS** *(Stunned, going up to her)*

You... You can speak! Oh god, oh god! She can speak! What are you trying to tell me?

**CHINKU**

Rraa...

## SCENE 8

*Evening. Table Down-left. The Man in the safari suit is seated with a Young Woman, well dressed, made up. He sits still, looking at her. She is slightly nervous.*

*The Woman from the earlier scene appears with a tray, which has a half bottle of whisky, an opened bottle of soda, a glass with ice cubes, and a saucer of pakodas. She sets the tray down on the table and takes a good look at the young woman.*

**WOMAN**

What will the princess have?

**MAN**

Chai, I think.

**WOMAN** *(To Young Woman)*

I take your order from him?

**MAN**

Yes, you do. Chai.

**WOMAN**

Have it your way.

*(Calling off)* One special chai!

Cup and saucer or regular? We have Chinese tea things, you know.

*(To Young Woman)* It will take a few minutes. Fresh batch being put on.

He doesn't have to wait for your chai to come. *(He doesn't)*
All that is only in the big hotels.
*(To the man)* So... What are you looking for?

**MAN**
Up market. No cheap service station.

**WOMAN** *(To Young Woman)*
He will do all the talking. You see what it's going to be like?

**MAN**
A hotel job should be all right? Lots of new spas coming up.

**WOMAN**
What about training?

**MAN**
She is trained. Same people.

**WOMAN**
Red or white?

**MAN**
Who cares? As long as there is good work for her.

**WOMAN**
Maybe she has a choice?

**MAN**
She can have an opinion. The choice is not hers.

**WOMAN** *(To Young Woman)*
There are two kinds of spas. In one, the girls wear red miniskirts. Everything happens right there. Everybody knows. In the other kind, they wear white coats over their dresses. There is a madam at the front desk, also in a white coat. It's all white-white drama in front. It turns out red in the end anyway. You pay double for the drama. So, what are you good at?
*(The Young Woman blushes.)*
*(To Man)* Look at her blushing! They'll love her! You will have to decide. Quick. Red or white? We have to make arrangements.

**MAN**
I think red.

**WOMAN**
I think white. Small numbers and large packets is any day better than large numbers and small packets. She is delicate in looks. That is a major attraction for those people. She will be a killer in a white coat.

**MAN**
You can try her out.

**WOMAN**
She should get to know the red anyway – part of the training.

*(To Young Woman)* You should see the men, I mean. They come in all shapes and sizes. Knobby knees, pot bellies, gunny-sack chests, drooping tits and all. Not to mention the overpowering foul breath, stained teeth, hairy ears... Wait till you see our police inspector coming for his weekly ration. But they expect a Miss India in bed. Not everybody is a mastan like this one here.

**MAN**

Right, let's get down to business.

**WOMAN**

Yes, it's white for her.

*(To Young Woman)* You will like it there. Easy work, good pay. The people who come there drive fancy cars, drink only foreign whisky, work out in gyms, paying through their nose, but that's all. They come there because they are losers. They are losers in their own bedrooms, so they create a dream world for themselves in the little dark room of the spa.

**MAN**

She is trained.

**WOMAN**

She will have to be retrained for the white coat. The village people teach all the wrong things. They don't know. It's all changed in the city now. The people in that village, it's gone to their heads, they think they are some kind of experts.

**MAN**

She is not from there.

**WOMAN**

No?

**MAN**

She is from further West, about fifty miles.

**WOMAN**

Supply dried up or what?

**MAN**

No, not at all. There are any number waiting to be brought to the city.

**WOMAN**

Why the change, then?

**MAN**

Good to have a second line. A little competition is always good. Keeps the prices in control.

**WOMAN**

She is good, but we have to work on her. Also, we will do something about those boobs. One day at the clinic and about five-six days at home. It will cost a little more than the last one.

*(Continuing, to Young Woman)* Your training is meant to get a man to believe that he is a man. The people here have problems being men. They need help. You need lots of patience with them. They are not real people, they don't live real lives.

**MAN**

They pay well.

**WOMAN**

They need you. You will be doing a great service to them. Maybe that's why they want to see you in a white coat. All right, they pay well too.

**MAN**

When can you take her?

**WOMAN**

The supply side is becoming a problem. They keep bringing girls from the North and dumping them here. Finding places for them takes time.

**MAN**

Give me a date.

**WOMAN**

I will call you tomorrow. Can you keep her with you till then?

**MAN**

All right, but no more than two nights. You have to act fast. The boss has a special interest in her.

**WOMAN**

I will need an advance.

**MAN**

It is possible. I will arrange it.

**WOMAN**

All right, you can leave her here tonight. I will inspect her and tell you all that has to be done by noon tomorrow.

**MAN**

You have room?

**WOMAN**

Yes, I have room now. Thank god. I got fed up waiting for the last one to be taken away. I finally found another place for her.

*(Continuing, to Young Woman)* Go in and wait. I will join you. You can get your chai inside. *(The Young Woman leaves.)*

*(To Man)* Tell him I will pay tomorrow. Tell him I will deduct the advance from the payment. Fair and square.

*(The Man pats the woman on the cheek and leaves. The Woman clears the table humming a tune to herself. As she is about to leave, Chakra enters. He goes up to her and holds out his hand.)*

## SCENE 9

*Dark stage. Loud pulsating disco music accompanied by flashing lights. If there is a cyclorama, it can be put to good use in the scene.*

*After a while, the sound and the lights begin to fade out, lap dissolved with the same music coming from a portable player. The disco lights are replaced with two flashlights, switched on and off, keeping time to the music.*

*We see the dimly-lit figure of Ji-mashi, flashlights in her two hands, swaying to the music herself. In front of her are two make-shift poles for dancing, with Nimi and Pipu at them, barely visible. They are attractive, skimpily clad, and are struggling with the dance. Ji-mashi is instructing them over the music.*

### JI-MASHI

Your legs, your legs... They are not moving enough... Free your legs, loosen them up... The legs should move the rest of your body, not the other way about... Don't try too hard to wriggle your boobs, you overdo it... You will look silly... Cheap... You want them to imagine what's in there... Too much wriggling shows what's not in there... Use your legs, it works much better... They may talk about boobs all the time, hundreds of jokes, but what really gets them going are your legs... You can have so-so boobs and great legs, you are a winner... Great boobs and skinny legs, you are nowhere... Right, move your legs, move your legs... That's better, move them, move them... Hug the pole, you're a snake, a snake... That's the way, that's the way... Keep that up, keep that up...

Nice... Very nice... You are doing fine... That will do for today... Bring it to a close... Done!

Take a break now. Clear up. We meet in front of the hut in fifteen minutes.

*(Fade out. The girls shift the poles and put on wrap-around skirts.)*

## SCENE 10

*Day time. The village home. Ji-mashi is seated with Nimi and Pipu. Mama is standing and watching. Ji-mashi speaks with great poise.*

### JI-MASHI

All right, it is almost time for you to leave. Another week and Chakra will be here. You are ready for the city. You have worked hard, you have been good learners. You are good. You heard what I said?

*(The girls smile. So does Mama.)*

You are good. But... There is a long way to go. The real journey begins next week. There is only that much you can get from me. The rest will come from practice. And experience. You will learn something new every day. You will understand why it is important to never stop learning. Just as no two men are the same, no two relationships are the same. You must make every man believe he is different, special. He must go back with a new faith in himself.

Remember that every relationship is important. It is always a give and take. Never forget that. He has something to give, something you want. You have something he wants. Give and take in all relationships. It has to be. In all jobs, all professions. It is what makes your job respectable.

Oh yes, there are men who don't see this. But they will, if you hold your ground. It is up to us – up to you – to make them see. Don't ever throw yourself away. Give respect, demand respect. Hold your head high, always. Never stoop. A smile looks brighter when the head is held high.

Remember your home and your village with pride. There are villages famous for their potatoes and their corn and their chickens. We can do better than that.

*(A long pause. The girls are not sure she has finished. Nimi raises her hand.)*

**JI-MASHI**

Yes.

**NIMI**

Can we take our embroidery with us?

**JI-MASHI**

I think so. We will ask Chakra when he gets here.

**MAMA**

Of course you can! You must.

**JI-MASHI**

Still – we will ask Chakra.

**PIPU**

I did a skirt for Nimi. Can't she take it with her?

**JI-MASHI**

All right. We'll find a way.

**MAMA**

What about you, Pipu? What do you want to take with you?

**NIMI**

I did a hand bag for her!

**PIPU**

I'd like to take the bag.

**JI-MASHI**

You will both have things to remind you of each other.

**NIMI**

As if we can ever forget!

**PIPU**

Chakra said we may be at the same place – or at least close to each other.

**JI-MASHI**

If you are not, you should not let that bother you. Chakra may have no way of making sure you are together.

**NIMI**

Will you come and visit us?

**MAMA**

We would like to...

**JI-MASHI**

But we may not be able to. Now, if there are no more questions, you could go inside and help Mama with her evening cooking.

**MAMA**

I have something special for you girls today!

**JI-MASHI**

All right, class dismissed. Off you go. And spend some time with your other friends before you leave home.

*(Nimi and Pipu go into the house. Mama and Ji-mashi remain outside.)*

**MAMA**

You brought tears to my eyes. You are so good with them.

**JI-MASHI**

They are so good with me.

**MAMA**

All that you said to them... I never knew... I had not seen things that way.

**JI-MASHI**

Neither had I.

**MAMA**

You were so good.

**JI-MASHI**

I did what little I could, standing on the shore. They will be thrown into the river now. They will learn to swim by themselves.

## SCENE 11

*The lone street light comes on Up-centre. The street is empty.*
*We hear whispered voices of a woman and a man over the house system.*

**VOICE 1 (WOMAN)**

The street lamp is the contact point. It is some kind of standard practice in every part of the city.

**VOICE 2 (MAN)**

The street is deserted. I see only the lamp post.

**VOICE 1**

Check the camera. It will be any minute now. You can start rolling when you see a man in a red shirt go to the lamp post.

**VOICE 2**

Who is handling the second camera?

**VOICE 1**

Veena and her boyfriend. All set in front of the tea shop.

**VOICE 2**

You will take care of messaging them when it starts?

**VOICE 1**

I will do that. The meeting is supposed to take place here first. They will go to the tea shop from here.

**VOICE 2**

I see somebody coming. I think it's him. *(Jagga enters and positions himself at the lamp post, cigarette in hand. Presently the Man and the Woman enter from opposite sides and meet Jagga. There is a brief exchange that we do not hear. The Man takes out a plastic pouch and gives it to the Woman.)*

**VOICE 2**

What is he giving her? Money?

**VOICE 1**

Nah! The daily fix for the girls.

**VOICE 2**

They are on drugs?

**VOICE 1**

You could say that. It's Dex... Dexamethasone... They all call it Dex

**VOICE 2**

What does it do?

**VOICE 1**

It's a steroid, meant to give them an appetite. They put on weight rapidly. Makes them look bigger, older. What the customers want. Not the malnourished teenagers they really are.

**VOICE 2**

Is it... safe?

**VOICE 1**

Dangerous... our staff are trying to educate them... it doesn't work. Women like her will beat them into taking the tablets.

**VOICE 2**

The man there – he gets it for them?

**VOICE 1**

From across the border. Costs five to six times more over the counter.

**VOICE 2**

Make them look bigger... hell!

**VOICE 1**

In Europe the drug is used to fatten cattle and pigs for the meat market.

*(The Woman walks away, and the Man and Jagga move in another direction together. The street is empty once again.)*

**VOICE 1**

Got them?

**VOICE 2**

Yes! There are shadows over their eyes because of the lamp above, but their meeting is all there.

**VOICE 1**

Doesn't matter. We have the basics.

*(Crossfade to Down-left, empty, dimly lit. We hear a pair of whispered voices over the house system, another woman, and a man.)*

**VOICE 1 (WOMAN)**

Stand by. They are on their way.

**VOICE 2 (MAN)**

Standing by. Just for you!

**VOICE 1**

You are sweet! You can't imagine how important this is to us.

**VOICE 2**

I can, I can. I got sucked into this, na?

**VOICE 1**

We can move a case only when we have a proper lead.

**VOICE 2**

Super sucker, that's me.

**VOICE 1**

This can be the breakthrough.

**VOICE 2**

We are shooting men. How does that help? Where are all the girls?

**VOICE 1**

Shhh! I think that's them. Ready to roll? *(Jagga and the Man enter and sit across the table. We do not hear their exchange.)*

**VOICE 2**

You think the girls are in the tea shop?

**VOICE 1**

Of course not. They are spread all over the place.

**VOICE 2**

What do you think they are talking about?

**VOICE 1**

You can guess what – there is a bada political rally next week.

**VOICE 2**

They have to be entertained!

**VOICE 1**

What else! Mr Safari Suit is given the job of organising a party for the rally.

**VOICE 2**

I get it. The girls will have to be brought in from different places by Mr Red Shirt there.

**VOICE 1**

The venue, the venue – that's what we've got to find out.

**VOICE 2**

You think they are deciding that now?

**VOICE 1**

We have a tip off. It could be a farm house owned by a businessman close to the minister. Wait... They are leaving...

*(Jagga and the Man rise and leave. The Down-left area is empty once again.)*

**VOICE 2**

You think they'll go to the farm house now?

**VOICE 1**

Can't say. Have you got it all?

**VOICE 2**

I think so. But it's only the two men.

**VOICE 1**

Good. We wait a couple of minutes and then call the car.

**VOICE 2**

If you ask me, you'll have a solid case only when you catch them with their pants down. You've got to get them with the girls.

## SCENE 12

*Night. Jagga is with Chinku.*

**JAGGA**

Get ready in ten minutes. We are going for a ride. That fellow from near the airport, he always wants it in his car. Maybe that's why he still keeps his Ambassador. Same car, same parking spot, under the tamarind tree. I will be on the scooter behind. As usual.

Not much traffic nowadays, na? Hardly two to three a day. Not even that college boy hero of yours. He has not come this week – third day today. Otherwise eight o'clock sharp and he is here, like a dog at feeding time. Eight sharp. Maybe he had enough. He must have found another one that side of the railway line.

Anyway, he is not the only one who has stopped coming. It is time for you to move on. We have to think of another place for you.

I have found a good place. Nice people, good place. They were renovating the rooms two weeks ago. It is ready now. They want to have a puja there tomorrow evening. We will go. You will come with me. If everything is ready, you can even shift tomorrow.

Don't look so frightened. They are good people. I chose the place for you myself. I will take you there. You have been good for us. But now you have to go. *(The sound of a car horn off.)*

He is early, the son of a pig! Can't wait. Get ready quick. I will keep him engaged for some time.

Ay! Don't worry. Everything will be all right. *(He starts to leave.)*

I will be thinking of you after you go.

*(He leaves. Chinku is frozen.)*

## SCENE 13

*Day time. The tea shop Down-left. The Police Inspector is seated with the Woman across the table. The Woman is speaking on a mobile phone, occasionally looking at the Inspector.*

**WOMAN**

Thursday... I have it straight from the station itself... About ten at night... They will come in two jeeps, about eight-ten men. There will be one woman constable and one woman inspector. As usual... Send the girls out by nine-thirty to be on the safe side. Send them to Appu's garage, off Highway 6... Let them be there all night. They can come back in the morning... I don't care about the khadi kurta people. I want the girls safe.

Of course we have to take care of him... No, no packet-wacket. He wants the usual... He is sitting right here, he is laughing... No hurry. Just make sure it is as soon as possible.

One more thing. When the police party comes for the raid, they will bring... Exactly! She will be there in one of the jeeps, her moon-sized bindi and the malli-poo bun... What else? She has no idea herself. She has filed the FIR thinking she is doing god's work... You know who is behind it!

The bastard is trying to wipe us out of business... We will deal with him later. Right now, we must deal with goddess Amma... Tell the boys to make some good biriyani – veggie only... And arrange some ghazal-wazal and put pictures from the Tours and Travels office on the wall... Not the Khajuraho one... Keep a big pot of mollagatanni soup at the entrance.

Tell the boys to be very, very polite... Ask Amma to come in... Be nice to her. Ask her to come again... Yes, he says you can call him if there is any trouble.

She disconnects. The Inspector motions to the Woman to make another call. She dials and tries to give the phone to the Inspector. He motions again.

**WOMAN**

Sir... It is done.

*(The Inspector signals that she may serve him now. The Woman gives the Inspector the phone and goes inside.*

*The Inspector lights up. He takes a drag or two.*

*Jaaga enters anxiously, goes up to the Inspector and whispers in his ear. The two leave quickly.*

*The Woman enters with the whisky service as before, finds the table empty.)*

## SCENE 14

*Day time. The sound of a van pulling up in the distance and toots of the horn, lap dissolved with the soulful rendering of a folk tune on a single-stringed instrument.*

*The Village farewell.*

*Chakra has entered and is standing by, while the two girls are with Mama and Ji-mashi at the home Down-right. The two girls have bags packed and ready. Food parcels and a basket of fruit are added to them by Mama.*

*The scene is without words except at the end. The scene is short but played unhurriedly, a poignant mix of sadness and joy.*

*The performing group can improvise to include the appropriate expression of love, affection, and warmth in the village community, and add rituals of a parting from a humble home. There is no wailing.*

*At last... The girls are ready to leave for the city with Chakra.*

**JI-MASHI** *(To Chakra)*

It is a long journey. Make sure they eat on the way. Drive carefully.

**MAMA**

Chinku can come back now. Tell her, I am waiting.

## SCENE 15

*In the dark we hear the sound of a speeding train in the distance.*
*Early morning, the sunlight slanting into the stage.*
*Music from a temple nearby.*
*The tea shop Down-left. Rags is seated, waiting.*

*The scene below is described for its bare essentials. The performing group is free to play it any way it wishes. The only advice to the group would be: Capture the pervasiveness of violence in the system, rather than the sensational in this one scene.*

» *Jagga enters from Right, dragging Chinku,*

» *Chinku is in her embroidered skirt. Her wrists are bound behind her.*

» *Jagga has changed his jibba. His face is covered, revealing only his eyes, but the length of cloth is the same.*

» *He stops and allows Rags to take in the scene.*

» *Rags moves instinctively to rescue Chinku.*

» *Jagga reveals a knife – halting Rags in his tracks.*

» *Rags tries to escape – finds two men blocking the path. They have their faces covered too. They have spars of wood in their hands.*

» *Rags is helpless. The two men close in on him.*

» *In a desperate bid, Rags tries to attack Jagga. One of the two men grabs him and throws him on the floor.*

**RAGS** *(Wildly)*

RANI !!! *(Jagga drags Chinku closer to Rags.)*

**JAGGA**

The Rani can watch as her Raja collects his tax.

» *The two men beat up Rags, attacking savagely.*

» *They finish and leave him in a heap.*

» *Jagga pushes Chinku against the table.*

**JAGGA**

As for you... You will never want to undress for a man ever again!

*(He raises her skirt and slashes her thigh with the knife. Chinku collapses at the foot of the table.*
*The three men stand still.*
*Fade out)*

## SCENE 16

*The village home Down-right. Mama and Ji-mashi are seated attending to a daily chore. The sound of a van offstage, drawing to a halt, horn tooting. Cheerful voices of girls, excited, the van horn tooting in response.*

*Mama and Ji-mashi look up expectantly. Chakra enters and stays at the edge.*

*All three freeze.*

*Crossfade.*

*Night. The street lamp Up-centre. The Police Inspector walks up to the lamp post. Jagga arrives, goes up to the Inspector. He takes out a large bulging envelope and gives it to the Inspector, who pockets it and walks away, leaving Jagga there.*

*Crossfade.*

*The Inspector crosses over to Down-left, where the Man is seated. The Inspector takes out the envelope, hands it over to the Man, and exits.*

*Blackout.*

***Close of play***

# UNTITLED

The transgender person has both a biological identity and a social identity. While the biological seeks definitions in fine sub-categories, the social identity is largely omnibus, and mostly unhelpful. The identities in India have no exact match in the modern Western taxonomy of gender and sexual orientation, and are often at variance from Western ideas of sex and gender.

In India, some transgender groups do not define themselves by specific sexual orientation, but rather by renouncing sexuality altogether. Sexual energy is often sublimated into roles with sacred associations. However, these notions can be contradictory in the everyday needs of survival. They often dress as women and act in a feminine manner in public spaces, even using feminine language to refer to themselves and each other. While there is inevitably a great deal of confusion about identity (accompanied by conflict) in the formative years, the transgender person arrives at a balance for oneself sooner or later.

The Indian parliament passed a bill supported by all political parties to ensure transgender people get benefits akin to other communities eligible for affirmative action privileges. In the implementation of the bill, all States are required to take steps to see that they get enrolment in schools and jobs in government institutions, besides protection from sexual harassment. While there are success stories of transgenders reported from here and there, it is clear that social prejudice and stigma will continue to come in the way for a very long time.

This play examines the complexity of the issue. It is the story of a success, against all odds, of Indira alias Indranil. It is also a story that ends in an almost predictable tragedy. On the other hand, the fate of Yamuna, the mother, can too easily be stereotyped. It should be entirely possible for her to be also seen as one requiring sympathy – first not wanting a child, then finding it is a girl child, and then finding that she is not really a girl.

## CHARACTERS IN THE PLAY

INDRANI .................... *Brown skinned, good looking, always well dressed, usually in a sari, but may also be in clothes viewed traditionally as women's wear. She always wears make-up, but never too heavy. She carries herself well, which is a part of her attractiveness. Her voice is in the lower register, a contralto, and her speech is pleasant sounding. She sings flawlessly.*

INDRANIL ............... *This part is played by the same actor playing Indrani. He is always in well-pressed, light-coloured, full-sleeved shirts and elegant trousers, with socks and shoes. He wears an elegant pair of spectacles.*

VOLUNTEER ......................... *A survey research interviewer engaged in door-to-door studies. The first time it is connected with a forthcoming election. The part is played preferably by a woman, but it can be a man.*

YAMUNA ................................. *A woman in her early fifties. Although from a conventional lower-middle-class upbringing, she has settled into a nuclear family with her husband and is determined to live her own life. She is mostly expressionless, perhaps emotionless. She displays a non-sentimental, assertive, and no-nonsense approach to life, which includes the relationship with her husband.*

NANDAN ........... *Yamuna's husband, about the same age as Yamuna or two years older. Also from a lower-middle-class family. In contrast to Yamuna, he is outgoing and talks more, but is a simpleton, naïve on many counts.*

YAMUNA 2 ................................................... *Twenty years younger. It is recommended that the same actor play both the Yamunas.*

NANDAN 2 ................................................... *Twenty years younger. It is recommended that the same actor play both the Nandans.*

BITTU ........................................ *A little girl, about ten years old. The young Indrani. She speaks little, mostly in single words. She is pretty, dressed simply, and is clean and neat. She has an enquiring look on her face.*

MONA ................................. *A seasoned sex worker, who later becomes a madam, shifting to another city. She brings up the abandoned Bittu.*

CLIENT ........................................... *Mona's client, a truck driver*

CLIENT 2 .............. *Mona's client in her new location. Well-dressed, middle-aged, appears well-off. May be played by the same actor as the first Client.*

MAMMA .............................. *A social worker and activist lawyer in her late forties. She has adopted Bittu, now Indrani, abandoned as dead twenty years ago. She has not gone through the due process of adoption, believing strongly that it was her moral duty to bring up Indrani as her own child.*

JUDGE ............................................ *Senior judiciary, in his fifties. Well-informed, sympathetic to genuine social causes.*

TWO POLICEMEN

MEN ON THE STREET

## FIRST PERFORMED

By Bangalore Little Theatre at Alliance Francaise, October 2015

*Indrani/Indranil* .................... APARNA NORI
*Volunteer* .................... POOJA SHANKAR OR SHIBANI RAO
*Mamma* .................... ARCHANA KARIAPPA
*Yamuna* .................... ARCHANA MITTAL
*Mona* .................... SHATARUPA BHATTACHARYYA
*Nandan* .................... MOHAN RAM
*Bittu* .................... SUCHISMITA ROY
*Judge* .................... VIJAY SHANKAR OR MANOSH SENGUPTA
*Ensemble* .................... ADITYE NAIR, VIVEK PUNJABI, ANIRUDH ACHARYA

*Assistant Director* .................... ANJANA APPANNA
*Stage Manager* .................... SANDEEP JAIN
*Communication* .................... POORNIMA KANNAN
*Music design* .................... TEJAS SHANKAR
*Sound design* .................... CHRIS AVINASH
*Light design* .................... PRITHAM KUMAR
*Costumes* .................... PRIYA RAO
*Poster design* .................... AKASH
*Ticketing* .................... SUBODHA SUBRAHMANYA
*Backstage team* .................... SHIVANI SHAH, CHITRA

*Directed by* .................... SHASHANK PURUSHOTHAM

*There are three main action areas for the play. The first is the space used by Yamuna and her husband Nandan, and any others in the present. The second is the space used by them and others in the past, about twenty years ago. The third is the space used by Indrani and Mamma, only in the present, distinct from the space for Yamuna and Nandan in the present. There may be a fourth neutral space.*

## SCENE 1

### PROLOGUE

*Optional opener scene with song.*

*A dimly-lit stage with a streak of light. A funeral bier on the ground with the body covered. Two women and two men stand on two sides of the bier. A female voice over the audio system sings a soft, soulful opening ballad, with no accompaniment. The two women and two men carry the body off-stage through the end of the song.*

There's a time to open and a time to close,
A time to open and a time to close,
If you don't know the difference,
You don't know highs from lows.

> There's times when anything goes,
> All those times when anything goes,
> If you want the highs to move in with you,
> Make way for a cart full of lows.

Sing me a lullaby, your teeth shut tight.
Sing it soft, keep it hushed, keep it light.
Shut the windows, keep out the night.
Put those heartstrings out of sight.

> Take me on a train ride, take me far away.
> A night train and a day train, take me far away.
> There's a silver horse in the carnival,
> I am going to ride some day.

Sing me a lullaby, your teeth shut tight.
Sing it soft, keep it hushed, keep it light.
Shut the windows, keep out the night.
Put those heartstrings out of sight.

> There are times to dream and tears to stream.
> You'll find times to dream and tears to stream.
> If you don't know the difference,
> Make way for tears in every dream.

*(The main prologue begins after the optional opener above.*

*A tight spot Down-left, remaining empty. A female voice is heard over the audio system, preferably the same voice that sang the song.)*

**VOICE**

She could not say she was different. It was not the first time a woman had an unwanted child. Not the last either. There is one born every minute somewhere. *(A pause)* There is one brought to life every minute somewhere. *(Pause)* There are three hundred and sixty thousand births every day. That's fifteen thousand new babies off the assembly line every hour. Two hundred and fifty every minute. General Motors and Toyota combined can't match that. Four new units every second. Four every second. *(Pause)* New arrivals, they are called. Two hundred and fifty every minute. *(Pause)* Would it not be a fair guess that at least one of the two hundred and fifty is unwanted? One unwanted every minute? Maybe more? *(Pause)*

Wanted. Unwanted. Is it really like that? Black and white? Go, no go? Or are there shades of wanted? Shades of unwanted? Mostly wanted, mostly unwanted. Partly true, partly untrue. None of the above? Can't say? Couldn't care a damn? *(Pause)* Wanted by whom? Since it takes two to make the baby. Unwanted by whom? *(Pause)* It can't really be like that. Black and white. Go, no go. There have to be shades of... unwanted. *(Pause)*

I will never know. *(Pause)* What was it with my mother? Was I partly unwanted? Mostly unwanted? *(Pause)* I will never know. Never wanted to know. I guess I was totally unwanted.

## SCENE 2

*A house-to-house survey in progress. A volunteer is visiting Yamuna in her home. The volunteer carries a clip board and has a shoulder bag with papers and survey paraphernalia. There is an ID card worn in front. The survey is conducted in a friendly yet business-like manner, entries made through the questions and answers. The volunteer may be either a woman or a man. Yamuna tries to be helpful, but is not enthusiastic about her participation.*

**VOLUNTEER**

Who else lives in this house?

**YAMUNA**

Husband.

**VOLUNTEER**

Anybody else?

**YAMUNA**

No.

**VOLUNTEER**

Nobody else? Only the two of you?

**YAMUNA**
Two of us.

**VOLUNTEER**
How long have you lived in this house?

**YAMUNA**
Ever since...

**VOLUNTEER**
Yes? Ever since... ?

**YAMUNA**
Ever since we left the old house near Cottonpet. About twenty years.

**VOLUNTEER**
Twenty years... Did you have the same address in the last two General elections?

**YAMUNA**
Yes.

**VOLUNTEER**
Did you vote in the last elections? I am not asking who you voted for. But did you cast your vote?

**YAMUNA**
Yes

**VOLUNTEER**
The election before that? Ten years ago?

**YAMUNA**
Yes.

**VOLUNTEER**
Do you have any proof of residence? *(No response)*
Anything to show you live here? Do you have any of these? *(Showing papers)* Electricity bill? Water bill?

**YAMUNA**
Must be somewhere. He will know.

**VOLUNTEER**
Telephone bill?

**YAMUNA**
No phone. Only mobile.

**VOLUNTEER**
Aadhar card?

**YAMUNA**
No.

**VOLUNTEER**
No Aadhar?

**YAMUNA**
No Aadhar.

**VOICE** *(Off stage)*
Applied. Not received till now.

**VOLUNTEER**
That is... ?

**YAMUNA**
Him.

**VOLUNTEER**
He is home?

**YAMUNA**
You heard him. *(Nandan walks in. He has a half-finished tumbler of tea in his hand. He is in home clothes, a lungi, a worn-out, half-sleeved shirt not fully buttoned, revealing a vest and a gold chain. )*

**NANDAN**
Took two months to first find the office. Go to the post office, they said. The post office sent us to a bank. The bank sent us to the Corporation School. They said, no, no, no, not this school, and sent us to another Corporation School. From there, to the Corporation office. It was like chasing a man who has taken your money and is on the run. Finally, we got the man. Standing in three long lines, one after the other, we got the man. He had his cell phone between his head and shoulder and was talking continuously. I saw him finishing five people in the line still talking on the cell phone. Including me. God knows how many more after me. You are... ?

**YAMUNA**
Election next month. Voter list.

**NANDAN**
Haan. Election, election. Will they ask for Aadhar?

**VOLUNTEER**
No, it won't be necessary.

**NANDAN**
Who knows when the card will reach us. Maybe before the next election.

**VOLUNTEER**
I suppose there is a rush for Aadhar cards now, before the election. But it has no connection with the voter registration survey that we are doing.

**NANDAN**
Just checking up, na? Are these people really there? How many people in the house? Children, parents, grandparents, guest-vest – things like that, na?

**VOLUNTEER**

Something like that. I have got everything.

**NANDAN** *(To Yamuna)*

Did you tell her about... ?

**YAMUNA** *(Cutting in)*

No need. Not connected with this work.

**NANDAN**

But still...

**YAMUNA**

You heard. Everything done. You can get back now.

**NANDAN**

Some chai-pani...

*(The volunteer shakes her head to decline. Nandan shrugs and leaves.)*

**YAMUNA**

Problem when you don't have a daytime job anymore.

**VOLUNTEER**

You said he retired a year ago.

**YAMUNA**

After retirement, you don't know what to do with your time.

**NANDAN** *(Off)*

I did not retire. I took voluntary retirement. They paid me well for it.

**YAMUNA**

Yes, yes, it was voluntary retirement. *(To Volunteer)* They made him take it. He was one of nearly two hundred who had to take it.

**VOLUNTEER**

I see. I must take your leave now. Four more streets to do before five o'clock.

**YAMUNA**

So, everything all right, na? We can vote.

**VOLUNTEER**

Yes, everything all right. Only remember to carry your Voter Card. Both of you.

*(The Volunteer leaves. Yamuna sits still a few moments. Nandan peeps in.)*

**NANDAN**

Gone?

**YAMUNA**

Maybe hiding inside the modha mudda there!

**NANDAN** *(Entering)*

Didn't she ask you about children?

**YAMUNA**
She did. I answered.

**NANDAN**
You didn't tell her we had...

**YAMUNA**
Had? Had when? They only want to know about now.

**NANDAN**
Yes, but...

**YAMUNA**
Do-you-have-any-children? Yes. No. The answer is No. Buss.

**NANDAN**
The fact is...

**YAMUNA**
Buss. *(She stares at him. A pause.)*

**NANDAN**
If you say so. But we did have a child once. A girl.

**YAMUNA**
Twenty years ago.

**NANDAN**
Still...

**YAMUNA**
She is no more. It means nothing today.

## SCENE 3

*A tight spot Down-left. Indrani steps into the spot. It is the voice in the prologue.*

**INDRANI**
You cannot say she was different. It was not the first time a woman had an unwanted child killed. Not the last either. Some do it when it is unborn, some after a while. Is there a difference? I don't know. There are people who have views on this question. Killing the unborn, killing after birth. They are called expert views – by people in high places. Mostly men – high priests, high court judges, high flying social workers, people who have not had babies – girl babies.

Do they kill boy babies? Only when they are grown up and fall in love with girls from another caste. Boy babies? I don't know. Boy babies can be unwanted too. Or seen as bad luck. Or a threat. A threat to the family, to the kingdom. They are then sent to the woodcutter for speedy and needful action. The boy survives because woodcutters are gentlemen. They float the baby downstream in a straw basket, which is then picked up by a cowherd or a kindly childless couple who bring up the boy as their own.

Girl babies are not so lucky. If there are fewer women than men all around us, it is because there are fewer girls than boys. And that is because... All around. Punjab and Haryana, about 875 girls to 1000 boys. UP, Gujarat, Maharashtra. All same. China... On par with most of India.

Girl babies are not so lucky. The services of gentlemen woodcutters are not available for them. It is a hands-on job for the mother. She is dumped in a well. Or chopped to fine pieces and buried or placed on a railway track in the dead of night or tossed into a lime pit or mixed with the firewood in a brick kiln. Or simply snuffed out by a pillow and a strong arm.

Putting out the life is not complicated at all. Every civilised society has invented its own one million ways to do it. It is getting rid of the body after death that poses the greatest challenge. This is where our creative energies are most needed.

## SCENE 4

*Twenty years ago. Bittu is by herself, absorbed in a game of Ludo, playing for two persons on her own. Yamuna enters with Nandan. She waits at the edge as Nandan goes up to her with a small stick of chocolate. She accepts it happily and returns to the game.*

**YAMUNA**
Ludo again?

**NANDAN**
Playing by yourself again? You like that, na?

**BITTU**
Yes.

**YAMUNA**
Homework over?

**NANDAN**
She always finishes her homework before play. Don't you, baby?

**BITTU**
Over.

**YAMUNA**
Not going out to play with your friends?

**BITTU**
No.

**NANDAN** *(To Yamuna)*
Let her play the way she wants.

**YAMUNA**
You need at least two to play Ludo.

**BITTU** *(Pointing to the other side)*
Santa.

**NANDAN**
You are playing with Santa? Santa kaun?
*(Bittu has crossed to the other side by now.)*

**BITTU** *(Pointing to the first side)*
Banta.

**NANDAN**
Achcha! You are playing for both Santa and Banta. So, who is winning?

**BITTU**
Both losing.

**YAMUNA**
You can go in now, Bittu. It is almost time for dinner. Go in and wash up. Wash your hands and feet.

**NANDAN**
Or you can go out to your friends for fifteen minutes. Wash up after that. What would you like to do?

**BITTU**
Out. Friends. *(She starts to pack up the Ludo set.)*

**NANDAN**
Theek. Fifteen minutes, okay?

**BITTU**
Okay. *(She rushes out.)*

**NANDAN**
She is growing up so nicely! *(Nandan goes inside.)*

**YAMUNA**
Yes. That is the problem. *(A long pause)*
The whole family must be waiting for the day. The whole neighbourhood. Ta-daa! Bittu is a grown-up girl now!
It is not going to be like that. Bittu will remain... Bittu.

## SCENE 5

*Indrani at Down-left. The tight spot is now expanded to reveal a small desk and an empty chair. Indrani is seated on the other side, talking to the empty chair. She rises and moves about occasionally.*

**INDRANI**

She was growing up so nicely! But she could not be allowed to. Sooner or later, they would find out that Bittu was not a girl. She would not become the grown-up girl they expected her to be.

Bittu knew this as much as her mother. She had stopped playing with the girls in the housing colony, because she could not take part in the games behind closed doors... The game of Show... Doctor-doctor... The oldest girl in the group, just over twelve, had already got her first monsoon, and had shared the secrets of padding up with the others. It was a wondrous new world. The girls couldn't wait for the doors to be opened to them... not without some trembling. *(Pause)*

Not Bittu. She knew it was a No Entry zone for her.

The mother... She had made up her mind long ago. It was unwanted. It was only a matter of when – and how. It could have been eleven years ago, when it was still unborn. It could have been just after the birth, when half the babies die anyway. She went along with it year after year. She knew the right moment would come along. It could be any time.

*(Crossfade to Yamuna. Twenty years ago. She is putting Bittu to sleep, covering her up. Next to her is a small tray with an empty glass.)*

**YAMUNA**

They say that when a woman is with child, the goddess of procreation descends to the earth and blesses the womb of the mother, placing within it a drop of nectar, drawn from the fragrances of twenty-four blooms from all the six seasons. This creates a lifelong bond between her and the child that holds them together through all the trials and ordeals that either of them may encounter at any time, the rest of their lives.

I have to say things like that. The fact is there was never any bond between us. The goddess must have made a mistake with her injection. It was a drop of a concoction drawn from the venoms of the deadliest twelve serpents of this land. I never once knew what a bond must feel like.

*(Through the following passage a man enters covered in a thick sheet or blanket. His head is wrapped with a length of cloth that leaves only his eyes uncovered. He approaches Yamuna and Bittu. Yamuna gestures in Bittu's direction. The man picks up the bundled Bittu gently and walks away, leaving Yamuna alone. She picks up the tray and the empty glass.)*

**YAMUNA** *(Continuing)*

But I was a good mother. The family said so. The neighbours said so. I brought her up with all the care any mother can give a daughter. But the time had come for us to part. It was time for her to go away. It's too bad it had to happen this way... *(A pause)* When Nandan was away. It was best with him away. *(Crossfade to Indrani)*

**INDRANI**

It was best that way. She was not his child anyway. She never let him know. There was no need for him to know. It was – as they say – thrust upon her. Hers was not the first time. Not the last either. When it was announced that she was going to present the family with a baby, she had already resolved firmly... He would never know... it had to go. *(Crossfade to Yamuna.)*

**YAMUNA**

Nobody can say I did not bring up Bittu well. I did everything by the book for her. Right up to her last glass of milk. *(Crossfade to Indrani.)*

**INDRANI**

She brought her up with all the care any mother can give a daughter, the same care with which you sweep and mop the floors and remove cobwebs in the corners of the ceiling. It was a job to be done. And she did it well. *(A pause)*

But the time had come for her to go away. It was a job to be done. And she had prepared well for it. *(A pause)*

But she did not die. Bittu lived. The story of the baby surviving was not the first. It will not be the last. *(Crossfade to Yamuna. She is standing exactly as she was earlier, the tray in one hand, the empty glass in the other.)*

**YAMUNA**

It is done. Tomorrow... I will go to the school at 4 o'clock. I will wait at the gate. I will chat with the girls on their way out. One of them will ask why Bittu didn't come to school today... It will take its course there on... We will send a telegram to Nandan to return immediately. We will book trunk calls...

*(Crossfade to Indrani. The lights expand to reveal a divan next to the desk. Indrani is seated at the desk. She is making entries in a large and thick notebook or diary. Mamma enters. She is carrying a small tray with a glass of milk. She keeps it on the desk, strokes Indrani's back and shoulders, caresses her.)*

**MAMMA**

It is late. Have your milk and go to sleep now.

**INDRANI**

There is work to finish. The case tomorrow is important.

**MAMMA**

I know. But your health is important too. All these late hours at the desk... It's becoming a habit. Not good for you.

**INDRANI**

And from where did I get these bad habits?

*(Mamma keeps the tray down and sits.)*

Who taught me never to put self above duty?

*(Mamma smiles, does not reply.)*

Silence – assent – case rested! Mamma, mamma, you know how important this is. Not just for me. You are part of it too. You are the one who put us on to this in the first place. It is going to be a game changer. It will be the precedence that gets into the law books for future generations to quote.

**MAMMA**

I know, beta. We have waited for this a long time. I never imagined then that you would be into it yourself.

**INDRANI**

Mamma's kid after all!

**MAMMA**

Leading it yourself.

**INDRANI**

Not without you by my side.

**MAMMA**

You were not named Indrani for nothing.

**INDRANI**

The Rani of Indra. With no face of her own! In the shadow of her male god husband. As with all the goddesses.

**MAMMA**

A mind of her own. Unlike other goddesses, she possesses an independent character.

**INDRANI**

Goddess of jealousy and wrath.

**MAMMA**

The goddess to dispel wrath and destroy jealousy.

**INDRANI**

Daughter of a demon.

**MAMMA**

The role model of all later goddesses.

**INDRANI**

Faceless, one among seven matrikas, with no place of her own.

**MAMMA**

Chosen over all others by Indra for her magnetic beauty.

**INDRANI**

The wanderer, the forest dweller.

**MAMMA**

Lions and elephants for companions. The white elephant, her vahana.

**INDRANI**

A white elephant... *(She breaks down, sobs. Mamma consoles her.)*

**MAMMA**

Indrani the strong... Determined... Resilient Indrani... Persevering... Shakti personified... Anointed by Indra himself.

## SCENE 6

*Twenty years ago. A secluded spot outside the city, dimly lit. A man and a woman on the ground. He is working class, a truck driver. She is an experienced sex worker, later known as Mona. Sounds of occasional highway traffic in the distance. She is faking an orgasm. It stops. The client buttons up (or covers up, if in a lungi) and rolls over. She sits up, tidies up. The following passage may be in colloquial Hindi or any regional language.*

**WOMAN**

Ah... ha... ha... ha... ha, what a setting! Straight from a Bombay cinema. You and I here. Millions of twinkling stars in the sky. The snow-covered hills of Switzerland in front of us. The moon peeping out between two peaks. Wah! *(There is no response)*

You like this Switzerland very much, na. *(No response)*

Look at the snow! Want to play in the snow? Throw snow on each other? Roll in the snow? *(No response)*

No danger of the snow melting away in summer here. It is there all the time. The mountains keep growing year after year. *(No response)*

Saala! Brings me to a landfill every time! Can't even afford a khatiya behind the dhaba. That Punjabi dhaba next to the petrol pump, run by a Nair, it has a nice shed behind with a steel khatiya and a durry. No, he must have his landfill Switzerland. Just look at the snow-covered slopes! Just smell it all!

**CLIENT**

Chup! If you have to go, just fuck off. You've got your payment. No need for speech-veech. Bombay cinemawaali!

**WOMAN**

That's what I was waiting for, your permission. Your command to get going. You can roll around in the snow here as long as you like. *(She stops, looking away)*

Wait! There's somebody behind that big pile there... Get up, quick! It may be a police party! *(He does. They hide.)*

It's a single person... A man...

**CLIENT**

Must be relieving himself.

**WOMAN**

He is clearing the pile... No, he is putting something into it... Covering it up... He is burying something in the landfill.

**CLIENT**

Let the bugger be. We mind our own business. My next trip this way will be on Monday. Same time. I am telling you in advance.

**WOMAN**

Oh my god, it's a... *(She cries out)*

**WOMAN**

Oy! Stop! Stop it at once! We can see you! Don't try to run! We have people all around... That's right... Come forward... You are safe... You will be safe if you come forward.

*(The man from the earlier scene enters. He is carrying Bittu, wrapped. He places the girl on the floor and stands motionless, frightened. The woman rushes to the girl and examines her. The Client holds the Man, preventing an escape.)*

**WOMAN**

She is alive!

*(To the man)* You were burying her alive! What sort of monster are you?

*(To Client)* We must get her to a hospital! Your truck! Let's go!

**MAN**

We can't do that. They will have hazaar questions at the hospital.

**WOMAN**

All right! To our own Lady Doctor then! She looks after all the girls. She will not ask questions. Quick!

**CLIENT**

This man? What do we do with him?

**WOMAN**

There is no time to lose! We can't waste time on this lump of shit. *(She walks up to him)* You've seen the lake on the other side of this landfill? Tie rocks to your hands and legs and jump into the lake! Monster! If you don't have the balls to do that, just stick your head into the hole you dug there.

*(The Woman and the Client rush out with the bundled girl. The man stands frozen. Fade out.*

*The following sequence of scenes is without words. The mime is best underplayed, accompanied with appropriate lighting to communicate effectively. If there is to be an audio accompaniment, it should be kept low and unobtrusive. The scenes begin twenty years ago and build up to the present.*

- *Young Yamuna. She is seated with a Police Inspector, Nandan standing. He is carrying a file, referring to pages in it once in a while. There is no trace of their daughter. It is looking hopeless.*
- *Crossfade to the Woman, who we know now as Mona. She is with Bittu, who is in new clothes, her hair done up, looking a bit older. Mona, better dressed now, is fixing flowers in Bittu's hair. Mona has graduated into a Madam, and Bittu is being groomed.*
- *Crossfade to Indrani's corner. Mamma is alone, at the same desk, working late at night. A lawyer's black coat-gown is draped over the second chair. She is an activist lawyer, working tirelessly for the underprivileged.*
- *Crossfade to Yamuna, Nandan, and Police Inspector. She is silent. Nandan appears agitated, frustrated. The Inspector closes the file and starts to leave. They have given up.*
- *Crossfade to Mona and Bittu. She stands Bittu up, looking at her admiringly. A Client enters and waits. Mona sends Bittu to him. They leave.*
- *Crossfade to Indrani's corner. Mamma is alone, at the same desk, working. Her telephone rings. She listens. She picks up a file and rushes out.*
- *Crossfade to Mona. There are sounds of doors being forced open and screams of protest. Two policemen lead a group of women out, all their heads covered. They signal to Mona to follow. She does. As the group leaves, Mamma steps in and shows the policemen a sheet of paper. They step aside and allow her to lead the women out. Mona stays behind with the policemen. She admonishes them.)*

**MONA**

Lost my phone number or what? You are supposed to call at least one hour before a raid. Always prompt in calling when you want favours, when you want service for your MLAs. What happened today? Raising your hafta or what?

*(The policemen and she follow the girls out.*

- *Crossfade to Yamuna and Nandan. They are seated in front of a framed photo of a girl. There are flowers, an oil lamp... After a few moments Nandan begins to sob. Yamuna remains motionless.*
- *Crossfade to Indrani's corner. Mamma enters, followed by Indrani. Mamma motions to her to sit. She doesn't. Mamma puts her papers on the desk and gets Indrani to sit on the divan.)*

**MAMMA**

You are safe here. You can stay as long as you want... I know they don't have an address for you. No family, no address, they don't know where you came from... You are safe here... Nobody can take you from here. Nobody can come here to see you... It is all right if you don't want to meet anybody... Want to eat something? No? I will get you some buttermilk. Go to sleep after that. We will talk in the morning tomorrow.

*(Mamma leaves. Indrani remains seated, staring ahead.*

*Crossfade to Yamuna and Nandan. He is sobbing. Yamuna rises, puts out the lamp, and watches Nandan. She picks up the photo frame and other puja things and leaves. Nandan is left alone.*

*Crossfade to Indrani. Mamma is interviewing Indrani.)*

**MAMMA**

What else do you remember?

**INDRANI**

That is all. I don't remember anything before that.

**MAMMA**

Does Mona madam know anything more?

**INDRANI**

No. Whatever she knows is what I know. She told me everything.

**MAMMA**

And Dr Vimaladevi.

**INDRANI**

Yes. Doctor-amma attended all the girls with Mona madam. She gave them regular check-ups. I was taken there by Mona madam. I was treated by her.

**MAMMA**

Anybody else? Any other doctor called by Vimaladevi?

**INDRANI**

I don't think so. Maybe some consultation on phone. Doctor-amma kept the case a tight secret. She said saving my life was the most important thing.

**MAMMA**

That was for more than five weeks according to Mona madam. You woke up only after two weeks. *(No response)*

**MAMMA** *(Continuing)*

For two weeks it was only Mona madam and doctor-amma, who looked after you.

**INDRANI**

That is what I was told.

**MAMMA**

And then?

**INDRANI**

I don't know. I don't remember. They looked after me well... They loved me.

**MAMMA**

Mona madam says you could not talk when you woke up.

**INDRANI**

They talked to me... I could not answer. They were new faces. I did not know who they were.

**MAMMA**

They thought it was a problem with language. Mona madam wanted to get somebody from the other side of the city to talk to you. Dr Vimaladevi said no. She was sure it was not a language problem. You had lost your memory.

**INDRANI**

I still don't...

**MAMMA**

It was like a new life, starting on a clean slate. Mona madam wanted to take you to her house.

**INDRANI**

I know she could not. It would be too risky, too complicated.

**MAMMA**

That's right. That is when Mona madam took the decision to leave the city.

**INDRANI**

And come here?

**MAMMA**

Six hundred miles away. To start afresh. The boss of her circle there arranged an introduction. It was an old Nepal connection. He and Dr Vimaladevi arranged for money too. Mona madam was respected.

**INDRANI**

I remember doctor-amma's face, her house, the room where I was kept. I don't remember much else.

**MAMMA**

Do you remember the journey? You came by bus, changing twice. She was told not to take the train, you and she.

**INDRANI**

Yes, I remember. I was dressed as a boy...

**MAMMA**

You remember that?

**INDRANI**

Yes... I liked that. Mona madam was asked questions by friendly travellers. She would not say much. They would look at me. I had no memory of the past... Only some sort of excitement about the future.

**MAMMA**

It was a new beginning. Because of her experience she became a madam very fast. Six hundred miles away.

**INDRANI**

A new beginning... *(A long pause)*

**MAMMA**

When did Mona madam know about your...

**INDRANI**

My condition?

**MAMMA**

Un-huh.

**INDRANI**

Right in the beginning. Doctor-amma told her.

**MAMMA**

When did you get to know?

**INDRANI**

Just before we came here, before the bus journey. We had a talk about it.

**MAMMA**

And you...

**INDRANI**

I think I knew. But I had not thought too much about it then. What bothered me more was that I had no memory of a life before Mona madam and doctor-amma.

**MAMMA**

When did you start thinking about it?

*(Crossfade to Mona. She is dressing Bittu up and talking to her lovingly. The mime there is accompanied by the voices in Mamma's interview with Indrani.)*

**INDRANI**

Mona madam was the only person in my life.

**MAMMA**

She thought of you as her daughter.

**INDRANI**

I did not know what it meant... Daughter... Mother... What did they mean?

**MAMMA**

But she was close to you.

**INDRANI**

Yes. That I understood... Closeness... Trust... Care.

**MAMMA**

Tell me what you remember about that.

**INDRANI**

She said she was very, very happy that god had chosen her to have me. I did not understand god, but I understood her happiness. I had a good feeling all over me about that.

**MAMMA**

She sent you to men often?

**INDRANI**

No. Not often. Only in the beginning.

**MAMMA**

Later?

**INDRANI**

She explained to me that I was not like other girls. I was very special. She would send me only to very special people.

**MAMMA**

Did you have any feelings about that?

**INDRANI**

Some curiosity... Only in the beginning... Why... ? How... ? Later I did not care. I was happy that for Mona madam I was special. *(Mamma extends her hand. Indrani takes it. Mamma seats Indrani on the divan.)*

**MAMMA**

You are safe here. You can look at this as your home.

**INDRANI**

And you? I can look at you as... ?

**MAMMA**

A friend. Look at me as your friend.

**INDRANI**

Friend... I don't know what that means.

**MAMMA**

You will find out. There is lots of time to find out.

*(Crossfade to Yamuna and Nandan today. A reprise.*

*The Volunteer picks up her things and leaves. Nandan peeps in, enters. He and Yamuna mime the first part of the conversation from the earlier scene, followed by the short exchange below.)*

**NANDAN**

You didn't tell her we had...

**YAMUNA**
Had? Had when? They only want to know about now.

**NANDAN**
Yes, but...

**YAMUNA**
Do-you-have-any-children? Yes. No. The answer is No. Buss.

**NANDAN**
The fact is...

**YAMUNA**
Buss. *(She stares at him. A pause.)*

**NANDAN**
If you say so. But we did have a child once. A girl.

**YAMUNA**
Twenty years ago.

**NANDAN**
Still...

**YAMUNA**
She is no more. It means nothing today. Buss.

## SCENE 7

*A resemblance to an earlier Crossfade. There are sounds of doors being forced open and screams of protest. Two policemen lead a group of women out, all their heads covered.*

*Crossfade to Indrani. She is Indranil now, seated at the desk. He is making entries in a large and thick notebook or diary. Mamma enters. She is carrying a small tray with a glass of milk. She keeps it on the desk, strokes Indranil's back and shoulders, caresses him.*

**MAMMA**
It is late. Have your milk and go to sleep now.

**INDRANIL**
There is work to finish. The case tomorrow is important.

**MAMMA**
I know. But your health is important too. All these late hours at the desk... It's becoming a habit. Not good for you.

**INDRANIL**
And from where did I get these bad habits?
*(Mamma keeps the tray down and sits)*

Who taught me never to put self above duty?

*(Mamma smiles, does not reply)*

Silence – assent – case rested! Mamma, mamma, you know how important this is. Not just for me. You are part of it too. You are the one who put us on to this in the first place. It is going to be a game changer. It will be the precedence that gets into the law books for future generations to quote.

**MAMMA**

I know, beta. We have waited for this a long time. I never imagined then that you would be into it yourself.

**INDRANIL**

Mamma's kid after all!

**MAMMA**

Leading it yourself.

**INDRANIL**

Not without you by my side.

**MAMMA**

Your first case by yourself.

**INDRANIL**

Everybody knows that I am representing you. You will be there too, won't you?

**MAMMA**

I will be there. But all eyes will be on you. Are you nervous?

**INDRANIL**

You asked me the same question yesterday. No, I am not. Not one bit. The fact is I don't know what that is supposed to feel like.

**MAMMA**

Good. No need to think about it.

**INDRANIL**

Now I am wondering if I am supposed to be nervous. If that is what normal people should be feeling.

**MAMMA** *(Laughing)*

Normal people spend too much of their energies worrying about what is normal.

*(A pause)* What are you actually feeling? About the case tomorrow.

**INDRANIL**

You remember the cock fight we saw at the weekly market?

**MAMMA**

In our last rural field trip? Of course! There was one cock crouched next to the owner, waiting to be sent in when it was time. He remained there, inconspicuous.

**INDRANIL**

In the other corner was the super aggressive cock, jumping, tugging at the cord, restless. If he had fists, he would be thumping his chest.

**MAMMA**

People laid their money on that one.

**INDRANIL**

And when the fight was flagged off, the quiet one went in there and finished off the braggart within a minute. He was a bloody mess.

**MAMMA**

Now, if the quiet one had fists, he would dust his palms to say, 'Next...' So... You'll just step up there tomorrow and give it to them.

**INDRANIL**

And I will be looking at my Mamma through the corner of my eye... watching me all the time, and making notes to coach me at the end of the fight.

**MAMMA**

What is the main line of argument you have prepared?

**INDRANIL**

As I have learned from you... the main line of argument should not be revealed at the start. Allow the opposition to use up their ammunition, let them get spent, tire themselves. Have I got that right?

**MAMMA** *(Proud of Indranil)*

And then?

**INDRANIL**

I will get the Honourable Judge and all else assembled to question the assumptions with which the case is being presented.

**MAMMA**

It is being seen as a benchmark case. They are expecting senior observers from several ministries and departments – Health and Family Welfare, Women and Child Development, Social Welfare, even the Law Department.

*(Crossfade to Yamuna. She is with the survey Volunteer.)*

**VOLUNTEER**

You remember? You have a good memory.

**YAMUNA**

Of course I remember you. It was before the last election. I didn't know the next election would be so soon.

**VOLUNTEER**
No, there is no election. This time, it is a different survey.

**YAMUNA**
This is what you do? From one survey to another? You don't get bored?

**VOLUNTEER**
It is a job. I like survey work.

**YAMUNA**
Achcha, let's begin. What is it this time?

**VOLUNTEER**
This is about education – schools and education.

**YAMUNA**
I see. What is it about education you are studying?

**VOLUNTEER**
This study is about the girl child and education. The Department is trying to know more about the drop-out rate of girl children from schools.

**YAMUNA**
Girl child...

**VOLUNTEER**
The first stage of the study was looking at school records over the past twenty-five years – how many girls joined school, what ages, which class, how many dropped out, at what age, and so on.

**YAMUNA**
But we don't have...

**VOLUNTEER**
The records of Nirmala Jyoti School show that you had a daughter. She stopped going to school at the age of ten. No reason is recorded. I am here to find out more about that.

**YAMUNA**
It was so long ago. Why now?

**VOLUNTEER**
It is needed purely for the survey research. No names will be mentioned anywhere. There are just three questions connected with the drop-outs.

**YAMUNA**
I don't think I remember much about it.

**VOLUNTEER**
The questions are simple. They don't need much thinking.

**YAMUNA** *(After a pause, hesitant)*
Let me see if I can answer the questions. I don't promise...

**VOLUNTEER**

First question. What was her name? This is just to make sure it was the same person. In the school record it is given as Binita. *(Yamuna nods)*

Were there any other names?

**YAMUNA**

No. She was called Bittu at home. By her friends.

**VOLUNTEER**

What class was she in when she stopped going to school?

**YAMUNA**

I don't remember. It must have been Class 4.

**VOLUNTEER**

Why did she stop going to school? It was in the middle of the year, was it not? Before the school year ended.

**YAMUNA**

She died.

**VOLUNTEER**

Oh, I am sorry. *(A pause)*

**YAMUNA**

Anything more?

**VOLUNTEER**

Nothing more for now. We are just collecting the basic information. We may come back to you later for a longer meeting.

**YAMUNA**

I will make some tea.

*(Yamuna rises and leaves quickly. The volunteer waits a moment, takes out her cell phone, and keys in a text message. Nandan enters with a tray and two tumblers of tea. He sits next to her and offers her a tumbler and takes one himself. He mimes asking her to take down his phone number. She does.*

*Crossfade to Indranil's corner. He is working at the same desk. His phone beeps. He looks at the incoming message and puts the phone away. He rises, puts on the gown, and steps into a wider lit area which is the area for the defence counsel in a court. He takes his stand.*

*Mamma seats herself at a distance. Sounds of a crowded hall, a gavel beating, and cries for order, followed by a voice calling the counsel for defence to continue.)*

**INDRANIL** *(Waving a sheaf of papers)*

My Lord, Both the police record and the court record state that the women were rescued from a home in Radhakrishna Nagar on the night of Wednesday, August 28. The home is shown as located in a semi-residential area with the address GOKUL, Door No. 248, 13th Cross.

*(He seeks confirmation from the Court clerk and continues. He speaks in a confident, clipped manner)*

Thank you for the confirmation. There are two key words in the record, My Lord. The first is the word HOME. The second is the word RESCUED. Both these need re-examination. I seek the Court's permission to continue...

*(Acknowledging the Judge's consent)* Thank you, my Lord.

First and foremost, the premises raided cannot be called a home by any stretch of the imagination. It is an office. Nobody lives there. It is not a residence. The board outside clearly shows it is a commercial establishment with the name Silver Moon, which is the registered name of a Private Limited Company. Under the name is given the nature of the business the Company is engaged in – Concierge Services. The nature of the business requires a certain number of contracted employees to be women. It is a completely legitimate business, my lord, a point on which I seek the Court's permission to make a full elucidation.

The second objection is to the use of the word rescue, which denotes release from some bondage, a salvation, a liberation. The denoted meaning includes the condition of bondage being against one's will, imposed on one by force by one or more others who have the power to impose. The connotative meaning is equally important. It connotes both a position of superior morality by which the act of rescue is carried out and the right to execute the act of rescue.

I submit that the case against the Company and the individual women arrested for the avowed purpose of rescue is on entirely flawed premises. Indeed it is ironical that the same arrested women had to be rescued from the humiliation and trauma that resulted from their detention in police custody, a trauma they had never experienced in their professional lives.

*(Sounds of agitated voices in the hall, a gavel beating, and cries for order. Silence restored, all eyes are on the Judge. Indranil accepts the Judge's advice.)*

**INDRANIL** *(Continuing)*

Thank you, my Lord. The advice is accepted. We shall meet in your chamber tomorrow at 3:00 pm.

*(Sounds of people leaving the court room. Indranil sits. Mamma joins him.)*

**MAMMA**

Well done! Getting the Judge to order a closed door hearing was a good tactical move. It is an accomplishment.

**INDRANIL**

I suppose so. But the counsel for prosecution is also invited.

**MAMMA**

To be welcomed. A judgment that is not in favour of the prosecution will be received with less opposition if there is an understanding before it is pronounced in the court room. It is a face saver.

**INDRANIL**

We have not won the case yet.

**MAMMA**

But you have opened it up for a closer examination. The right signals have been sent out. The media is at it. People will talk about it. The ball is set rolling.

**INDRANIL**

What more preparation do I need? I have till three tomorrow.

**MAMMA**

Nothing. You can put forward the arguments you have already lined up. Chamber hearings are more relaxed. You will not be under pressure to excel over the prosecution, there will be no audience watching.

*(A pause. Indranil is staring ahead.)*

Not that you were under any pressure here. You were calm and unperturbed right through. Where do you get that from?

**INDRANIL**

I found out.

**MAMMA**

Found out... About... ?

**INDRANIL**

The mother. I found out who she is, where she is.

**MAMMA**

Indranil, Indranil, my dear, dear Indrani, where is this going to take you?

**INDRANIL**

Nowhere. It is certainly not going to take me away from you.

**MAMMA**

Was it necessary?

**INDRANIL**

I don't know. Maybe it was not necessary. Maybe it was. For the record, as they say. For a case to be closed.

**MAMMA**

What did you find out? How much?

**INDRANIL**

Everything.

**MAMMA**

It was over twenty years ago. How can you get all the facts?

**INDRANIL**

If you dig deep enough, the bones from two thousand years ago can tell a story.

**MAMMA**
If you dig deep enough.

**INDRANIL**
One thing leads to another. One person leads to two others.

**MAMMA**
Did you find out about... ?

**INDRANIL**
Yes. It is true. I was not supposed to be found. *(A long pause)*
I was not supposed to be found alive. But I was.

**MAMMA**
You were. And that is why you are what you are today.

**INDRANIL**
I should be thankful... to the mother... who got rid of me.

**MAMMA**
Are you planning to... ?

**INDRANIL**
No.

**MAMMA**
There will be grave consequences... Very complex.

**INDRANIL**
The case is closed. You need not worry. I am not going to do anything more.

**MAMMA**
Then why... ?

**INDRANIL**
The past was a great big void. It has been filled. It does not matter at all what fills it. It is not an album full of happy faces and scenic holiday spots and picnics and birthday parties. It was different. I was different. But it is restored. It is now complete. I was born at the age of zero, not at the age of ten.

**MAMMA**
They say that there is a lifelong bond between a mother and her child that holds them together no matter how far apart they may be.

**INDRANIL**
And the poor father?

**MAMMA**
They don't have much to say about the father.

**INDRANIL**
They say... what they believe they must say. I have no need for such declarations. My lifelong bonds are with my three mothers. I am three times more blessed than the garden variety child.

## SCENE 8

*The Judge is meeting Indranil in his chamber. There is a tea service on the table with a pot, two cups and saucers, jars for milk and sugar, and a tea strainer.*

**INDRANIL**
May I?

**JUDGE**
Just plain tea for me.

**INDRANIL**
Yes, sir.

**JUDGE**
Darjeeling tea should not be adulterated with milk and sugar.

**INDRANIL**
Noted.

**JUDGE**
It is a bigger crime than adulterating Scotch with soda.

**INDRANIL**
I shall remember when I get there, sir.

**JUDGE**
Why don't you try it plain yourself?

**INDRANIL**
I think I will... Thank you for the invitation.

**JUDGE**
You appeared to have something important to say. The crowded court room did not appear to be the right place for it.

**INDRANIL**
Thank you once again. I thought we were meeting together with...

**JUDGE**
I will meet the prosecution counsel separately – at least to start with. I may ask for a joint meeting later on with both of you present.

**INDRANIL**
So it is just the two of us now?

**JUDGE**
Your mother was welcome to attend, but she has chosen not to. Yes, it will be just the two of us.

**INDRANIL**
Where would you like me to begin?

**JUDGE**

Your two contentions – on the references to a home and to the rescue. Please elaborate the assertions.

**INDRANIL**

At a basic level, we can argue that since the terms used in the orders are factually incorrect, the case itself is invalid.

**JUDGE**

A brothel by any other name is still a brothel. A prostitute by any other name...

**INDRANIL** *(Correcting him politely)*

Sex worker.

**JUDGE**

By any other name...

**INDRANIL**

Sir, it is absolutely indisputable that Silver Moon is a concierge services business. The Company is registered, the conduct of business satisfies all statutory conditions, the accounts are audited and submitted to the Income Tax Office within the stipulated time, the last Annual Report is available for scrutiny.

**JUDGE**

Sex in the name of escort services is neither new nor ingenious. You will have to be honest with me. Is there sex in this concierge business or no?

**INDRANIL**

Not in the business, not on the premises. The address quoted in the order is strictly a business office. In fact the police party that conducted the raid searched every room to find some little incriminating evidence, a bed, a divan, a hiding customer, some tell-tale signs – they were so disappointed.

**JUDGE**

They filed a report nevertheless – as they were expected to. So... Not in the business, not on the premises, but they do offer sexual services, do they not?

**INDRANIL**

They do not offer the services, sir. The women are very strict about their conduct. The men seek these services.

**JUDGE**

And then the women consent. And it happens.

**INDRANIL**

As it happens in a hundred other places when a man is attracted to a woman – in a wedding reception, a navratri dance, a durga puja celebration, in a company picnic.

**JUDGE**

There is no fee for favours granted in these places.

**INDRANIL**

An expensive dinner outing, a bracelet, a shopping spree, a stolen weekend trip to Malaysia... No fee.

**JUDGE**

You are beginning to sound like your mother.

**INDRANIL**

I would like to believe you are paying me a compliment, sir.

**JUDGE**

The women in the business... They are all single I gather.

**INDRANIL**

And those seeking their services are mostly married men. If there is to be a case registered at all, it has to be against the men – for adultery.

**JUDGE**

Has the company not had instances of the women exploiting the men? Blackmail? Accusations of sexual molestation?

**INDRANIL**

It can happen both ways, sir.

**JUDGE**

Yes, I am sure it can. How would the company handle such instances?

**INDRANIL**

The concierge services are undertaken only after a contract is signed.

**JUDGE**

Sex with a signed contract. Tell me more.

**INDRANIL**

The women have to be protected, sir. There are clauses of indemnity, privacy, and non-disclosure, provision of two-way termination and damages on account of unforeseen accidents.

**JUDGE**

Is there a reference to sexual intimacy?

**INDRANIL**

Not in the service contract. If and when the woman finds herself confronted with an extension of the service sought by the client, a separate agreement is undertaken that it is entirely consensual.

**JUDGE**

Do you really think all this holds water legally?

**INDRANIL**

Sir, you are surely aware that the state of Gujarat has maintained the well-established institution of Maitri Karar for a man-woman relationship outside marriage. It has always had both a social and legal sanction. In recent times this has been converted into a Service Agreement.

**JUDGE** *(Concealing his admiration)*
You have done your homework.

**INDRANIL**
Thank you, sir. *(A pause)*

**JUDGE**
Legal but immoral nevertheless.

**INDRANIL**
Amoral, sir. Not immoral. The women have scruples. If I may take the liberty of suggesting it, it would be highly desirable for you to have a chamber meeting with some of them.

**JUDGE**
And the men? Are their acts not immoral?

**INDRANIL**
If the deemed immorality is indeed an offence as per the given laws, they should certainly be held to account and punished. Is it not a travesty of the law, sir, if the woman is punished and the man goes completely free?

**JUDGE**
It can be argued that the services made available off the shelf, so to speak, stokes the immorality of men, and increases the incidence of the offence.

**INDRANIL**
A hypothesis worth noting, sir, but at the moment it is just that – a hypothesis.

**JUDGE**
Worth noting, you admit.

**INDRANIL**
As much as another hypothesis, that the available service reduces the incidence of molestation and rape. *(A pause)*

**JUDGE**
You had a second contention.

**INDRANIL**
About the women being rescued.

**JUDGE**
I suppose the second follows from the first.

**INDRANIL**
That is correct, sir. The two points cannot be separated. We do not rescue people from positions of their choice, positions of respectability.

**JUDGE**
Would the women not have a sense of relief? Would they not be grateful that they were taken out of those positions?

**INDRANIL**

They resent being taken out, and they hate being given labels that they do not see applying to them. Rescuing them is so pompous, sir – so holier-than-thou.

**JUDGE**

I see.

**INDRANIL**

On the contrary, they will go right back when they are released. They will find one way or the other to do that.

**JUDGE**

You do not think the positions are traps?

**INDRANIL**

The traps, sir, are elsewhere. Why don't we think of rescuing the big businessmen from their traps? And the members of parliament and bureaucrats. And the police officers and the bankers and the income tax officers, and we all know how many others, including honourable members of our profession, we must admit, who have created a great big trap for themselves. All beautifully connected among themselves, all members of the same clubs, all with the phone numbers of all others, all coming to each other's aid readily when needed. *(Pause)*

Surely the need for rescue is far greater there, sir. *(A long pause. The Judge is looking at Indranil intently. Finally a smile. He rises and extends his hand.)*

**JUDGE**

Thank you. It was a pleasure discussing this with you. Your mother was right. She said you would be able to handle the case by yourself.

**INDRANIL**

Thank you, sir.

**JUDGE**

That is to be taken as a compliment. Not a judgment. I have still to meet the counsel for the prosecution. Please stand by for a call for a joint meeting next week.

## SCENE 9

*Mona's room. A simple two-seater, two armchairs, and a teapoy. The Volunteer and Nandan are with her. Mona is on her cell phone. She motions the two others to sit. The Volunteer does.*

**MONA**

She is not picking up her phone.

**VOLUNTEER**

But she does visit you every Saturday afternoon, you said.

**MONA**

Yes. Around four-thirty. Definitely by five.

**VOLUNTEER**

It is almost time. We can wait.

**MONA**

I still think it is better to meet her at her mother's place. Who am I? I just happen to know her because of the good work she and her mother do.

**VOLUNTEER**

Can we ask you a few questions while we are waiting for her?

**MONA**

Better to ask her. All questions to her or her mother. That is our understanding.

**VOLUNTEER**

We will meet the mother too. But since we are here already...

**NANDAN**

Her mother... She is a lawyer, no?

**MONA**

That's right. And Indrani is growing up to be fine lawyer too, just like her mother.

**NANDAN**

That is her name? Indrani?

**MONA**

Yes. As a lawyer she is Indranil. Didn't you know?

**VOLUNTEER**

He didn't. I just suggested that he should meet the mother and daughter to see if they can take up his case?

**MONA**

What is the case?

**NANDAN**

It is about... How to put it...

**VOLUNTEER**

It is difficult to explain.

**MONA**

It's all right. I understand if you can't talk about it. But how did you think of coming to me? You could have got in touch with them directly.

**VOLUNTEER**

You are well known. And we were told that you have known them well.

**MONA**

The second part is true. The first part, I don't know. I may be well known only to some kinds of people. *(Laughs)*

Now you will tell me you were sent here by the police people.

**VOLUNTEER**

You don't mind talking about it?

**MONA**

What is there to mind-wind? We all do our work, na?

**VOLUNTEER**

Yes, we all do.

**MONA**

Some people have respectable jobs but are rogues in real life. Others can have jobs that have low respect, but they can still live decent lives. That is possible or no?

**VOLUNTEER**

Possible, yes. And this is the place where you...

**MONA**

Used to. I am retired now. You are thinking about my age, no?

**VOLUNTEER**

You couldn't be any more than...

**MONA**

Early retirement. Voluntary. I do social work now. *(To Nandan)*

Why don't you sit? She will come any time now.

*(Crossfade to a street. Indrani is on her way to Mona's place. She is stalked by a group of three men. She tries to change direction. Too late. She is pounced upon by the three men. She screams, struggles wildly, but is overpowered and dragged out.*

*The sounds of a big car starting and zooming off.*

*Crossfade to Mona. She is on the phone. She moves to a corner to continue.)*

**MONA**

Yes... Yes, I follow... But, Mammaji, it is a big hospital. There will be questions – forms to be filled... Yes, I understand... Her life must be saved first... Are you sure you want me to... All right, I will be there... I am starting immediately. *(She returns to Nandan and the Volunteer)*

Sorry, I have to leave you. There is an emergency. I have to leave immediately. Very sorry. Please come some other time. As I said, you could have gone to their place straight... You should have gone there first.

*(She guides them out, returns to the two-seater and collapses on it.)*

Bitty! My poor Bittu! What have they done to you! Why do we have to go through this all over again?!

## SCENE 10

*Yamuna's corner. She is seated by herself, reading a newspaper, a tumbler of tea before her. The sound of a door opening and closing.*

**YAMUNA**

You are back? Get yourself some tea. There is more in the kettle. Then you can come here and tell me about your pilgrimage.

*(She returns to the newspaper. Nandan enters with a tray in his hand. On it is a leaf bowl and a stainless steel tumbler. He is dressed in a dark lungi, an orange kurta and a top cloth, with a jholi shoulder bag slung across. He has a large bindi and ash on his forehead.)*

**YAMUNA** *(Continuing)*

Did you get a good darshan? There must have been a huge swarm of pilgrims from all over.

**NANDAN** *(Keeping the tray down)*

Prasad.

**YAMUNA**

The kheer too?

**NANDAN**

Twenty rupees extra. They give it in a sachet. You can get the prasad with kheer. *(Yamuna eats the sweet from the leaf bowl.)*

**YAMUNA**

How was the journey? Train and bus up, and train and bus back, right?

**NANDAN**

It was all right. Not too hot luckily. I had company, so the time passed easily. Drink the kheer. It will not last long. *(Yamuna drinks the kheer.)*

**YAMUNA**

It might be spoiling already. Anyway, what else did you do there? Having gone six hundred miles. Just the temple and back?

**NANDAN**

We saw some interesting parts of the town. Met some interesting people.

**YAMUNA**

Good you had company.

**NANDAN**

Found out interesting things.

**YAMUNA**

Who was the person you had for company?

**NANDAN**

I will tell you.

*(Nandan picks up the empty tumbler and leaf bowl and carries them out with the tray. By now Yamuna is not quite herself. She calls after him.)*

**YAMUNA**

Get me some water when you come. This prasad and kheer...

*(She slumps forward. Nandan enters, surveys the scene, approaches Yamuna from behind, and props her up, his left arm around her neck.)*

**NANDAN**

You don't need water. What you want is some rest. A long rest.

**YAMUNA** *(Incoherent)*

Tell me... What... ? Found out...

**NANDAN**

Everything.

**YAMUNA**

You... Found out... What...

**NANDAN**

Everything that needed to be known... So you can rest in peace now.

**YAMUNA**

Good... Rest... Your arm... Strong... *(Nandan reaches into the shoulder bag and takes out a country-made pistol.)*

**NANDAN**

No failure this time. We have a backup. There are only two shots in this gun. They will both work. One for you. One for me. Share and share alike. Bound by the sacred vows of marriage.

*(By now Yamuna has gone limp. He places the gun muzzle at her temple.*

*Fade out. In the dark we hear a gunshot. After a few moments there is a second gunshot. [It would be good if the performing group can manage the flashes of a country-made pistol in the dark.]*

*Crossfade to Indrani's corner. Mamma is in her gown. She steps into a wider lit area which is for the defence counsel as in the earlier scene. She takes her stand. Sounds of a crowded hall, a gavel beating, and cries for order. Mamma takes her seat. All eyes are on the unseen Judge as he proceeds to pronounce his judgment.*

*A long freeze. Sounds of agitated voices again in the hall, a gavel beating, and cries for order. Silence restored. All rise. Mamma bows in respect. A long pause.*

*Sounds of people leaving the court room in some excitement. Quiet.*

*Mamma sits. She reaches into her briefcase, takes out a framed photo, and keeps it on the desk. She steps Down-left and stares ahead.*

*Mona enters and joins her. They stand still for a while, arms around each other. Finally, Mona speaks.)*

**MONA**

You won. You won the case.

**MAMMA**

Indranil won.

**MONA**

It is a very special day for many, many people. Who knows, sometime in the future, the date may be celebrated as Indranil day.

**MAMMA**

Indranil won. Indrani lost.

**MONA**

Yes… It was a heavy price to pay for this victory!

**MAMMA**

What next?

**MONA**

The press and TV people are waiting outside. Are you going to meet them?

**MAMMA**

I suppose I will have to. The counsel for prosecution can exhaust them first.

**MONA**

He has already announced that he has accepted the judgment. He is not going up with an appeal.

**MAMMA**

There is nothing more to do.

**MONA**

They will have other questions… About Indrani… About Indranil.

**MAMMA**

And they will have decided the answers themselves before I meet them.

**MONA**

What will you say to them?

**MAMMA**

I will say… Mission accomplished… It is time to retire now.

*(They look at each other. Mamma bends her head. Mona caresses her gently.*

*Fade out. A tight spot on the photo frame on Mamma's desk.*

*Crossfade to Down-left, now empty again, held for a while.)*

*Fade out.*

***Close of play***

# In Memoriam
## Addendum & Corrigendum

*A double bill laid by the stick*
***Vijay Padaki***

FOR
**DAVID SELVARAJ**

# INTRODUCTION

## Tales from the City

Excerpts from the general introduction at the start of *In Transit* are reproduced here. It is for the benefit of readers who choose to read *In Memoriam* first.

What started as ideas for a trilogy expanded into a set of five plays. All of them are presented in this volume. The 'trilogy of five plays' may be seen as the sociology of the city, especially the underbelly, uncovering the usually unseen occupations that remain integral to the economy of the city. The set was originally titled *Tales from the City*. All the tales have an inescapable tragic quality about them. Denial of the tragedy itself appeared to be a characteristic of the city.

We cannot help noting how much of the 'liberated economy' of developing countries has had compromises in so many different ways, especially with respect to human rights.

The concept of 'development' has steadily got equated with making more money. This pursuit has decorously been termed economic growth. The natural resources available for growth are finite, but the goals of growth are infinite. In a lot of the aspirations of growth, the most sought after resource is land. It is seen in a glaringly massive scale in the displacement of indigenous peoples for large development projects, for mining, dams, large manufacturing complexes, the benefits of which reach people other than the displaced. Displacement – and the resultant migration – is recognised widely as one the foremost hurdles in achieving Sustainable Development Goals proposed by the United Nations. It is also known that the acquisition of land and other needed resources is achieved through a blatant combination of political manoeuvring and brute force. The game of development is not played on a level playing field.

# ADDENDUM

It is no different in the microcosm of the city. Land assets here are even more precious than gold reserves. The acquisition of land for one aspiration or the other is often by means that are located in a parallel system of enforcement. The beneficiaries do not get their hands dirty. There are ready service providers. It can get violent. The two plays in this double bill have characters who find themselves sucked into the system they have unwittingly stepped into. Yet, it must be said at the start that the two stories are different. The characters are different, their circumstances are different, and the directions taken in the two stories are distinct. The only thing common to them is the tragic ends.

## Language Notes

*Devadasi:* Literally servant of God. A hereditary occupation of women in Hindu temples in some parts of India.
*Bilkul:* Absolutely.
*Vijayadasami:* The tenth day of the Dasara festival, considered auspicious for new ventures.
*Vastu:* Dwelling. Short for Vastu Shastra, the traditional system of ensuring favourable qualities in architecture.
*Bechaara:* Poor fellow.
*Mausi:* Maternal aunt.
*Peda:* A milk-based confectionary.
*Badam milk:* A popular almond-based milk drink.
*Hajaar:* A thousand. Also hazaar.

## CHARACTERS IN THE PLAY

CHANDRASHEKHAR ................................ *Young man, late twenties, resident of Mysore, visiting his brother in Bangalore. He has a degree in Commerce and a temporary job in a car dealer's showroom. He is the third of five children, an older brother, an older sister, and two younger sisters. He helps in the family business of a small all-purpose grocery store. He is visiting his older brother, Raja, in Bangalore.*

RAJASHEKHAR ............................ *Chandru's older brother, early thirties. Moved to Bangalore for his college studies, was part of a student association working with slum children, and joined the project staff of an NGO soon after his degree, where he met his live-in partner. He joined her in co-founding an NGO to focus on the needs of battered women, mostly from poor households. He is cut off from the family in Mysore, not estranged, and stays in touch with them through Chandru. He is called Raja.*

RADHA ..................... *About the same age as Raja. The only child of a civil servant father, born in Bangalore, widely travelled through her school and college years through her father's postings. She is distanced from her parents and committed to an activist life. She adores Raja from their first job together. The live-in relationship with him is on her insistence, although it is by moving into his apartment, which is small, functional, and neatly maintained at all times. She does not protest when referred to as Raja's wife.*

THE BOSS ................................ *A local dada and petty criminal with ambitions of making it big in the underworld. He is well connected and is seen as a reliable organiser by politicians and businessmen. His mainstay is a bootlegging and illicit liquor business which serves many. He is never seen. We only hear his voice, perhaps over the house system.*

THE AGENT ........................ *The right hand man and faithful attendant of the Boss. He takes care of most business dealings on his behalf. He has acquired much street wisdom over the years.*

CONTRACTOR .................................... *He is given the job of erecting a building on a small plot of encroached land. It is meant to be an outlet for the liquor business of the Boss, among other things.*

THREE HOODLUMS ............................ *They are hired now and then by the Agent for extortion jobs and any enforcement of his word.*

INSPECTOR ...................................... *A Police Officer of Inspector rank attached to the local Police Station.*

OFFICER ............................................ *A Police Officer of higher rank in another Station of higher standing.*

WOMAN ........................................... *A Devadasi being rehabilitated by the NGO run by Raja and Radha.*

*The play offers much scope for innovation in stage design that combines the interior of a humble home and the encroachment on a small plot of land on which the home rests. The action keeps alternating between these two areas on the stage. The 'outdoor' suggests that the encroachment has already taken place. It has a menacing presence. It appears only a matter of time for it to grow into swallowing up the home itself. The menacing quality of the space is complemented by the physical violence that takes place in the spaces. No description of the stage is given here. The action areas explain themselves. The performing group can design the stage as it chooses. The only advice is to keep it simple and suggestive, and to not resort to a heavy set.*

## SCENE 1

*A tight spot Down-right. Chandru enters the spot and speaks to the audience.*

**CHANDRU**

You will not know left from right, they said. You will not know if you are coming or going. Bugger off. Go back to your hole. You have three days, they said.

*(Raja's bedsitter is lit. A gang of three hoodlums are confronting Raja. He is holding on to his leg in great pain. One of the hoodlums has an iron rod in his hand.)*

**CHANDRU** *(Continuing)*

Don't poke your nose in things of no concern to you. *(Chandru's spot off.)*

**HOODLUMS** *(Speaking in turns)*

» When was the last time you had broken bones? In school, huh? Fell off a bike, no?

» Ever seen blood gushing out of somebody's belly? Like a tap open?

» Ever looked inside an open skull? Like checking a cauliflower in the veggie market?

» All right, your leg is hurt today. Tch, tch, tch, it's swollen bad. How did it happen?

» Aah, you slipped and fell down the stairs? Banging against the railing? Tch, tch, tch!

» That's how it happened, right? You will remember, when people ask you, right?

» It could have been worse. You will be more careful in future. Right.

» Right?

*(There is no response from Raja. The hoodlum raises the iron rod to strike but brings it down gently for a short tap on Raja's hurt leg. The three of them laugh and exit quickly.*

*Crossfade to Chandru's spot. Empty.)*

**CHANDRU'S VOICE**

Don't poke your nose in things of no concern to you...

I just wanted to see my brother. He hadn't been home for over two years. I came to Bangalore to see him. I was carrying gifts from his sisters, his favourite sweets, a message from Amma.

*(Raja's bedsitter. Radha is with him, wrapping a crepe bandage on his leg. She finishes and sits next to him. He puts his arm around her. She rests her head against his shoulder. Long pause.)*

**RADHA**

Like they said... It could have been worse. You got away with a hairline crack. *(Pause)* What next?

*(The doorbell rings. Radha rises and starts to put things away.)*

Come in! The door is open! *(To Raja)* As always.

*(Chandru enters. He has an old tote bag in one hand and a box of sweets in the other. He stops at the entrance, seeing Raja with a bandaged leg.)*

Chandru! Come in, come in! What a surprise! What brings you... Oh, Rajanna's leg? Come and sit down. We will tell you about it

**RAJA**

It was an accident. Nothing serious.

**RADHA**

Fell down the stairs. Banged his leg against the railing.

**RAJA**

Lost my balance and fell down the stairs.

**CHANDRU**

You didn't inform us... When did it happen? What was actually... ?

**RADHA**

Close the door and come in. *(He does)*

Sit down. *(He sits next to Raja and gives him the box of sweets. They hold hands.)* When you were coming up here, did you see any men hanging about? Near the stairs? In the passage? No? You are sure?

**RAJA**

RADHA...

**RADHA**

We can't keep this bottled! We have to do something. And we have to begin by talking about it. Who do we talk to? Not the police! Not just now anyway.

**RAJA**

The poor boy has just got in. Let him get some rest. What do we have for dinner? Chandru, you just go in there and wash up and change. It is almost dinner time. We will have a long chat after dinner.

**RADHA**

You should know that Rajanna did not fall down the stairs.

**CHANDRU**

He didn't? You mean this is some kind of...

**RADHA**

Game? Yes, it is!

**RAJA**

It is a long story.

## SCENE 2

*Construction activity, silhouetted against a cyclorama. Materials being carried, empties returned, bricks being passed, etc. A construction site din. A whistle blows. People stop work and take a lunch break. Quiet.*

*Two men enter in the downstage area with papers. They carry folding chairs/stools and sit. One is a contractor. The other is an agent of the person getting the building erected. They have papers and files in their hands.*

**AGENT**

On schedule?

**CONTRACTOR**

Bilkul. Maybe three-four days behind to finish the inside, but on track.

**AGENT**

Won't do. He is very, very clear, he wants to enter the place on Vijayadasami day. Very auspicious, you know.

**CONTRACTOR**

I will try my best.

**AGENT**

Trying-frying will not do. The vastu date was fixed long ago. You know that. The invitations are being printed right now. He has fixed up the priest.

**CONTRACTOR**

Bhai saab, you must understand. I can never say what will be done the next day. There is nothing certain about the supplies.

**AGENT**

He will cut off your balls. That is certain. You will see what happens then. The place will be ready the day before Vijayadasami and handed over. That's it.

**CONTRACTOR**

Have you not told him about... ?

**AGENT**

About what? *(The contractor refers to papers)*

That letter of objection? He will deal with it. That is why he wanted you to put up the wall first before this building. Have the same design of wall on the outer side – where the fence is just now. Take down the fence and put up the wall. The new building will have walls on all sides.

**CONTRACTOR**

Sir, the letter of objection is addressed to the Municipal Commissioner. Copy to me, copy to you.

**AGENT**

So? Anybody can send a letter to the Commissioner. Anybody can send a letter to the Chief Minister, to Mr Narayana Murthy, to Madhuri Dixit. It is a free country. The question is, Has the Commissioner sent a letter to you? No? Then nothing can stop you from your targets.

**CONTRACTOR**

It can happen any time. He can issue a stay on the construction.

**AGENT**

It will not be before Vijayadasami. We will occupy the building on Vijayadasami day. That is final.

**CONTRACTOR**

He can send a party to inspect the site.

**AGENT**

The party will have to meet him, no? Leave it to him. He will take care of it.

**CONTRACTOR**

I could lose my licence...

**AGENT**

You could? Ah, yes, you could. That is possible, isn't it? You could lose your licence. For what reason?

**CONTRACTOR**

For this, this...

**AGENT**

For this what? You are trying to say something? *(The contractor is silent)* Are you by any chance suggesting that there is something wrong with this construction? *(He laughs)* Something... not done? What is the word? Illegal? *(He laughs again)* Is that it?

**CONTRACTOR**

The Corporation...

**AGENT**

The Corporation will decide if it is legal or illegal, right? Of course! That is the correct procedure. That is what the corporation is supposed to do. So, let them do what they are supposed to do. Why should that worry you? You just stick to your job. And stick to the target – Vijayadasami day.

**CONTRACTOR**

The letter... My name is in the letter.

**AGENT**

Ohho, bechaara, your name is in the letter. So? It means you are mentioned. So it means it is too late. You have taken up the work and you are party to the construction. And if the Corporation decides it is illegal, then tch, tch, tch, tch, you are in trouble.

**CONTRACTOR**
Sir, for you it is a joke. For me...

**AGENT**
Don't worry. Leave it to him. He will take care of all your troubles. He is a good man.

## SCENE 3

*A tight spot with a single folding chair/stool Down-left. The Agent walks into the spot, carrying an opened bottle of rum and a glass. He speaks to the Boss who is unseen, as he sits and pours himself a drink.*

**AGENT**
Cheers, sir. *(He takes a long sip)*
We have found out that the Commissioner has drafted a stay order, but it has not been posted yet. The office is verifying some more documents.

**VOICE OF BOSS**
Call Acharya. His private cell is 98457-27330. Tell him it is a message from me and that I will talk to him later. Xerox the letter of objection and send it to him.

**AGENT**
I can scan it and send it by e-mail.

**VOICE**
No! Send a Xerox copy by hand delivery. Send the pooja invitation with it. Add two bottles of the fifteen-year stock. Gift wrap them.

**AGENT**
The couple run an NGO. They have connections in the Social Welfare Ministry.

**VOICE**
Call Naidu in the Home Ministry. Tell them we see foreigners coming to the NGO every now and then.

**AGENT**
Yes, sir. Straight away.

**VOICE**
The contractor fellow – is he behaving all right?

**AGENT**
He is all right, sir. Just nervous.

**VOICE**
They are the dangerous ones. They can crack up under pressure. Show him how to handle his nervousness.

**AGENT**

Right, sir.

**VOICE**

Is he sticking to the targets?

**AGENT**

I am taking care of that, sir.

**VOICE**

Good. And take care of yourself. God bless.

*(Crossfade to Down-right. There is a small desk and chairs. A Police Inspector is on one side. Raja and Radha are on the other side. The Police Inspector is reading a handwritten FIR.)*

**INSPECTOR**

Are you submitting this FIR jointly, or by yourself?

**RAJA**

Which is better, sir? What is your advice?

**INSPECTOR**

It can be jointly too, since you are a married couple living in the house.

**RADHA**

Well, the house is registered in his name. So, I suppose it will be by himself?

**INSPECTOR**

The complaint refers to encroachment of the premises occupied by both of you. But it is all right if you prefer only one person filing the complaint.

**RAJA**

We will go with that.

**INSPECTOR**

Also, you will have to add a line to say whether the premises are used only as your home or if there is any other use.

**RAJA**

You mean...

**INSPECTOR**

Your NGO – what's it called – the Centre for Distressing Women...

**RAJA**

Women in Distress.

**INSPECTOR**

Same thing. Does it have an office on the premises?

**RAJA**

We have some meetings there.

**INSPECTOR**

Is there an office there?

**RADHA**

There is no office there.

**INSPECTOR**

Add a line here to say that. What is the compound space used for?

**RAJA**

There is not much compound space.

**INSPECTOR**

Whatever. What is the space used for?

**RAJA**

Right now it is used as a small playground by the slum children.

**RADHA**

We are going to convert it into a vegetable garden.

**INSPECTOR**

So there will be fertilizers and chemicals stored in the compound?

**RAJA**

Not at all. It will be completely organic.

**INSPECTOR**

Worms and garbage and all that.

**RADHA**

No chemicals. Why are you asking?

**INSPECTOR**

There may be questions. Just two of you in the building, compound space, materials stored... Why so much farming activity? There may be questions.

**RAJA**

The Corporation people have already visited the place. That is how...

**INSPECTOR**

I know. They have issued a stay order, no? So why this FIR now?

**RAJA**

The two things are different.

**INSPECTOR**

They are different, but they are the same. A case of encroachment is not an easy matter. You should know that.

**RADHA**

How can they be the same? The FIR is a complaint about a criminal act that has to be brought to the attention of the Police. The stay order...

**INSPECTOR**

You are trying to teach me something?

**RAJA**

Not like that. Sir. We are only doing what we believe is the correct thing to do.

**INSPECTOR**

All right. Make a fresh copy with the corrections. Sign on both pages. I will look into the case. We may have to inspect the premises.

*(Crossfade to Agent in the spot. He is looking anxious. A pause.)*

**VOICE**

The mother fucking bastard has guts, huh?

**AGENT**

It is his wife, sir. She is behind him.

**VOICE**

We will have to call Narasimha. You will find the number in my diary. He is listed as Nari. Tell him I expect urgent action from him.

**AGENT**

Right away, sir.

**VOICE**

Tell him the lorry with his consignment is on its way, but there are chances of it being held up.

**AGENT**

The lorry has already arrived, sir.

**VOICE**

You heard me. It is on its way. Remind him about the pooja. Tell him it is a personal invitation from me.

**AGENT**

Meanwhile, the FIR, sir...

**VOICE**

We will see.

*(Crossfade to desk. Raja and Radha are waiting. Presently the Inspector walks in.)*

**INSPECTOR**

Yes?

**RAJA**

We have come to enquire about the FIR, sir.

**INSPECTOR**

What FIR?

**RAJA**

The one we filed last week. On the 5th of October.

**INSPECTOR**

You filed an FIR? Here?

**RAJA**

On the 5th of October. You said we should...

**INSPECTOR**

I don't know what you are talking about. Do you have a copy?

**RAJA**

Copy? You said we should make some changes. We did that and we submitted it to you. Right here.

**INSPECTOR**

You must have a copy with the Police Station's seal of acknowledgement.

**RADHA**

You didn't tell us at that time...

**INSPECTOR**

I have urgent work to attend to now. If you have some complaint, please go to the duty constable at the entrance.

**RADHA**

Sir! We have work with you. We have waited forty-five minutes for you. You can't just ignore our enquiry.

**INSPECTOR**

I can't?

*(Crossfade to the Agent. He is laughing.)*

**VOICE**

I say, as civilised people, and as peace-loving citizens of this city, we must invite them to the pooja and vastu.

**AGENT** *(Laughing)*

As god-fearing people of the city, we all love...

**VOICE**

We must be good neighbours, no? Cooperative, helping each other at all times.

**AGENT**

We can even buy the vegetables from their garden regularly. It will be very convenient once the bar is opened.

**VOICE**

Tell Acharya to be ready to file our FIR anyway.

**AGENT**

Done, sir.

**VOICE**

One more week. Pooja at 6:00 pm. Opening ceremony at 7:30 pm sharp. Have they got the signboard ready?

**AGENT**

Very nice lighting. It will look high class at night. 'Shri Maruti Community Centre'.

**VOICE**

You have enough stock for the opening function?

*(Crossfade to desk. An officer of senior rank has replaced the Inspector.)*

**OFFICER**

Please sign here to acknowledge that you have seen this document.

**RAJA**

I can't believe this. An FIR against us.

**RADHA**

We filed an FIR two weeks ago.

**OFFICER**

I don't know about that, but I should tell you that this one is serious business.

**RADHA**

And ours was non-serious business!

**OFFICER**

That is not my business.

**RAJA**

What course of action is available to us now? Can we consult a lawyer?

**OFFICER**

Of course you can settle the matter out of court.

**RAJA**

And if we don't want to do that?

**RADHA**

It is simple. The land is ours. The construction is an encroachment.

**OFFICER**

It is not that simple.

**RAJA**

The court can decide how simple or complicated a case of encroachment is.

**OFFICER**

You saw the names in the FIR? Mr Acharya is a Corporator. He has attested that the strip of land is allotted for community purposes.

**RADHA**

But it has to be officially taken from us before it is officially given to someone else. That has not happened.

**OFFICER**

It is also noted that you are using your home premises to run an office. The corporation office does not have any record of permission for office use or property tax for that.

**RAJA**

The Registered Office of the NGO is in Mahadevnagar. We can show you the document for that.

**OFFICER**

We also have a noting from Mr PK Narasimha in the Home Ministry. It states that you have foreigners coming and going at your premises.

**RADHA**

One foreigner. She is a volunteer from a respectable university in Canada.

**OFFICER**

Ah, so you admit there are foreigners visiting.

**RADHA**

One foreigner. One woman student – whose papers are all completely in order, and who reports at the Police Commissioner's Office on the first day of every month. You can meet her if you like.

**OFFICER**

That is not part of my job. I am only telling you as a friend, and as someone who knows about the work you are doing, that the Home Ministry is watching you.

**RAJA**

You know about our NGO?

**OFFICER**

Yes, something with women, I believe.

**RAJA**

Yes, women. The NGO is called...

**OFFICER**

That is why there is a constant flow of women in and out of the place.

**RADHA**

Mostly battered women, mainly from within the city.

**RAJA**

And yes, some destitutes.

**OFFICER**

Prostitutes?

**RADHA**

Some of them, maybe. If there is violence against them.

**OFFICER**

I suppose all these women are from the poorer class – living in the slums, house maids. All this domestic violence business.

**RADHA**

You will be surprised, sir. We sometimes have wives of people who carry a totally different image in public. Saints!

**OFFICER** *(Smiling)*

I know what you mean, believe me. But Rajashekhar-ji, the point here is not what you are doing as an NGO. The point is about the premises.

**RAJA**

It is our land.

**RADHA**

We have all the papers.

**RAJA**

Should we go to a lawyer?

**OFFICER**

Go to the vastu pooja. I will also be there. I can introduce you to Mr Narasimha and Mr Acharya.

**RADHA**

That will be something!

**OFFICER**

They are good people, you will like them. They are co-brothers, you know. Their wives may also be there, the two sisters. Of course they may not stay for the party after the pooja. It will be mostly, you know...

## SCENE 4

*Link.*

*The vastu function silhouetted against a cyclorama. Decorations, lights, music, guests arriving and leaving. Flashing lights around an illuminated signboard with the name, 'Shri Maruti Community Centre'. Fireworks, if possible.*

*The last of the guests leaves. As the lights fade out on the cyclorama, we hear a chorus of boisterous male voices, raising toasts, making merry: 'Cheers', 'Shri Maruti Zindabad', 'Make it bada', 'Soda, soda', 'On the rocks', etc.*

*Gradual fade out.*

## SCENE 5

*Raja's bedsitter. He, Radha, and Chandru are gathered after their meal. Raja is seated with his bandaged leg resting on a foot stool or low hassock. Chandru is seated next to him. Radha is standing apart.*

**RADHA**

You must be tired. Tell us when you want to go to bed.

**CHANDRU**

It's all right. I am not tired. We were going to talk after dinner.

**RAJA**

Good Dharwad peda. After such a long time. Picked it up from Swami's?

**CHANDRU**

Where else?

**RAJA**

Did you know that Vani-mausi used to make Dharwad peda herself? Always. Never got it from outside.

**CHANDRU**

I remember.

**RAJA**

People placed orders with her. She was very busy before festivals.

**CHANDRU**

Nobody makes peda at home anymore.

**RAJA**

I know. A pity. Vani-mausi's peda was a different class.

**CHANDRU**

Times have changed.

**RAJA**

I know. It's all so different now.

**RADHA**

Anyway, it was very thoughtful of Amma to have sent the Dharwad peda.

**RAJA**

Good old Swami's. His badam milk still selling by bucketloads?

**CHANDRU**

We were going to talk about... Not about Swami's. *(Long pause)*

We were wondering why there was no news from you for a long time. But now... After all that you have told me, I am really worried. I am frightened. I can't think what I should tell Amma?

**RADHA**

Nothing! Not just now. We will stir up unnecessary panic.

**RAJA**

Radha is right. There will be too much confusion.

**RADHA**

Also, we can't have too many people know just now, too many people getting involved... There is a case on hand. We will take it one step at a time.

**CHANDRU**

One step at a time? Look where the last few steps landed you!

**RAJA**

Chandru, now you are getting panicky. Easy. We have to take these things in stride.

**CHANDRU**

Encroachment, threats, physical assault – in your stride? Criminal acts of others to be tolerated and taken in your stride?

**RADHA**

Chandru, please listen to me. Will you listen? *(Pause)*

We can only hope that you will understand. Nobody in Rajanna's family understands what he is doing with his life. Nobody in my family knows what I am doing with mine. It is a path we have chosen and we must accept everything that comes our way. We have come to accept that. We never expected it to be easy.

We have also come to realise that it is too much to expect our families to understand. Why did he not join the IAS and make money and live a comfortable life? Why could she not have taken the CAT exam and got an MBA? They will not understand, they cannot understand. They have enough problems of their own in life – the price of dal and rice going through the roof, the servants getting haughty and talking back, the garbage piling up outside their very gates...

Chandru, you know that we both are very fond of you. You are Rajanna's favourite. And I love you like my own younger brother. Is it possible that you at least will understand a little bit about what we are doing? And why?

*(A long pause. Chandru wipes away a tear.)*

**CHANDRU**

You have to believe that I do. At least I try to.

**RAJA**

Chandru...

**CHANDRU**

What I have not fully understood is why the people who stand up for justice for others must get hurt.

**RAJA**

Neither did we, when we started.

**RADHA**

We cannot say we have the answer today. But we must go on.

**CHANDRU**

You can expect more trouble. This is only the beginning.

*(The doorbell rings. Raja motions to Chandru to go inside. He chooses to stay. Radha goes to the door. The Agent and the Contractor enter. They are carrying a bottle, gift wrapped, a box of sweets, and a small bag with a coconut and betel leaves in it.)*

**AGENT**

Namaskar! Namaskar! We hope we are not disturbing you.

**RADHA**

Not really. We have Mr Rajashekhar's brother visiting us.

**CONTRACTOR**

A relaxed family evening, I see.

**AGENT**

The boss was disappointed that you did not come to the vastu pooja function.

**CONTRACTOR**

He was keen that all neighbours must be present. Yes, he was disappointed.

**AGENT**

You could have brought your brother along. No problem. We are all one family here, you know.

**RAJA**

It's not that. You see...

**RADHA**

He has hurt his leg, you see.

**RAJA**

It was an accident.

**RADHA**

As you probably know.

**CONTRACTOR**

Ohho, we could have arranged a car. My car was making trips all the time.

**AGENT**

Anyhow, the boss has sent some gifts for you. Pooja prasad, some sweets for the occasion, and this.

**CONTRACTOR**

He was keen that we should come personally to give you these – on his behalf. He sends his regards.

**AGENT**

We will take your leave now. Sorry if we disturbed you. Please take care, sir. I will drop in tomorrow to discuss another matter. No urgency. You take rest now. Madam, any help you need – please call. No hesitation.

*(They leave. Raja, Chandru, and Radha are speechless.)*

**CHANDRU**

I am staying back. You need help.

## SCENE 6

*The spot with the Agent on a stool.*

**VOICE**

So… The bastard will not budge. Stubborn.

**AGENT**

Both of them. They were not interested in discussing the matter.

**VOICE**

He thinks it is his father's property or what?

**AGENT**

He is going to court, sir.

**VOICE**

I know, I know. His lawyer has already sent me a notice. Wants to see if things can be settled without the case admitted in court.

**AGENT**

Should we inform Acharya sir?

**VOICE**

He knows already. He is mentioned in the case.

**AGENT**

Who is the lawyer, sir? I can see if…

**VOICE**

It is another NGO. It works like a cooperative. About fifteen advocates giving time to the office. They enjoy the confidence of the Lokayukta.

**AGENT**

But sir, the Lokayukta has a lot of enemies too.

**VOICE**

That is not the point. It is not a power game now, not who knows who. It is who knows the other's moves first.

**AGENT**

It looks like they are trying to reach all NGOs for sympathy. They are trying to mobilise the support of this city's hajaar NGOs.

**VOICE**

They can try. The fucking NGOs are too busy fighting each other to be mobilised.

We don't have to worry about them. We have to prepare a favourable opinion in the high court in advance.

**AGENT**

One of them came to the vastu pooja, sir, Justice Prabhu.

**VOICE**

And public opinion. Who is approachable in the Times? What is the name of the silly girl in that buk-buk TV channel? She is always shouting that her channel was the first to report every minister's sex adventures.

**AGENT**

I will line them up, sir. Straight away.

**VOICE**

And get someone to watch all movements around the house – who is going in, who is going out.

## SCENE 7

*Raja's bedsitter. Chandru is alone, absorbed in a book, and making notes. The landline rings. It is Raja.*

**CHANDRU**

Hello? Oh, Rajanna... No, nobody so far. I will call you when they come. Yes, on your mobile... I will ask them to wait... Right, I will make tea for them... I was reading... Oh, about Habeas Corpus rights, how to demand court action against improper detention... Yes, I think I have found an angle... She is resting... All right, I will look into that.

*(He puts the receiver down. He peeps into the adjoining room, returns to the book, and begins to write. The doorbell rings. He goes to the door. Two men and a woman burst into the room. One of them has a still camera and starts to click away. The other has a compact video camera. The woman moves about making notes.)*

**WOMAN**

This is the home of Mr Rajashekhar, right?

**CHANDRU**

Yes, you must be from the Rehabilitation Centre.

**WOMAN**

In a way, yes. You could say that. We are from the media. I am from the New Times. My colleague is from New Times TV.

*(The men move into the adjoining room.)*

**CHANDRU**

Wait! You can't go in there!

**WOMAN**

Don't worry! They are not burglars. Nothing will be touched.

**CHANDRU**

There is a lady sleeping there.

**WOMAN**

We know. That is why we are here.

*(The two men bring a woman out of the room, half asleep. The cameras are blazing away. Chandru rushes to protect her, covering her face, not realising it is all caught on camera.)*

**CHANDRU**

I thought you were from the Rehab Centre. She is waiting for them to come and take her. She was resting.

**WOMAN**

She is not Mrs Rajashekhar, I suppose.

**CHANDRU**

No, Radha is out with Raja... Rajashekhar. This is a woman...

**WOMAN**

A prostitute.

**CHANDRU**

Not really. She is a Devadasi – one of the women brought into the city from –

**WOMAN**

There are others? Where are they kept?

**CHANDRU**

You don't understand! They are rescued from unlawful detention – the exploitation, humiliation. They are rehabilitated in a respectable centre in this city, found respectable jobs.

**WOMAN**

I do understand, believe me. I have seen a lot of them in respectable jobs. And you are... ?

**CHANDRU**

I am a visitor here. I have come from Mysore.

**WOMAN**
Very interesting. A visitor. This house is put to some very interesting uses. Thank you very much.
*(The three of them leave quickly.*
*Chandru is shattered, speechless. The woman stands beside him, bewildered. He motions her in, suggesting she go back to rest. She does.*
*Chandru sits, his head in his hands. A long pause.*
*The doorbell rings.)*

## SCENE 8

*Link*
*Spot on the police station desk. Chandru is waiting. He is alone. He rises, takes a step or two, and sits again. A long wait.*

## SCENE 9

*Loud music, a filmy disco number. Party sounds. The spot on the single stool. The Agent walks in as the music fades out. He is in a jolly mood, carrying a bottle and a glass as in the first scene in the spot.*

**AGENT**
Sir, you are a genius! Every paper and every TV channel is now rushing headlong into the story!

**VOICE**
As I have always said – you must strike first. It is the other bastard's job to prove his innocence then.

**AGENT**
Every channel is claiming to have found something new – reported for the first time.

**VOICE**
All you have to do is drop one pebble. The ripples will go on and on. You just sit back and enjoy the scenery.

**AGENT**
The panel discussions, expert comments, letters to the editor, the call-ins – Wah! They are doing a fantastic job.

**VOICE**
They are doing what they are supposed to be doing.

**AGENT**

The tip of the iceberg, they call it. You know what that means! They are dying to know how much more lies underneath.

**VOICE**

The public has a bottomless appetite for scandal. They want more and more all the time. All that holiness shit outside, but craving for more sleaze all the time. The bastard hypocrites!

**AGENT**

The dirtier, the better.

**VOICE**

Just drop the pebble, buss!

**AGENT**

The public will invent the dirty picture themselves.

**VOICE**

The public will believe what they want to believe.

**AGENT**

They believe every little thing reported. The media have more detectives than the entire Police force and CBI combined.

**VOICE**

All of them equally shit-headed.

**AGENT**

No doubt about it, sir!

**VOICE** *(Turning serious)*

What news of our good neighbours?

**AGENT**

No news, sir. The house remains locked. Nobody coming or going. It looks like they moved out immediately, in the middle of the night. That is good, no sir?

**VOICE**

You can't say. You can't be sure. The case is still on, right?

**AGENT**

Yes, sir.

**VOICE**

Has the lawyer sent any message?

**AGENT**

Only to say that the date of the hearing has been put off by a month.

**VOICE**

Must be getting a judge of their choice.

**AGENT**

Also to revise the case, sir. They are adding some details, some alleged activities...

**VOICE**

Some so-called anti-social activities at the Community Centre.

**AGENT**

Yes, sir. That is what they are calling it.

**VOICE**

So, you see what I was saying? It is too early to celebrate. The serpent is wounded, but not dead. We have to use a heavier stick to finish it off.

**AGENT** *(Looking off)*

Sir! It is the brother, Mr Chandrashekhar. He is heading this way.

**VOICE**

You handle him. *(Chandru enters the spot. The Agent rises to greet him.)*

**AGENT**

Ohho-ho-ho, Chandrashekhar sir! What a pleasant surprise. What an honour! How can I be of service to you?

**CHANDRU**

I want to talk to your boss.

**AGENT**

He is not available just now. But that does not matter. You can talk to me. I will take care of whatever you wish to discuss. Here, please be seated. I will get another seat. *(He picks up the bottle)*

Can I serve you one? Chota? No? Some tea-coffee? Later maybe, any time you say. This is like your house, you know.

*(The Agent steps out of the spot. Chandru remains standing. He takes out a slip of paper from his shirt pocket, glances through it for a few moments, and puts it back. The Agent reappears with a second stool.)*

**AGENT**

Please! Please be seated. Here. That's better. *(He sits anyway)*

Now, tell me, what can we do for you? Is it about... the case that is coming up in the High Court? It is so unfortunate it had to go so far, no? The boss was very upset. It could all have been sorted out simply, you know. *(Pause)*

By the way, how are they – your brother and sister-in-law? We have not seen them for some time. All well, I hope. The media people, I tell you... Anyhow, what can we do for you now? *(Pause)*

About the case, are you by any chance... ?

**CHANDRU**

The case is on. The hearing is on November 30th

**AGENT**

I see. Are you sure you do not wish to reconsider your decision? A rather unwise decision, as you know – as the events of the last few days have shown.

**CHANDRU**

The events of the last few days have strengthened the case.

**AGENT**

The bogus NGO that your brother and his woman friend have been running – yes, it is known that they are not married, but are simply partners – in crime. It is known that they have been engaged – in illegal activities.

**CHANDRU**

It is also known that the only illegal activities in this area have been on this illegally occupied piece of land in this illegally constructed building.

**AGENT**

You are referring to... ?

**CHANDRU**

You know very well what I am referring to.

**AGENT**

This Shri Maruti Community Centre?

**CHANDRU**

This bootlegging centre at daytime, boozing centre after sunset, and screwing centre after ten.

**AGENT**

You people have a fertile imagination, sir.

**CHANDRU**

Yes. It is extremely useful in our work. You will see that it is a very imaginative file of evidence submitted to the court.

**AGENT**

What I see right now is that you insist on being unreasonable.

**CHANDRU**

What you do not see may be more important.

**AGENT**

What are you proposing?

**CHANDRU**

That you still have time to do something about it – if you want to, of course.

**AGENT**

You are right. We should do something about it. Very sensible. Why allow things to get unnecessarily complicated.

*(We see the three hoodlums from earlier forming an arc around Chandru. They close in. Chandru sees them, but too late. They grab him and drag him out.*

*The Agent freezes. A long pause.*
*The Contractor joins the Agent.)*

**CONTRACTOR**

It was an accident. Looked like a hit-and-run case. Some people sleeping on the pavement thought they saw an SUV speeding away, but were not sure. He was rushed to the hospital in an auto rickshaw. But it was too late.

## SCENE 10

*There is a funeral pyre on the cyclorama. Seated before it are Raja and Radha, backs to the audience, silhouetted.*

*The tight spot Down-right comes on as at the start of the play. It is empty. We hear Chandru's voice.*

**CHANDRU'S VOICE**

You will not know left from right, they said. You will not know if you are coming or going. Bugger off. Go back to your hole.

*(The spot and the cyclorama go off. Raja and Radha rise, step downstage, face the audience, and freeze. Held long.)*

*Slow fade out*
***Close of play***

# CORRIGENDUM

Those who have read the three earlier plays will recognize the continuing thread, which should really not need explanation. *Corrigendum*, in particular, is seen by many as a companion piece to *Addendum*. On the other hand, precisely because there are some apparent similarities, the two plays may be separated into different programmes. The 'new economy' has led to a great deal of investment in real estate. This is largely from rising incomes in the middle and upper classes. It is seen as an investment, with the returns better than from the stock market or fixed deposits or even gold. Owning two or more homes is often 'the done thing', even if the additional homes are to be kept locked.

### Language Notes

*Charpoy:* Simple cot
*Sholapur:* Town in Central India, famous weave of bed linen.
*Chup:* Quiet
*Kali-mata:* Goddess Kali
*Haldi-kumkum:* Turmeric and vermillion – two coloured powders used in many traditional rituals.
*Karpoor:* Camphor
*Rasoi:* Traditional kitchen
*Jhadoo-pocha:* Broom and mop
*Lathi:* Staff, pole
*Satsang:* Gathering of seekers.
*Arati:* Ritual by oil lamp, followed by offering of flame to others. Refers both to the ritual and to the lamp.
*Puja:* Ritual worship
*Pranam:* Bowing in reverence.
*Odhni:* Length of cloth worn by women to cover the head, upper half of the body.
*Bhajan:* Religious group singing.
*No dum:* No spirit, no kicks

## CHARACTERS IN THE PLAY

MANYA ........................... *Caretaker-watchman of a Hindu burial ground*
BHANU ........................................................................ *His wife*
MAN 1, MAN 2 .............................. *Henchmen of an unseen builder boss*
SANTOSH .......................... *A successful corporate executive on a fast track*
DEEPA ....................................................... *His wife, riding the wave*
A SPIRITUAL GURU ............................... *Religious affiliation undefined*
TWO GROUPS OF MEN ................ *May be played by the same ensemble*

*The set for this play has a raised area upstage with an ultra-modern kitchen platform running Up-left to Up-right: a gleaming hood, sunken burners, sleek cabinets above and below, the newest models of appliances on the platform, and bright floor tiles. It is a narrow strip and brightly lit, as if revealed through a shaft of light coming in from a window. The strip is lit briefly in some scenes and remains in the dark at other times.*

*The strip serves as a backdrop. It is never used for any action in the play.*

*Stage Left has the front of a hovel, a gravel path reaching it from the Left wing. The front entrance has a make-shift curtain strung across. There is an old charpoy in front with some clutter around it. There are two stone tablets off the path. One has a hooded serpent, the other has the figure of goddess Kali, with the remains of flowers and vermillion on them*

*Stage Right and Centre are used for different spaces in a flexible way – a corner of a living room, the audience space in the premises of a spiritual guru, a police station, and so on.*

*The upstage set is seen before the play begins, with the rest of the stage unlit. The lighting upstage is subdued and gives the set a cosmic sci-fi look. The stage turns dark before the play begins.*

*There are several Hindu communities that bury their dead. It is not uncommon to see funeral processions led by a decorated hearse making their way to such burial grounds. The grounds are usually caste-specific locations.*

## SCENE 1

*In the dark we hear the sound of a car approaching. It halts. Two doors open and close. There are approaching footsteps on a gravel path. The lights open on the charpoy. Manya is asleep on it, covered fully with an old Sholapur sheet. Two men enter and stop before the charpoy. Man 1 has a baton in his hand. He taps the leg of the charpoy with the baton. Manya stirs, but does not rise. The man uncovers Manya with the baton and then taps his back side with it. Man 2 has a large carry bag that is bulging. He shouts 'Oy!'. A head appears at the entrance from behind the curtain. It is Bhanu. She is alarmed, but appears accustomed to intrusions.*

*The entire conversation below may be done in street Hindustani or any other regional language.*

**BHANU**

Who?

*(Man 2 puts his finger to his lips with a 'Shhh'. Man 1 moves the baton between Manya's legs. Bhanu tries to protest, but Man 2 moves swiftly to hold her still and cup her mouth. Man 1 and 2 laugh. There is no response from Manya. Man uses his baton to turn Manya over on to his back. He begins to stir. Man 1 strokes Manya's crotch with the baton. Man 2 releases Bhanu and thrusts her towards Manya.)*

**BHANU**

Manya!

*(Manya wakes up. Seeing Bhanu and the two others he sits up immediately.)*

**MAN 2**

Two weeks up.

*(Manya tries to rise. Man 1 holds him down with his baton.)*

Everything exactly as it was, we see. Both of you still here.

*(A dog barks from offstage.)*

All three of you.

**BHANU** *(To offstage)*

Kalu! Chup!

**MAN 2**

Kalu! Chup! We have visitors. They are here for darshan.

**MANYA**

Saheb...

**MAN 2**

What did you say?

**MANYA**

Saheb... Please...

**MAN 2**

Two weeks up. Everything exactly as it was.

**BHANU**

Saheb, it is not as if...

**MAN 2**

Are you talking to somebody?

**BHANU**

Saheb!

**MAN 2**

Is somebody talking to you?

**BHANU**

No, saheb.

**MAN 2**

Then keep all the openings in your body tightly shut – for now. And sit there, on the ground. You are coming in the way.

*(To Manya)* Is somebody talking to you?

**MANYA**

Saheb, I talked to the priest about it first.

**MAN 2**

Priest... What priest?

**MANYA**

The one who does the last rites.

**MAN 2**

Last rites... This place has not had a burial in the last six years. You think we don't know?

**MANYA**

Still – the burial ground is a sacred place, saheb.

**MAN 2**

The only thing buried here is tons of shit every morning. Sacred first rites before sunrise. Every morning.

**MANYA**

Saheb, the priest said...

**MAN 2**

The priest said. *(To Man 1)* The priest said.

**MAN 1**

The priest said.

**MAN 2**

The priest said. The priest who has no more last rites to do here. Does the priest come here still? When? Every morning before sunrise?

**MANYA**

Once a month. He comes to worship Kali-mata and pray for the departed souls she has taken away.

**MAN 2**

And you? What have you to do with his monthly shit?

**BHANU**

It is his job. He has to make preparations for the puja – wash and clean the line of idols, bring flowers, haldi-kumkum, coconuts, karpoor, he does all of that.

**MAN 2**

*(To her)* Still talking?

*(To Man 1)* Still talking.

**MAN 1**

Still talking. We have to do something about that. *(He starts to move)*

**MAN 2**

Wait. There is time.

*(To her)* Sooo... he prepares the puja for the priest. And what do you do for the priest? Once a month?

**BHANU**

Saheb...

**MAN 2**

You have no place here. Not you, and not you. No puja, no shit. No place here. You have to vacate this place immediately.

*(He takes out a sheet of paper and waves it before Manya.)*

**MANYA**

Saheb, you know that we are caretakers of the Kali shrine here and the burial ground.

**MAN 2**

Caretakers? What is that?

**MANYA**

The people who bury their dead here, they gave us the job of looking after the place.

**MAN 2**

The people who bury their dead...

**MANYA**

We are from the same caste.

**MAN 2**

I see. You were appointed. You got an appointment letter from these people, I suppose... You want to show me that.

**MANYA**

I have asked the priest to get me a copy from the caste headman.

*(A pause. Man 1 and Man 2 exchange glances.)*

**BHANU**

His father before him was in the same house that we are in.

**MAN 2**

House? You have a house here? Ohho, you mean this thing here, this shed put up illegally on public land. Tch, tch, tch, tch. It has to go.

*(Man 2 takes out a carboy from the carry bag. He unscrews the cap and begins to squirt the contents on the charpoy and on Manya. Bhanu, realizing what the men are up to, rises and rushes towards them. Man 1 holds her back. Man 2 squirts her too, and then starts to pour the liquid into the shed. He puts the carboy down and takes out a box of matches. Bhanu screams. Manya is petrified. Man 2 plays with the matches, lighting them one by one and tossing them in different directions. He holds the last match lit in front of Manya for a while, then blows it off. The match box is still in his hand. A long pause.)*

**MAN 2**

We will be back on Tuesday. Auspicious day.

*(Man 1 pushes Manya back on the charpoy with his baton.)*

**MAN 1**

Go back to sleep. The shit line starts only after an hour.

*(The two men drag Bhanu away offstage. Spot on Manya. Slow fade out.)*

## SCENE 2

*The kitchen platform strip is held for a while and fades out.*

*Deepa and Santosh are seated before a coffee table in their living room. There are architectural drawings and pamphlets on the table. Santosh has just returned from work and appears a bit tired, the tie loosened, and the cuffs folded up. There is a mug of coffee on the table. Deepa is energised.*

**DEEPA**

This will be the most important part of the house. A proper modern kitchen at last.

**SANTOSH**

Apartment. We are in a house now. We are buying an apartment.

**DEEPA**

Our own apartment. This old house...

**SANTOSH**

Is your Mom's. There is a line waiting to move in when we vacate it.

**DEEPA**

Vacate we will. I am tired of this old kitchen and dining, the bathroom, so primitive, ancient electric fittings, the flooring, everything.

**SANTOSH**

The other side being greener. You know how many of our friends love our red oxide flooring.

**DEEPA**

Okay baba, we will get those tiles that look like red oxide just for your den. You can keep rubbing your feet on the floor sitting there.

**SANTOSH**

Anyway, there's a long way to go before we choose tiles and fittings. You know there is a delay in the project.

**DEEPA**

Doesn't matter. Whenever that happens we will choose the very best fittings – especially for the dining room.

**SANTOSH**

I thought the most important part of the apartment was the kitchen. You wanted to show me the kitchen designs.

**DEEPA**

Same thing. The dining and kitchen areas are the same. The kitchen is part of the dining room. The platform with the cooking range will be between the drawing and dining rooms. As shown here. Look, the dining area overlooks the drawing room.

**SANTOSH**

And these are the pamphlets for the cooking range?

**DEEPA**

Yep! Aren't they smart? When people enter the house, the first thing that should strike them is a modern kitchen range stretching from here to here. Not a rasoi! You know, another room through another door, as we have everywhere, with a clutter of pots and pans and buckets and jhadoo-pocha and all.

**SANTOSH**

I see a step there. The kitchen and dining area, a little higher than the sitting room.

**DEEPA**

That's right. It must stand out just that bit.

**SANTOSH**

Wow! The kitchen platform as the altar!

**DEEPA**

Are you making fun of me? You don't like the design?

**SANTOSH**

No, no! Nothing like that. It's just that it will take some time for me to absorb it. When we enter this house, we see the puja room first.

**DEEPA**

Look, this is very important for me. The first two flats, you invested in, were not so important. Smart buildings in their own way, but we were not going to live in them. We just went with the schemes, two BHK, three BHK, or whatever. This time, it is different. You understand, no?

**SANTOSH**

Of course, I do. It's just that...

**DEEPA**

It's just that you don't think the kitchen is so important.

**SANTOSH**

Of course the kitchen is important! What gave you the idea... ?

**DEEPA**

My kitchen!

**SANTOSH**

Your dining!

**DEEPA**

Your den!

**SANTOSH**

Our bedroom! *(The kitchen platform strip fades in and is held for a while.)*

## SCENE 3

*Manya's hovel. Seated on the charpoy is an elder, his head and body covered with a chaddar. On the floor is huddled a small group of men, backs to the audience, their faces unseen. All of them have their heads and bodies covered. There is a pile of lathis on the ground. Manya is seated on one side.*

*The group sits still, pondering. Bhanu enters with a kettle and a wire basket with small glass tumblers of tea. She serves the group silently. She sits at a distance.*

*The elder bows his head. The rest follow. He raises his head, sits still for a few moments, rises, and steps up to Manya, who also rises. The elder places his hands on Manya's shoulders, blesses him, and leaves. Other members of the group rise and do the same one by one, picking up a lathi each as they leave.*

*Manya and Bhanu remain. Manya moves to the charpoy and sits, staring ahead. Bhanu moves to him and sits at his feet.*

## SCENE 4

*Crossfade to Right. A small group of men enters singing a bhajan. They sit, backs to the audience, before a spiritual guru who is concluding a satsang session. Santosh and Deepa are seen on one side. The group rises, takes the arati one by one, and leaves. Deepa bows in pranam, picks up the arati and other puja paraphernalia, and exits. Santosh and the guru remain.*

**GURU**

You appear troubled.

**SANTOSH**

It's nothing. We are happy that you came to this house for the satsang.

**GURU**

I go wherever I am called. Today it was your home.

**SANTOSH**

My humble home.

*(The kitchen platform strip fades in and is held for a while.)*

**GURU**

It is a beautiful home. We have had a beautiful satsang today, here, in the serene atmosphere of your home.

**SANTOSH**

I am glad you honoured us with your presence. Deepa and I are very happy that you accepted. I hope the arrangements were to your...

**GURU**

But you are not happy with what is happening in your life. What is it? Something not going right at work? Is it domestic? *(A pause)*

I can see that it is troubling you. Not Deepa-behn, only you.

**SANTOSH**

I did not think it was... You are right, guruji, there is something troubling me.

**GURU**

I know you do not have any children. Just the two of you. Is that... ?

**SANTOSH**

No, guruji, that is no problem at all. In fact it is a non-issue, so to speak. We agreed long ago not to have children.

**GURU**

Oh, is that so? It was your choice, then. Would you mind if I asked... ?

**SANTOSH**

Why we made that choice?

**GURU**

Not the choice, really. Your decision is to be respected. But whether it was one person's choice and the other went along... No need to tell me if you don't wish to.

**SANTOSH**

It's not something that seems important now. *(A pause)*

**GURU**

All right. It's something else, then. Do you want to... ?

**SANTOSH**

May I? If it is not...

**GURU**

Go ahead. You have been a gracious host. I am still enjoying your hospitality in your beautiful home. The least I can do is listen.

**SANTOSH**

We should have left this beautiful home some time ago. We are still here. God knows how much longer it will be.

**GURU**

Oh? So, it is something about your home that is troubling you.

**SANTOSH**

You could say that. It is about the flat that we are supposed to move into. We were expecting to take possession by next Diwali, just nine months from now. But the project is stuck.

**GURU**

I think you are referring to the Lake Shore project. I heard you had booked an apartment there.

**SANTOSH**

The project is stuck.

**GURU**

Some legal issues, I am told.

**SANTOSH**

The builder is not allowed to continue. There is a court order.

**GURU**

You have a lot of money blocked there, I suppose. *(Santosh nods)* Well, at least you have a roof over your heads now. You can continue to stay here, can't you? It is a family house, I believe.

**SANTOSH**

We can. Not forever, but we can for some time. It is from Deepa's family side.

**GURU**

Some pressure to vacate this house?

**SANTOSH**

Not directly. But yes, there are others who would be keen to move in.

**GURU**

We can pray that the legal issues will be sorted out in good time. *(A pause)*

**SANTOSH**

Builders have ways to sort out legal issues. They have the means.

**GURU**

Yes, I suppose they do. Any idea how long it is likely to take?

**SANTOSH**

It is not the time taken. We can wait. At least I can.

**GURU**

Look, son, it is completely understandable. Every man would like to be a good provider for his family. Every man would like to have a home that he can call his own. It is only a matter of time.

*(He notices Santosh is preoccupied.)*

It's something else.

**SANTOSH**

The means... When the construction starts again, and it is all done, and we do take possession, what is it that we will have possessed?

**GURU**

I see. Your conscience bothers you.

**SANTOSH**

Yes. That is not a home to be proud of.

**GURU**

Even if you have not spent a single rupee yourself on anything that can be called underhand.

**SANTOSH**

The papers will all be completely in order.

**GURU**

But tainted nevertheless.

**SANTOSH**

Yes. The legal issue that has got the project stuck... we didn't know about it when it started. That stretch of land was acquired by means that were completely illegal. And now that it has been challenged, the issue will be settled by... you know... other means that are...

**GURU**

I see. What do the other apartment owners think? What will they do?

**SANTOSH**

They don't care – as long as they can take possession.

**GURU**

But you do. It bothers you.

**SANTOSH**

I have not been able to sleep the last two weeks.

**GURU**

What do you think you should do?

**SANTOSH**

That is the problem. I don't know what to do. I don't know what to think.

**GURU**

Can't you pull out of the project? Take out your money? Or sell it to somebody else before completion. I hear the value has more than doubled already.

**SANTOSH**

It is not so easy. *(A pause)*

**GURU**

I see. May I tell you something? Only if you say yes. *(Santosh nods)*

It is one thing if you are bothered and are sleepless. Yes, one should go to bed with a mind that is calm and peaceful. But that you are sleepless because you have a conscience is nothing to be alarmed about. You should actually be proud of the fact that your conscience is alive and has not been blanked out by all that is happening around us.

**SANTOSH**

That is one way of looking at it.

**GURU**

There is another way of looking at it. May I? Again, only if you say yes.

**SANTOSH**

Please go on.

**GURU**

Do you really need the new apartment?

*(The kitchen platform strip fades in and is held for a while.)*

**SANTOSH**

Meaning?

**GURU**

Have you asked yourself the question? Do I really need a third apartment? What do I do with the two apartments I already have?

**SANTOSH**

Deepa-behn is very keen on this one.

**GURU**

I see. That is the connection, then? And that is what's troubling you.

**SANTOSH**

The two other apartments...

**GURU**

Just investments.

**SANTOSH**

Yes.

**GURU**

Investments for what? For whom?

**SANTOSH**

I don't know... The usual things... I suppose...

**GURU**

So, there are two different things on your conscience, not one. First, the means by which your new apartment will be – what do they call it – how it will be regularised. The second is whether you should have three apartments at all...

**SANTOSH**

I had not really...

**GURU**

When thousands upon thousands of people struggle to manage with a single room, paying half their earnings for it...

**SANTOSH**

I don't know how...

**GURU**

And millions of people have no roof over their heads at all.

## SCENE 5

*Manya's hovel. He is seated on the charpoy, Bhanu next to him. We hear the sound of a car approaching. It halts. Two doors open and close. Bhanu leaves hurriedly. Manya lies down and covers himself.*

*There are approaching footsteps on a gravel path. The two men enter and stop before the charpoy. The group of men from Scene 3 appears. They line up above the charpoy, facing the two men. They are armed with lathis. The two men try to leave, but are quickly surrounded by the group. Bhanu enters and watches from the edge. Manya rises and steps aside. The elder gives Manya a carboy. The others make way, but hold the two men in their places. Manya steps up to the two men, opens the carboy, and squirts them with the liquid. He puts the carboy down and takes out a box of matches. Man 1 and Man 2 are terror stricken. Manya plays with the matches, lighting them one by one and tossing them in different directions. He holds the last match lit in front of*

*Man 2 for a while, then blows it off. The match box is still in his hand. The two men are thrown on the ground. Manya and the others surround them, look down on them, and ready their lathis.*

*We hear the sound of three to four cars approaching. They halt. Doors opening and closing in quick succession. Bhanu enters and gestures in alarm. The group leaves hurriedly, leaving Man 1 and Man 2 on the floor.*

*There are sounds of several footsteps on the gravel path. Man 1 and Man 2 sit up.*

*Fade out.*

## SCENE 6

*Deepa and Santosh are seated at the coffee table in their living room. He is dressed for the day and is busy with last minute preparations on his laptop. She is reading a newspaper. There is a tea service on the table.*

*The kitchen platform strip fades in and is held for a while.*

**DEEPA**

All set for the presentation today?

**SANTOSH**

More or less. Just a bit of tidying up. The theme is innovation. The innovation culture needed in everything we do, in all departments.

**DEEPA**

Is the Company's Accounts Department listening?

**SANTOSH**

Maybe it will rub off on them some time... somewhere down the line.

**DEEPA**

Another hundred years maybe. A law unto themselves, aren't they?

**SANTOSH**

They are doing their job. I suppose that's the way to look at it.

**DEEPA**

Your travel bills of last year – when do you think they will be settled? Doing their job, doing their job... Taking their time over it.

**SANTOSH**

Let me just put the finishing touches here. The presentation must also be in line with the theme of innovation, no!

**DEEPA**

See if this will help. *(Tapping a column in the papers)* It says here that mankind will have to stop burying its dead by 2020. There simply is no more space for graves. So they are thinking innovations. Going six storeys downwards or going upwards in high rise graveyards.

**SANTOSH**

Upwards?

**DEEPA**

Why not? If we can have terrace gardening, we can have multi-storeyed tombs as well.

**SANTOSH**

I suppose the wisdom of cremation will be rediscovered.

**DEEPA**

Or also lost as a thing of the past. There may be no electricity for them in crematoriums.

**SANTOSH**

And no firewood for them on river banks.

**DEEPA**

And no rivers and no river banks.

**SANTOSH**

Anyway... I think I've got what I wanted as an opener. Here, take a look. It begins, 'Keeping our 2020 vision... beyond 2020.'

**DEEPA**

Neat!

**SANTOSH**

By the way, our building project has hit another road block.

**DEEPA**

Again? What is it this time?

**SANTOSH**

No water.

**DEEPA**

What! We were promised round-the-clock supply. Non-stop supply of water and electricity.

**SANTOSH**

The builder made those promises. The electricity and water supply people did not.

**DEEPA**

How can they do this? We've waited so long for our dream house! The Lake Shore Manor Homes!

**SANTOSH**

It was a lake some time ago. More like a puddle now.

**DEEPA**

What are we going to do about it?

**SANTOSH**

The apartment owners group is meeting the builder next week. There will be some hard talk – some hard bargaining.

**DEEPA**

Where's the question of bargaining! You better insist that they deliver every little detail promised in the sale deed.

**SANTOSH**

Or else!

**DEEPA**

Or else!

**SANTOSH**

Or else what? What if he says take it or leave it? What do we do?

**DEEPA**

I don't care about the others. What about us? What will you say if he takes that position?

**SANTOSH**

I'd say... Leave it. In fact, I say we should leave it even before we are driven to that point.

**DEEPA**

You must be out of your mind! Why leave it?!

**SANTOSH**

Because, it's not getting us anywhere. There has been one problem or the other with this building project. *(Pause)*

**DEEPA**

With the project? Or with you?

**SANTOSH**

I don't know what you...

**DEEPA**

You have been avoiding talking about the new apartment for some time. Behaving funny. Don't think I haven't noticed.

**SANTOSH**

I suppose it's the pressure in the office. I am handling the work of two departments the last few weeks.

**DEEPA**

I don't think it's the office. You love challenges at work.

**SANTOSH**

If you could explain what you mean... Behaving different...

**DEEPA**

Behaving funny. Behaving odd. Not yourself. You here, your thoughts elsewhere. There is somebody else in your life.

**SANTOSH**

Deepa, I swear there is no...

**DEEPA**

I think it's that swamiji. He has some hold on you, I think.

**SANTOSH**

He is an enlightened person. There is a lot to learn from him.

**DEEPA**

He has seduced you. I have heard of swamijis seducing women. But this one – is he gay?

**SANTOSH**

Deepa!

**DEEPA**

Are you turning gay?

**SANTOSH**

Deepa! For god's sake! There is no need to jump to wild conclusions. Yes, he has had an impact on me. But it is nothing like what you are imagining. We can talk about it when I am back from work. I will need some time to explain – to talk about this calmly.

**DEEPA**

You will be late getting home. You will drop into his ashram on the way back! For a quick consultation!

**SANTOSH**

I am getting late now. I have to leave – I have to be in time for the conference. I promise I will get back home directly. *(He packs up)*

**DEEPA**

Wait. *(A pause. She stands in his way. She dials a number)*

Mr Anand Mehta, please... Anandbhai, good morning. You will have to excuse Santosh for a slight delay. He has had a flat... Yes, he had to change the tyre... Took a little longer than usual. Aadat nahin hai, na... Washing up after that... He will be there soon. Give him a few minutes to get his breath back... How is Ashabehn? All well, na? Yes, we must meet. We keep saying that... Achcha, bye. *(Disconnects)*

You have to tell me this before you leave. *(Pause)*

Whatever your relationship with the swamiji... I don't care. If it's a men's thing, so be it. I don't care. What I want to know is what it has to do with our new apartment. *(Santosh returns to his seat, puts the briefcase down, sits.)*

**SANTOSH**

Now that I have got nicely late, changing a flat and all... Let me think where to begin.

**DEEPA**

Not interested in the beginning. What is the end?

**SANTOSH**

I am not for it. I want to pull out of the project.

**DEEPA**

Why?!

**SANTOSH**

I am not sure it's worth all the trouble.

**DEEPA**

What trouble? Instead of the promised eighteen months, let them take thirty months. They will find ways to fix the water and electricity problems. It can't be the first time they are doing this. It's their job! There must be something else on your mind.

**SANTOSH**

Maybe.

**DEEPA**

And you are not telling me.

**SANTOSH**

Not because I don't want to... I just haven't got down to it... Not knowing how you will take it. Will you try to understand?

**DEEPA**

Try me.

**SANTOSH**

Your graveyards going up into the sky... Why do you think it has come to this?

**DEEPA**

More people to bury! More people born, more people dead, more bodies to get rid of. What does it have to do with our apartment?

**SANTOSH**

It is part of the eighty-twenty thing. *(Santosh starts on a long, rambling explanation, hunting for words. She listens, incredulous, rises slowly towards the end, and exits.)*

**SANTOSH**

I had to ask myself... I asked myself if I really needed three apartments... What would I do with them... ? Is that me? Who am I? What is my job? What is it all about? I asked myself... There were no ready answers... All I got as answers were images of childhood... A happy childhood... My first bicycle... The family waiting to receive me when I had circled the maidan... The picnic by the riverside... Gathering jamoon and bel and anjeer and guavas in season and covering up in layers of woollens in winter... I cycled to school, I cycled to college... I got a two-wheeler only when I got my first job, a moped... And my first watch... From my uncle... Growing up in a small town and having everything... Not wanting anything else...

Not knowing what else to want... My first proper motorbike when we got married... Presented by your father... Our first car... Only two years after we got married... A flat... A second flat... A third... What next? If we had children... We would reserve places in the play school... We would reserve a place as soon as the pregnancy was confirmed... Primary school... Secondary school... College... We were wise not to have children... We celebrate our decision every time we see the children in our neighbourhood... the cousins and friends and their children... Sweet kids, but what a legacy left to them... Graveyards... No place... People reserving space on the twentieth floor...

*(Deepa has left the scene by now. Santosh is still explaining to her)*

**SANTOSH**

It is all the eighty-twenty thing really... 80 per cent of the land occupied by 20 per cent of the people... 20 per cent of the people served by the 80 per cent others...

**DEEPA** *(Off)*

You are late! Remember to pick up the lunch box.

*(Santosh picks up his briefcase and leaves. Scene empty for two beats. The kitchen platform strip fades in and is held for a while)*

## SCENE 7

*A desk in a police station. A sub-inspector is examining a sheaf of papers. (Called Police here.) Manya and the elder are standing. They are accompanied by a social activist member of an NGO. (Called Social here.) He serves as a go-between, interpreting statements, and consulting the two others, now and then, before responding to the sub-inspector.*

**POLICE**

Who will sign the FIR? *(Consultation)* Both of them? *(A nod)*

Let me repeat the main points here before they sign. It happened three hours ago, you say. *(A nod)* About eight to ten men came there. *(Consultation. Social corrects the number.)* Eighteen, you say. *(Consultation)* Are you sure? You counted? Can we put it as six to eight? Are you sure? You counted? All right, eighteen. Now, this is important – they attacked. *(A nod)* They attacked first. They came in attacking, you say. *(A nod)* Any proof of the attack? *(The men show parts of their bodies)*

**SOCIAL**

Sir, they were all taken to the Corporation hospital immediately. The report is there – lacerations, contusions, broken bones, two head injuries. One dead. Fortunately no more.

**POLICE**
So they attacked. What else?

**SOCIAL**
The woman, Bhanu by name, Manya's wife...

**POLICE**
She is reported missing.

**SOCIAL**
She was abducted. First, raped in front of the group by two men, then, carried away.

**POLICE**
Do you want to report rape? There will be complications...

**SOCIAL**
Sir, this is an FIR. We have to write what we...

**POLICE**
All right, have it your way. You say they witnessed the rape.

**SOCIAL**
All of them. They were forced to watch it. Only two are filing the FIR.

**POLICE**
Forced to, you say. How? What weapons were they carrying?

**SOCIAL**
Mostly iron rods and chains. Two had choppers. And two had guns.

**POLICE**
Guns? *(Consultation)*

**SOCIAL**
One hand gun, maybe revolver. One big gun, like what guards carry in front of banks.

**POLICE** *(Writing)*
Guns... one revolver... one shotgun.

**SOCIAL**
And the choppers.

**POLICE**
Two choppers. What happened afterwards?
*(Manya and the elder break down. They sit on the floor sobbing.)*

**SOCIAL**
It is there, sir. Bhanu was carried away. Then the men set fire to Manya's shed. They threw Bhanu's odhni into the fire before leaving. They shouted abuses at the group, calling them low caste pariah dogs. They ordered them to stay there without moving, then drove away.

**POLICE**
I see... How did you happen to go there? When?

**SOCIAL**

It was after about one hour. Their children attend our school. Four of them came running to my house with the news. I rushed there immediately. There was still a lot of smoke coming from a heap where the shed was. There were zinc sheets on the ground, all black, but everything else was ash.

**POLICE**

Sir, you should know that a case like this will become very complicated – weapons, fire, rape, abduction... Like some filmi masala thing. You can see that, na?

**SOCIAL**

But all true. Very unfortunately for them.

**POLICE**

And your getting involved in all this...

**SOCIAL**

So? Are you saying it is better if they don't register a case when something like this happens?

**POLICE**

Sir, you don't know how it works. You think you know everything, coming here with them, big hero and all, maybe standing for elections. But you don't know anything. These people are very good in cooking up cases and registering FIRs.

*(Telephone rings)* They do it all the time. Very good actors. *(Takes call)*

Hello? Speaking... Just a minute... I will write it down... Please give me the exact time... How many in the group... ? I see. I see.

*(He disconnects and looks at Social)*

There is an FIR registered at the Ring Road Police Station. It says a small group of four men parked their vehicle and stepped outside to buy cigarettes. They were attacked by this group here. Their vehicle was smashed and set on fire. They have recovered the lathis used in the attack.

*(He looks knowingly at Social and smiles)*

I have to detain you here. You people can't leave the station now.

*(He picks up the phone, dials an extension.*
*Fade out)*

## SCENE 8

*Santosh's living room. It is dark. Santosh enters, puts his briefcase down.*

**SANTOSH**

It went very well. They really liked the opening. I told them at coffee break where I got the idea from... Deepa?

*(He looks about. He switches on a light [A standing lamp]. He notices a letter on the coffee table. He picks it up and reads it. He sits down, frozen.)*

## SCENE 9

*The area where Manya's hovel used to be. There are corrugated sheets cordoning the area. There is a sign that says PVT. PROPERTY. TRESPASSERS WILL BE PROSECUTED. Manya and the group are huddled before a small table and chair. Presently Man 2 enters, very business-like, and takes the chair. Man 1, accompanying him, places a briefcase on the table, takes out several large envelopes, a register, and a stamp pad. The huddle rises in respect. Man 2 motions to the group and they form a line. One by one, they step up and receive an envelope from Man 2 after Man 1 has got an inked thumb impression in the register. Manya is the last to receive the envelope. Man 2 signals the group to move along. Manya remains. Man 2 pulls Manya's face close to him and speaks.*

**MAN 2**

You don't deserve this, you lump of pariah dog shit. You are lucky the saheb came into the picture and settled things. Another two hours and you would have been finished – all of you – in one stroke. No fuss, no sign of any of you anywhere. Lucky bastards! Thank the saheb in your prayers. You can all start a new life now. Who knows, the saheb may also give you work on the site. Lucky bastards! My advice to you, go away. Go far away. If you hang about in these parts, you may cross my path. I cannot be so nice to you then. Pariah dog shit. Go! Why are you standing there, staring? Go!

**MANYA**

Saheb...

**MAN 2**

You insist on opening your mouth?

**MANYA**

Saheb... Bhanu...

**MAN 2**

Bhanu?

**MANYA**

My wife...

**MAN 2**

Aah, that woman who used to be here. What do I know about her? What do I care? Go! Go, start a new life. Saheb will be very pleased.

## SCENE 10

*A small group of men enters, singing a bhajan. They sit, backs to the audience, before the spiritual guru who is concluding a satsang session. Santosh is one of the group. He is in a simple white dhoti, a top cloth over his bare chest. The group concludes the bhajan, bows to the swamiji, resumes seating. The guru passes a silver tray filled with flower petals to all gathered and motions Santosh to come forward and sit by his side.*

**GURU**

I want you all to join me in welcoming a new follower of the path. He has chosen to renounce his worldly attachments and seek the higher truth by taking this path. The higher truth that resides in all of us, waiting to be found, the truth to be found by taking the path. Please join me in blessing him as he starts a new chapter in his life. *(Santosh prostrates before the Guru. The others toss flower petals on the prostrate Santosh. He remains prostrate as the others take their leave and depart. Santosh sobs, still prostrate. Guru raises Santosh and seats him on a cushion. Santosh hugs the standing Guru and continues sobbing. Guru strokes his head patiently and finally raises his head, looking deeply into his eyes. Santosh stops sobbing.)*

**GURU**

It has passed.

*(Guru moves away, putting things in place, rolling up mats, and clearing the floor. Santosh attempts to help. Guru keeps him seated. Guru speaks to Santosh on the move, taking time between sentences.)*

Your new life has begun... Untying oneself from the old life is never easy... The attachments... An image beckoning... The memories of sights... sounds... The pain of knowing that they are not real anymore... All you need to know is that memories are gifts of nature, gifts of god... It does no good to deny them... Pain too, is a gift of god... How can we deny it...? Who are we to deny it... ?

*(By now he has cleared up and is standing next to Santosh again)*

You have done well, surprisingly well. You have moved fast, you have been firm. You have a god-given strength within you that you might not have known. This is indeed your first discovery of truth.

**SANTOSH**

It is all on account of you, guruji.

**GURU**

I know well what you have gone through. It was a trial of fire. But look at yourself now. You have come out of it strong and firm. It has passed. Do you not feel a lightness of being? A great invisible burden lifted off you? An eagerness to pick yourself up and walk towards the sun? *(Santosh nods in agreement)*

**GURU**

Shall I make some tea? *(Santosh nods again)*

It will be green tea. No milk, no sugar.

*(He moves to fetch the tea. The kitchen platform strip fades in and is held for a while. He returns with a pot and two mugs and sits next to Santosh.)*

**GURU**

So... What are they going to do with the house now?

**SANTOSH**

I don't know. She may not want to live there by herself. Very unlikely.

**GURU**

One of your other...

**SANTOSH**

She can always move into one of them. She is a joint owner.

**GURU**

There should be no bitterness about the decision you have taken – both of you have taken.

**SANTOSH**

We are still man and wife... after all.

**GURU**

Very beautiful house. I remember the satsang you had organised there.

**SANTOSH**

Yes, it is a beautiful house. Old world, but beautiful.

**GURU**

You were very generous in transferring the new apartment to the Trust for our use as a guest house. It is ideally situated.

**SANTOSH**

That was the best thing to do... Instead of pulling out of the project and losing a lot of money... Not that the money means anything now.

**GURU**

I understand the project is likely to pick up once again. It may be ready within a year it seems.

**SANTOSH**

I suppose so.

**GURU**

Your putting in a word must have been important.

**SANTOSH**

I did not do anything more than...

**GURU**

You did the right thing at the right time. The authorities were convinced. The idea of creating a meditation and satsang hall on the East side of the project was yours. All they had to do was reduce the area for the club house – it was a needless extravagance anyway – and create the satsang hall for us... a civic amenity for the locality. It was very farsighted of you.

**SANTOSH**
All I did was suggest the idea. They did all the work with the authorities.

**GURU**
All working out to everybody's satisfaction. You are truly god-sent.

**SANTOSH**
A humble disciple. I have a long way to go, the journey has just begun. *(Pause)* I hope you will reconsider the decision to turn the apartment into the centre's guest house. I would dearly wish to see you stay there yourself. I can serve you there readily.

**GURU** *(Looking at him fondly)*
We shall see. *(Pause)* It is large enough.

**SANTOSH**
I can be at the satsang hall and still serve you. I will be happy to be there as a caretaker, in one corner of the hall.

**GURU**
What have you decided about your stocks in the Company?

**SANTOSH**
I need time to think about it. Whatever I do, it must be for the greatest good. It must benefit all.

**GURU**
Yes, it must.

**SANTOSH**
I wish I could have arranged something more than a meditation and satsang hall. We need a proper spiritual centre.

**GURU**
It is very thoughtful of you. Very noble.

**SANTOSH**
In time we should have an International Centre in this city.

**GURU**
How your mind dances! A butterfly!

**SANTOSH**
Always at the service of my guru. If I have your consent, I can start scouting for opportunities.

**GURU**
I understand there is another building project that has stalled – somewhere in the Southern extension of the city.

**SANTOSH**
I can find out.

**GURU**
On account of some dispute over the land.

**SANTOSH**
Same story. It is always a dispute over land. We can never tell who is right and who is making false claims.

**GURU**
As in your own project.

**SANTOSH**
As long as the project is put to good use at the end...

**GURU**
As long as some innocent people are not exploited – poor people, homeless people, people in need.

**SANTOSH**
A proper spiritual centre is the greatest need of people today. This city needs spiritual enlightenment very badly. Most of our troubles arise out of this deficiency.

**GURU**
The enthusiasm of my disciple pleases me! But you need rest now.

**SANTOSH**
I will find out more about this project.

## SCENE 11

*The project site where Manya's hovel used to be. Man 1 and Man 2 escort Santosh in and seat him at a table.*

**MAN 2**
I am sure the General Manager will be pleased to see you. Please be seated. We will tell him about your visit.

**MAN 1**
You will have some tea?

**SANTOSH**
Thanks. *(Man 1 leaves)* Plain lal chai if possible.

**MAN 2**
It is an honour to have the Guruji take interest in this project. Next time he must visit us himself.

**SANTOSH**

Why not? He always takes interest in public welfare and anything that can serve the people.

**MAN 2**

Please wait here. I will inform Manager-saheb. Tea will be here soon. Is there anything else... ? We have tea service twenty-four hours!

*(Man 2 leaves. Santosh sits, takes out a small book, and begins to read. Bhanu enters with tea. She is looking cleaner and better dressed. She keeps the tea on the table. Santosh notices her. Bhanu smiles.)*

**BHANU**

Never take milk or sugar?

**SANTOSH**

Avoid it if I can.

**BHANU**

No dum in this. Plain watery chai.

**SANTOSH** *(Sipping)*

It is good!

**BHANU**

Come to buy a flat?

**SANTOSH**

They must all be sold out.

**BHANU**

That's what they say. But they'll have a way to find one for you.

**SANTOSH**

So, not all sold out?

**BHANU**

So, you've come to buy a flat.

**SANTOSH**

Not really. Just finding out more.

**BHANU**

Then they'll say they are all sold out.

**SANTOSH**

You seem to know them well. Are you part of the office?

**BHANU**

You could say that.

**SANTOSH**

Working with them from the start?

**BHANU**

From long ago... from very long ago.

**SANTOSH**

You stay here?

**BHANU**

You could say that.

**SANTOSH**

Behn... Are you trying to... ?

*(Manya has entered quietly and is taking in the scene. It is possible that he has had a drink or two to prepare himself. The confrontation between Manya and Bhanu has physical handling that reveals Manya's desperation and Bhanu's dilemma. The details are best left to the ingenuity of the actors. The exchange between them may be in the local language. )*

**MANYA**

Bhanu!

**BHANU**

Manya! What are you doing here? Go away. They will kill you if you are seen here.

**MANYA**

You are coming with me.

**BHANU**

No! I cannot come with you. Go away now!

**MANYA**

You will come!

**BHANU**

No! I cannot. Please leave now. They will be here any moment.

**MANYA**

Why can't you? What has happened to you?

**BHANU**

Nothing. I can't explain. But I can't come with you. You will die if you are found here. Go now. Go!

**MANYA**

You will die before they can get their hands on me. So... That's the way it is!

*(He has drawn out a large knife by now.)*

You slut! You filthy bitch! They call us pariah dogs and drive us out. But they don't mind housing a pariah bitch! So that's where you have ended up!

**BHANU**

Manya! You will never understand. I beg you please go now. I may have had to leave you, but I don't want to see you hurt. No, you won't be hurt. You will be killed.

**MANYA**

So this is what you are down to? Your line of work? Miserable eunuchs like this for clients! I can chop off his prick and he will ask his god to forgive me.

*(Manya lunges at Santosh. Bhanu rushes to hold him back and places herself between them. Manya grabs her and throws her on the ground. He pounces on her, strangles her to death. He then stabs her several times. Finally he breaks down and sobs over her dead body. Santosh kneels beside him, taking the knife away, placing his arm over his shoulder. Manya rises abruptly, hearing footsteps. He rushes off.*

*Man 2 enters and freezes in shock at the sight – Bhanu dead, in a pool of blood, Santosh kneeling beside her, the knife in his hand.)*

*Fade out.*

*The kitchen platform strip is held for a while.*

*Fade out.*

***Close of play***

# In Absentia

*The body in question*
***Vijay Padaki***

FOR
**PAUL GREENOUGH**

## INTRODUCTION

In Absentia was the second play in the series that came to be called *Tales from the City*. The seeds for the play were tossed while I had a visiting assignment at the University of Iowa in 2011. A group meeting at the International Writing Program went, not surprisingly, into the many paradoxes that constitute contemporary India. Much of the discussion was about the dizzying pace of economic growth that coexisted with the most degrading levels of poverty. The 'Bangalore phenomenon' could not escape attention. The information technology hub of India had clearly contributed hugely to the transformation of India. In the process, the city had transformed itself. The 'sociology of the city' appeared a very fascinating subject indeed. It could be examined through a body of available hard statistics, demographics, consumption patterns, habitat, traffic density, the addition of cars and two-wheelers to the roads per month, the migration to the city from other States, the emerging social institutions and demand-supply chains to serve the needs of change, and so on. It could also be examined through the lives lived by people in the new city – in roles unimagined just fifteen years earlier.

Unlike the other four plays in the set, *In Absentia* is a 'white collar' tale, set among occupations of the new Bangalore. The migration from poorer, more conservative communities in other parts of India has presented new experiences to the workforce – both new opportunities and new challenges in realigning their lives. As with all the plays in this volume, the play is based on real characters I came to know as part of my professional work. The narrative is fictional, with three storylines running in parallel. It is an attempt to capture an elusive whole over the parts.

The action of the play takes place in multiple spaces, and is best accomplished through a lean and mean stage design. The characters in the different threads of the story cross over to other spaces as needed.

The play may be combined with any other in the set of five for a double-bill. In an evening of readings in Canada, it was combined with *Untitled.* The double-bill was titled *Judgement* as both the plays were exploring frontiers of jurisprudence.

### Language Notes

*Kab se shuroo kiya?:* When did you start on this?
*Achcha nahin laga toh theek hai:* It's okay if you didn't like it.
*Zara bold lagta hai:* Seems a bit bold.
*Sach baat kahoon?:* Should I tell you the truth?
*Ab tak jhoot baat bol rahe the?:* You were telling lies till now?
*Isko dating kehte hain na?:* This is called dating, no?
*Haalat:* State, condition, plight.

*Vagairah:* Etcetra.
*Kuch agenda hai kya?:* You have some agenda, or what?
*Sachmuch:* Quite true.
*Matlab?:* Meaning?
*Kirana shop:* Small all-purpose shop.
*Baahar khana pani:* Eating out.
*Thali:* Traditional meal with several dishes in one large plate.
*Rasam:* South Indian broth, had with rice or sipped by itself.
*Do minute ke liye:* For two minutes.
*Dhamaal:* Ruckus.
*Mangetar:* Fiancé.
*Lafda:* Scam.
*Shaadi:* Marriage.
*Maaro goli!:* Shoot it down!
*Mujhe toh yeh kuch blackmail jaisa lag raha hai:* It looks like blackmail to me.

## CHARACTERS IN THE PLAY

JUSTICE KRISHNAMURTHY
(KNOWN AS MURTHY) .......................... *Old school, preparing to retire, but always learning*

VIMALA, HIS WIFE ....................... *Traditional and devoted to the home*

A WOMAN LAWYER ................................ *Young, smart, contemporary*

A WOMAN CLIENT ........................... *Seeking an exit and a fresh start*

VISITOR AT THE COURT/MAN .............................. *A troubled soul*

A COUNSELLOR ......................................... *Professional in procedure*

GIRL IN OFFICE ....................................... *Migrant from a small town, unsophisticated but smart*

BOY IN OFFICE ............................................. *Brought up in the city, but middle-class upbringing*

TEAM LEADER .................................. *Career oriented, business savvy*

## SCENE 1

***Justice Krishnamurthy's home***

*An old sofa with a small coffee table. Sound of a door opening and closing. Voice of Vimala, wife of Justice Krishnamurthy, offstage.*

**VIMALA** *(Off)*

There is a courier letter for you on the table... I'm bringing tea in five minutes.

*(Krishnamurthy enters, keeps his briefcase on the coffee table, sits, and closes his eyes. He opens his briefcase, takes out a folder, and leafs through the papers. He stops and stares ahead.)*

**VIMALA** *(Off)*

There was a call asking if the courier letter had come... I said yes... They requested you read it soon. At your earliest convenience she said... it was a woman on the phone... I didn't get the name.

*(Krishnamurthy notices an envelope on the table, picks it up, and puts it back. He goes back to the folder, puts it down, and covers his eyes again.)*

**VIMALA** *(Entering)*

I tried to get her name, but she seemed to be in a hurry... Is something wrong? *(No response)* Bad day at court? Politicians poking their noses into petty cases again?

**MURTHY**

No, no, I was just... I was just thinking about a case... and wondering... Nothing special. What's for dinner today?

**VIMALA**

Nothing special! But your tea must be ready. Let me get it.

**MURTHY**

Wait! No hurry... We can... Why don't we go out for dinner tonight? They say there is a very good thali at the new Krishna Sagar off Netaji Road. What do you say? We can start early to avoid the rush.

**VIMALA**

Hmmm... You need that cup of tea! There is something on your mind. I will be back in a minute.

(*Exit Vimala. Murthy picks up the papers again. He turns to the unseen audience in the court and speaks above their heads.*)

**MURTHY**

Court adjourned! *(Pause)* The cup that cheers needs a pinch of masala!

## SCENE 2

***The City Court***

*It is the last case of the day. There is a young woman seated at a desk with a lawyer, also a woman. There is a visitor standing at a distance, a Man, not clearly seen. He appears in a later scene.*

*The Judge is wrapping up. He is not seen, but may be imagined seated at a height above the front row of the audience.*

*The sound of the gavel striking. The lawyer and the young woman rise.*

**MURTHY** *(Voice)*

In the absence of the respondent in person or by representation, and after a full examination of the petitioner's case claiming incompatibility in marriage, the evidence appears sufficient to establish that the petitioner is justified in seeking dissolution of the marriage by decree of divorce. This court hereby passes the order as follows. The marriage of the petitioner and the respondent is to be dissolved with the decree of divorce. There are no costs claimed by either party and there is no settlement of claims. The case is closed.

*(The sound of a gavel striking. The woman and the lawyer bow. They shake hands. The woman is joined by the visitor. A brief hug. The two of them leave, leaving the lawyer alone, facing the judge. She bows once more to leave.)*

**MURTHY** *(Voice)*

Wait. That was the last case for the day. Can you stay back a minute?

**LAWYER**

Yes, sir. *(Pause)*

**MURTHY**

Divorce within a month of marriage...

**LAWYER**

Yes, sir.

**MURTHY**

Are we not expected to first make an effort to save the marriage?

**LAWYER**

Yes, sir, but the petitioner's claim of incompatibility...

**MURTHY**

Counselling? A period of trial separation?

**LAWYER**

The petition was uncontested, sir. The court went through the due process of notice to both parties.

**MURTHY**

So I noted.

**LAWYER**
There was no respondent, no defence...

**MURTHY**
I know. I was compelled to issue the decree.

**LAWYER**
We had no choice, sir.

**MURTHY**
Do you remember her answer to my last question?

## SCENE 3

***Justice Krishnamurthy's home***
*Murthy is at the coffee table on a comfortable chair. His wife, Vimala, has drawn up a hassock or modha and is also seated. There is a cup of tea on the table.*

**MURTHY**
It was a mistake... That's what she said. Just like that. Like she had just got the spelling wrong, or got the total wrong in her monthly grocery accounts.

**VIMALA**
Or got on the wrong bus.

**MURTHY**
It is something new, this incompatibility.

**VIMALA**
The husband... didn't he contest the petition for divorce?

**MURTHY**
No.

**VIMALA**
Strange.

**MURTHY**
He had the right to a defence. He could have asked for a lawyer.

**VIMALA**
You would think... married just one month, you say?

**MURTHY**
First time in my court. There have been cases before the other judges. First one for me... in all my years.

**VIMALA**
And not the last, I am sure.

**MURTHY**
It's on the increase, they say. The number of cases coming up...

**VIMALA**

One month marriages – why get married at all? As if there isn't enough freedom for youngsters to do whatever they want to?

**MURTHY**

It is not for us to deny the freedom today even if we did not have it in our time. People still get married.

**VIMALA**

The marriage certificate is some sort of licence then? You know – letting people know you are occupying one half of a bed legally?

**MURTHY**

People still get married. People still think they made a mistake. People still get divorced.

**VIMALA**

You know, our Cheenu used to go all over the place with Ratna before they married. We didn't object, did we?

**MURTHY**

Of course we did, but only between you and me, here, at home. We put on a different face for people outside. We had to be seen as modern parents, no?

**VIMALA**

Anyway, it was still a proper marriage.

**MURTHY**

Properly arranged in the end.

**VIMALA**

Ratna is such a sweet girl. She is so good for Cheenu, a really good find, don't you think?

**MURTHY**

It does not help.

**VIMALA**

Huh?

**MURTHY**

The change of topic.

**VIMALA**

I am sorry, I didn't mean to...

**MURTHY**

We both know you are very good at it.

**VIMALA**

You looked disturbed, so I just...

**MURTHY**
My getting disturbed is not important. I am not supposed to let my personal feelings get in the way. The facts are what matter.

**VIMALA**
And the facts are... ?

**MURTHY**
As of now, a strong impression, till somebody has the statistics right. The impression pointing to a trend – a rapid increase in the number of cases.

**VIMALA**
Increase in divorce? I thought that was well established already.

**MURTHY**
Increase in the grounds cited... incompatibility

**VIMALA**
Is that new?

**MURTHY**
Cases moved by women, citing incompatibility.

**VIMALA**
What is this incompatibility business anyway?

## INTERLUDE 1

*The stage is dark, except for a dim spot picking up an easy chair with a man's clothes tossed on it. In the background we hear a woman moaning expectantly. The moaning stops. A man rushes in, bare, wrapped in a towel, and collapses on the chair, holding his head in his hands. He takes out a cell phone from below the pile of clothes, dials a number, and turns away, cupping the phone and speaking in a whisper. We do not hear his words. He puts the phone away, picks himself up, dresses hurriedly, and rushes out.*

## SCENE 4

***The Lawyer's Chamber***
*The lawyer and the woman are seated at her desk.*

**LAWYER**
It will be very difficult, ma'am. It is all loaded against you.

**WOMAN**
I see. So what's the way out? I go my way and he goes his way, but remain Mr and Mrs on paper?

**LAWYER**

You could put it that way. You could try again after six months or a year. An appeal for divorce one month after the marriage date... the court will not touch the case.

**WOMAN**

Is that the law?

**LAWYER**

Not really. It is the convention. The court is expected to give first preference to reconciliation by any means.

**WOMAN**

Not law, but legal.

**LAWYER**

All judges are bound by the convention. The judge who hears this case will be obliged to prescribe corrective measures – marriage counselling, for example. In any case he will ask for both of you to be present. He will insist on a defence by your husband.

**WOMAN** *(Pause. Rising)*

What if he is not present?

**LAWYER**

The husband?

**WOMAN**

If he is not interested himself, there is no room for defence is there? No need for defence.

**LAWYER**

Technically, yes, it can happen that way. The judge will still want to know why. Why is the husband not contesting the case? Why is he not available? Why is the case presented ex-parte? Unless...

**WOMAN**

Unless what?

**LAWYER**

There are grounds that can be called truly rare...

**WOMAN**

So, it is possible?

**LAWYER**

You will have to satisfy the court that the incompatibility you claim may be deemed truly extraordinary grounds.

**WOMAN**

I see... *(Moving away)* In an open court...

**LAWYER**

If it is difficult for you... we can arrange a private hearing.

**WOMAN**

And his lordship will understand?

**LAWYER**

We can only hope he will. Now... shall we proceed with your statement? I will be obliged to ask you for details as required.

**WOMAN**

I don't know where to begin.

**LAWYER**

Begin anywhere. Whatever you think is important.

**WOMAN** *(Long pause)*

Incompatibility is not something one talks about every day. It is not...

**LAWYER**

Not easy to talk about it. I understand. Your hesitation is quite natural. Let me see how I can help. (*Taking out papers from a briefcase*)

We have here the six most common categories of incompatibility in case of divorce. The illustrations are meant for our less-educated and non-literate clients. Each figure here is followed by a short definition.

*(She pauses. The woman steps up to the desk to see.)*

**LAWYER** *(Continuing)*

You can choose any category you consider as being closest to your case, and then we can go into it in detail according to your own experience.

*(The woman does not respond)*

It is also possible for it to be a combination of two or three.

**WOMAN**

None of the above.

## SCENE 5

***The City Court***

*The woman takes her place at the desk. The lawyer takes her place pleading to the judge, who is not seen.*

**LAWYER**

Sexual satiation, my lord. It is not ordinarily cited as an area of incompatibility, that is to say, the woman experiencing intense frustration and therefore incompatibility in the marriage relationship on account of the inability of the husband to provide the needed satisfaction in their sexual relations.

**MURTHY** *(Voice)*

That may be admitted as a complaint peculiar to this couple. It could be either on account of the woman or the man. Does it qualify as a case of incompatibility?

**LAWYER**

It must be so, my lord – not because it does not happen, but because married couples find it difficult to talk about it. Nevertheless, it must be accepted as incompatibility.

**MURTHY**

You used the word satiation. Are we not then dealing with the phenomenon of appetite?

**LAWYER**

It is the term used by medical science, my lord.

**MURTHY**

Satiation... You propose that if a man cannot satiate the sexual appetite of a woman who is his lawfully wedded wife, it is grounds for incompatibility.

**LAWYER**

I have here a copy of a research study along with an attestation from the Head of the Department of Reproductive Health at St Theresa Institute of Medical Sciences. With your permission... *(Taking out a sheaf of papers from a folder)*

It shows that over 65 per cent of women in marriage report incomplete satiation in a sexual engagement. That is to say, about two out of three women, my lord. Within that number, over 55 per cent report incomplete satiation a 100 per cent of the time.

**MURTHY**

They conduct studies like that?

**LAWYER**

Nearly three thousand women took part in the study in seven cities of India.

**MURTHY**

Please leave a copy of the report at my chamber. What is the date of the report?

**LAWYER**

It is just a month old, my lord. The study was conducted over an eighteen-month period and concluded three months ago.

**MURTHY**

Are there corresponding statistics for men?

**LAWYER**

Yes, my lord. It's there.

**MURTHY**
What does it say?

**LAWYER**
The incidence is less than 3 per cent.

**MURTHY**
Just that? What is the explanation given?

**LAWYER**
They are more easily satiated. That is to say... they finish faster.
*(The woman turns to the unseen audience in the court and admonishes them.)*

**WOMAN**
Shhh! The court is in order!

**MURTHY**
Thank you, ma'am. Although that prerogative is mine.

**WOMAN** *(Resuming, to the Judge)*
And then they fall asleep, almost immediately, leaving the woman staring at the ceiling.

**MURTHY**
A case is being made to include incomplete satiation as grounds for incompatibility.

**LAWYER**
Non-satiation as well as incomplete satiation, my lord.

**MURTHY**
Non-satiation and incomplete satiation... Under what principle of jurisprudence are you claiming the inclusion?

**LAWYER**
Rights, my lord. Satiation as a right, my lord. The court already accepts the principle of conjugal rights. The satiation of sexual needs must be regarded as a necessary and integral part of conjugal rights.

**MURTHY**
I see. *(Pause)* The case is adjourned for five days. This hearing shall be resumed on the following Monday at 3:00 pm.
*(The sound of a gavel striking. The woman rises. She and the lawyer bow. The sound of footsteps receding.)*

**LAWYER** *(To woman)*
He is at least willing to listen. But it is too early to say.

## SCENE 6

***The Counsellor's Clinic***

*The lights open to reveal the office of a counsellor. Just two comfortable chairs should do. He is examining the papers in a folder. The man steps in cautiously and waits at a distance. The counsellor invites him in. The man walks across, hesitates, and sits.*

**MAN**

Thank you for agreeing to see me... At short notice.

**COUNSEL**

You are welcome.

**MAN**

You are a busy person. There must have been other...

**COUNSEL**

No problem. Where would you like to begin?

**MAN**

Since the last time we met... *(Long pause)*

**COUNSEL**

Yes?

**MAN**

It is getting worse... unbearable.

**COUNSEL**

What exactly happened? What made you call me for an appointment?

**MAN**

Last night... *(He struggles)*

**COUNSEL** *(Professional)*

Take your time... There's no hurry... You can begin when you are ready... wherever you like.

**MAN**

Last night... I tried a different approach.

**COUNSEL**

Uh-huh.

**MAN**

I thought there was something missing in our life, some romance. I did what I thought might be right... we went out for a nice dinner... relaxed, nice music... the wine... warm conversation. I could see that something exciting was coming...

**COUNSEL**

Uh-huh... go on...

**MAN**

She was really glowing... we went to bed... she was passionate... wildly passionate... she was taking the lead, talking, talking sexy... moaning... moaning passionately and calling out... Bobby! Bobby! Oh Bobby...

*(He stops)*

**COUNSEL**

Uh-huh... you really set up a great night for yourselves.

**MAN**

Sir... Bobby is not my name.

*(He turns to the audience and admonishes them)*

Shhh! You think it happens only to others!

*(A pause. He regains his composure)*

I have to find a way out. I don't know how to deal with this.

**COUNSEL**

Deal with what?

**MAN**

This mess!

**COUNSEL**

What is the mess?

**MAN**

A fucking Bobby mess!

**COUNSEL**

Who do you think Bobby is? Do you have some idea?

*(The man shakes his head)*

What do you think Bobby is?

**MAN**

I can't think! Is it worth all this... ? Can there ever be a solution to this? You think this problem has any... ?

**COUNSEL**

It depends on our getting at the cause.

**MAN**

Isn't it...

**COUNSEL**

The real cause – not what we think might be the cause – or what we would like to believe is the cause.

**MAN**

I have not brought this upon myself! Why the hell should it be my job to go looking for a cause?

*(The counsellor pats the man's hand.)*

## SCENE 7

***The Hive***

*In the dark we hear a telephone voice over the audio system.*

*'To continue in English please press 1.'*

*A short pause.*

*'For product enquiries please press 1. For service enquiries, please press 2. For any other queries and to speak to an executive please press 9.'*

*A short pause.*

*'This call may be recorded to aid our training and quality assurance programme.'*

*Lights up on an office setup. Two small desks with monitors, keyboards, and headsets neatly arranged. A third desk separately set.*

*A young man (YM) and a young woman (YW) enter carrying mugs or paper cups, chatting. They move to a corner away from the desks.*

**YOUNG WOMAN**

No, baba, no.

**YOUNG MAN**

Please, baby, you must. It's nothing, just a film and dinner.

**YOUNG WOMAN**

Yeh baby-waby kab se shuroo kiya?

**YOUNG MAN**

Just – achcha nahin lagta toh theek hai, I will not call you baby, baby!

**YOUNG WOMAN** *(Giggling)*

Not like that. It is just – zara bold lagta hai.

**YOUNG MAN**

Sach baat kahoon?

**YOUNG WOMAN**

Ab tak jhoot baat bol rahe the?

**YOUNG MAN**

No, really, suno. Kaan khol ke suno. I don't say baby to everybody. When I am with you it is different. I feel like...

**YOUNG WOMAN**

Feel like... ?

**YOUNG MAN**

You know what I mean, na!

**YOUNG WOMAN**

I am supposed to know?

**YOUNG MAN**

There are over thirty girls in this department.

**YOUNG WOMAN**
Thirty-two

**YOUNG MAN**
And twenty-four boys.

**YOUNG WOMAN**
How many films have you seen with them? How many dinners? Isko dating kehte hain na?

**YOUNG MAN**
Only one. She told me after dinner that she was married.

**YOUNG WOMAN**
What! What did she want from you? And you...

**YOUNG MAN**
Nothing happened. I never saw her again.

**YOUNG WOMAN**
What do you know about me? What if I am also married? Fixed up when I was sixteen, before I left for this job?

**YOUNG MAN**
You are not married. I found out!

**YOUNG WOMAN**
Oh, you have been finding out things. But what if I am fixed up? *(Short pause)*

Suno, I am allowed to take this job so that my father has enough money for my marriage.

**YOUNG MAN**
People know about this?

**YOUNG WOMAN**
The girls in my PG flat know. Four of them are in the same haalat. I suppose the whole office knows. You know.

**YOUNG MAN**
I only found out that you were not married. Nothing more.

**YOUNG WOMAN**
So this film, dinner, vagairah... Kuch agenda hai kya?

**YOUNG MAN**
What to say? Sach-much, I like to be with you. You are so...

**YOUNG WOMAN**
The other girls – they also have boys talking about film-wilm, you know.

**YOUNG MAN**
You girls never go anywhere from the PG flat?

**YOUNG WOMAN**

Anywhere matlab? I have to go out for so many things – to the kirana shop, to the laundry, to the courier-wallah.

**YOUNG MAN**

I mean to enjoy – like time pass in the mall, baahar khana-peena, multiplex cinema, yes?

**YOUNG WOMAN**

In a group, yes.

**YOUNG MAN**

Never by yourself?

**YOUNG WOMAN**

To visit my local guardian on Sundays.

**YOUNG MAN**

Never with a boy?

**YOUNG WOMAN**

No, baba.

**YOUNG MAN**

Chalo, I can at least have coffee with you here, na?

**YOUNG WOMAN**

Did I say I would not come to a film with you?

*(A buzz is heard. A slightly older woman steps into the room and waits at the edge. She is the Section Leader. She has a clipboard with sheets of paper attached to it. The young woman and young man hastily put their cups away and take their seats at the desks. They put on the headsets and get ready to start work. The Section Leader walks up to the two of them and speaks.)*

**LEADER**

You must be at your desk at 2:58. When the buzz goes you are at your desk. You start work at 3:00 sharp when the buzz stops. (*YW and YM nod in acceptance)*

Hari, the recorded log shows that some of your callers are still not fully comfortable when they are talking to you. I want you to sign off for ten minutes and come over to my desk. *(She walks up to her desk and waits. YM mumbles a request to his colleague over the headset phone, takes off his headset, and walks over to Leader. An awkward pause. She asks him to sit at her desk.)*

**LEADER**

Open the Incoming folder...

Don't take your eyes off the screen... Listen carefully to what I am saying... Your record is good on the whole... but erratic... *(She bends over him)*

What do we say in the quarterly report, huh?

Could do better. Tendency for distraction. Needs to concentrate.

*(A pause. She gets closer, her cheek brushing his.)*

Now... what did you say in the mail last week? Let's see... Hmm... You never thought I would become the Section Leader, na? Well, you should be happy to have a section leader who takes interest in your performance.

*(She turns his head to herself)*

You – will – come – when – I call for you. Understand? We can do something about your performance. *(She straightens.)*

Could do better.

## SCENE 8

***Justice Krishnamurthy's chamber***

*A small round table and two chairs.*

*Justice Krishnamurthy leads the woman lawyer to the table. They carry cups of coffee with them.*

**MURTHY**

Thank you for finding the time for this. I know you are a very busy professional. The practice is going well, I hear.

**LAWYER**

Okay. Keeps me going.

**MURTHY**

Satisfying? If not satiating?

**LAWYER** *(Laughing)*

On the whole, yes. It is a new field. Not much money in it. Not like those corporate law cases. But it keeps me busy.

**MURTHY**

You don't mind this... ?

**LAWYER**

Oh, not at all, sir. It is a pleasure. You are like a mentor for me – for so many of us.

**MURTHY**

Thank you. I am really grateful you came personally to give me the copy of the research report.

**LAWYER**

It's nothing, sir. It was an opportunity to see you in person. After a long time.

**MURTHY**

Yes, a long time.

**LAWYER**

And we get good coffee in the judge's chambers!

**MURTHY**

This report...

**LAWYER**

I managed to get an advance copy before publication. It was on the strict condition that I don't take out copies – not a single copy.

**MURTHY**

The research team will testify if needed?

**LAWYER**

If needed, yes, of course. It will be in their interest to do that.

**MURTHY**

So... I have some questions.

**LAWYER**

If they are technical... I will not be in a position...

**MURTHY**

Not technical, not about the medical science details. My questions are more about the social meaning, the legal implications.

**LAWYER**

Yes, sir, I understand. I can try... *(A pause)*

**MURTHY**

60 per cent, you said.

**LAWYER**

Sir?

**MURTHY**

You said that some 60-odd per cent of women in marriage report dissatisfaction...

**LAWYER**

Ah, yes, sir, with the...

**MURTHY**

'Incomplete satiation' is how you described it.

**LAWYER**

As described in the report, sir. The exact estimate...

**MURTHY**

It does not matter what the exact figure is, a few per cent points this way or that. What matters is the report itself.

**LAWYER**

The research team has impeccable credentials.

**MURTHY**

Not to be doubted. Do you see what the report means for us? In the legal community?

**LAWYER**
Sir?

**MURTHY**
It means – it could mean – any number of cases waiting to be brought to the courts all over the country.

**LAWYER**
Is that... wrong?

**MURTHY**
Not right or wrong, but the numbers!

**LAWYER**
It can be a large number, sir.

**MURTHY**
Look at it this way. What do you think is the incidence of dowry harassment in this country?

**LAWYER**
It is not precisely known, I believe.

**MURTHY**
Take a guess. In what percentage of marriages is there a strife within the first year in connection with dowry?

**LAWYER**
I suppose it depends on the demographics.

**MURTHY**
Spoken like a true professional – it depends.

**LAWYER**
What I meant was...

**MURTHY**
It does not matter. For the court, a dowry harassment is a dowry harassment, no matter what the demographics. And you know as well that there is harassment even in rich families.

**LAWYER**
Yes, sir. That is known.

**MURTHY**
I have it from the bureau of statistics of the High Court. Roughly half a per cent of all marriages end up in dowry harassment conflicts.

**LAWYER**
A mere half per cent?

**MURTHY**
A mere half per cent or a hefty half per cent. It depends on how you look at it. Now, out of the half per cent, an even smaller percentage actually comes to the attention of the police or civil courts.

**LAWYER**

That too is well known, sir.

**MURTHY**

And yet, the civil courts have their hands full with dowry harassment cases. Section 406, Section 498, and even dowry deaths under Section 304B.

**LAWYER**

Yes, sir, it is certainly on the increase. By no means in decline.

**MURTHY**

Would it be safe to suggest that the increase in the number of dowry harassment cases in our courts is not necessarily on account of an increase in dowry harassment cases in society... ?

**LAWYER**

But more women and more families bringing instances of harassment out in the open.

**MURTHY**

And more and more homosexuals coming out in the open does not mean...

**LAWYER**

More homosexuals in the population today.

**MURTHY**

It is all about coming out, right? *(She nods in agreement)*

So... 60 per cent. In a population of over a billion you could say about three hundred million of them exist in cohabitation as husband and wife.

**LAWYER**

Sir.

**MURTHY**

And about two hundred million in reasonably virile condition. Even with half the number of wives deciding to take a legal recourse, awakened to the possibility of a way out of a trap that they never intended for themselves in the first place, you know, the state of being chronically unsatiated as the report puts it, can you even begin to imagine the flood we will have to deal with in hundreds of lower courts all over the country? *(A pause. Turning to the audience)*

**MURTHY**

It is no laughing matter.

**LAWYER**

It can happen, sir.

**MURTHY**

Can you imagine what happens tomorrow? The report goes public. A weekly picture magazine does a cover feature – of course it is peppered with pictures of women in suggestive poses. A novel comes out, and goes on to win some award. A Booker or something like that? Then a movie is made from the book? We have millions of women flocking to see the film, somehow feeling liberated by the act of flocking... Hindi, Tamil, Kannada, Marathi versions of the movie...

**LAWYER**

The courts simply cannot handle it.

**MURTHY**

And why should it fall upon the courts to handle it? Our courts?

**LAWYER**

It is true there is no precedent, sir.

**MURTHY**

Ah, precedent, precedent! There is no legislation, no legal statute. Whatever we decide in this case becomes the precedent for all other courts in all future cases.

**LAWYER**

Would you rather not...

**MURTHY**

It is an onerous responsibility.

**LAWYER**

Somebody has to take the first step.

**MURTHY**

And we have been chosen, you and I, for the honour.

**LAWYER**

My client, but your judgment. If there is no appeal in a higher court, it can indeed become the reference point for others – the precedent.

**MURTHY**

But of course it will go to a higher court.

**LAWYER**

It may not, sir. You will remember it is not being contested.

**MURTHY**

That's right. *(A pause)*
I wonder why. Do you know why?

**LAWYER**

Perhaps an admission, sir...

**MURTHY**

How did we become this way?

**LAWYER**

Which way, sir?

**MURTHY**

The high appetite society. Unsatiated.

**LAWYER**

There is simply more of it available today, sir. More exposure, more opportunity, more freedom...

**MURTHY**

You are beginning to sound like somebody from a TV show.

**LAWYER**

More experimentation...

**MURTHY**

More experience.

**LAWYER**

More experience before marriage.

**MURTHY**

Before experimenting with marriage?

**LAWYER**

There is simply a lot more of it all around, sir.

**MURTHY**

I see... I think I do.

**LAWYER**

There is far more contact, familiarity. Just the proximity – it all leads to more close encounters...

**MURTHY**

Of the casual kind.

**LAWYER**

You could say that. And there are no regrets, no qualms about it.

**MURTHY**

Peculiar thing about human consumption, is it not? Increasing consumption has no connection to satisfaction. It only raises thresholds – only increases impatience with what you have.

**LAWYER**

You know, sir, with over a hundred channels available on TV, all we do is surf channels so much more frequently.

**MURTHY**

A demand-supply explanation, is that it? Is it the demand that creates the supply or the supply that drives the demand?

**LAWYER**

No TV show has the answer to that, sir.

**MURTHY**

I have to pass a judgment tomorrow. I can't wait for a bolt of inspiration from a TV show. *(A pause)*

**LAWYER**
Sir, may I ask a personal question?

**MURTHY**
Hmmm? Yes, go ahead.

**LAWYER**
A little quiz, sir. No offence meant.

**MURTHY**
Go ahead.

## INTERLUDE 2

***The Counsellor's clinic***

*The Man is at the table, his head buried in his arms. He is sobbing. The Counsellor is standing next to him. After a while, he takes his seat and watches the Man, detached. The man looks up. There is a long pause. The counsellor rises.*

**COUNSEL**
Do you want to be by yourself for a while? *(No response)*

**MAN**
I don't know. I feel...

**COUNSEL**
Yes?

**MAN**
It is confusing. I don't know how I feel.

**COUNSEL**
Something you haven't experienced before?

**MAN**
No.

**COUNSEL**
Can you describe it? In your own words?

**MAN**
I don't think so.

**COUNSEL**
You don't have to. It's fine if you don't.

**MAN**
Thank you.

**COUNSEL**
Feel free to stay here as long as you like. Make yourself comfortable. There's a coffee service in the corridor. You may... I will be in my office. Call me if there's any need.

*(The Counsellor leaves. The Man sits staring for a while. He rises quietly, making sure there is no sound. He looks in the direction of the Counsellor's office.)*

**MAN**

There will be no need, thank you. I think I can handle this. *(He scribbles a note hurriedly on a pad on the table)*

I am a man. *(He leaves quietly.)*

## SCENE 9

***Justice Krishnamurthy's home***

*Krishnamurthy is at the sofa, waiting. He is dressed to go out. Vimala enters, also dressed up. He rises, smiles. They look at each other across the coffee table and hold the glow between themselves for a few moments. He reaches out and strokes her cheek. She takes his hand and holds it close.*

**VIMALA**

Well, I am ready now to try that thali at Krishna Sagar.

**MURTHY**

You are beautiful.

**VIMALA**

What was that?

**MURTHY**

I said...

**VIMALA**

I haven't heard that in twenty years.

**MURTHY**

Beautiful. I said you are...

**VIMALA**

Now what? What sort of case in the court has brought this on?

**MURTHY**

No, really, I just said what came to my mind. Honestly.

**VIMALA**

As a good judge should. You weighed all the pros and cons, I suppose.

**MURTHY**

In half a second after you entered the room.

**VIMALA**

Very professional. And how many such cases have you handled in your long career, sir? The half-second cases, I mean?

**MURTHY**

I have lost count. But I do remember that all of them pertained to only one person, a woman of some substance, I believe.

**VIMALA**

I believe we are late already. We should have been at Krishna Sagar by now. Cold rasam in the thali is not something the good judge will approve. Not this evening.

**MURTHY** *(Sitting)*

Sit down. There's no hurry.

**VIMALA**

Now? Sit down for what?

**MURTHY**

I have phoned them to say we may be a bit late.

**VIMALA**

Oh?

**MURTHY**

Sit down… it is not often that we have the luxury of sitting and chatting in the evening.

**VIMALA**

Chatting? *(She sits)*

**MURTHY**

Yes, just sitting and chatting.

**VIMALA**

Is it about the case today?

**MURTHY**

No, about us.

**VIMALA**

Oh, ma! Now it is turning into a thriller.

**MURTHY**

You see? We simply don't have enough time between ourselves.

**VIMALA**

I will not disagree with that. So… what do we talk about? Cold rasam?

**MURTHY**

We could…

**VIMALA**

You started it, you lead the way.

**MURTHY**

May I begin with something we have never discussed before?

**VIMALA**
Like... ?

**MURTHY**
Something that might appear a bit personal?

**VIMALA**
Hmmm...

**MURTHY**
You don't mind?

**VIMALA**
Go ahead.

**MURTHY**
Like a little quiz?

**VIMALA**
Are there prizes?

**MURTHY**
It is meant to be an innocent question – no offence meant.

**VIMALA**
Go ahead.

**MURTHY**
Ready?

**VIMALA**
Ready.

**MURTHY**
It's something like a memory test.

**VIMALA** *(Closing her eyes)*
I am ready.

**MURTHY**
I am going to ask you to remember a date.

**VIMALA**
A date? Like in a history lesson?

**MURTHY**
Something like that.

**VIMALA**
Your birthday? Our anniversary? Oh my god, have I forgotten?

**MURTHY**
No, no, they are months away. I am going to ask you to try and remember – how shall I put it...

**VIMALA**
In simple language, please.

**MURTHY**

All right – do you remember the day of the week... the day of the week when you had your first intercourse?

**VIMALA**

My what?

**MURTHY**

Sex – your first sexual intercourse... the day of the week.

**VIMALA**

Oh my god, what a strange question!

**MURTHY**

Do you have an answer?

**VIMALA**

Of course I do! It was a Wednesday!

**MURTHY**

How wonderful that you remember!

**VIMALA**

It was the day I got married. To a handsome young lawyer who went on to become a respectable judge.

**MURTHY**

July 30...

**VIMALA**

1986 was a Wednesday.

**MURTHY**

You remember!

**VIMALA**

Of course! A very important thing happened on a very important day in my life.

**MURTHY**

Yes, yes, of course.

**VIMALA**

Have I passed? Do I qualify for the next round?

**MURTHY**

Oh my god! Oh my god!

*(He sits back, staring at Vimala, first in amazement, then in adoration. He rises, takes her in his arms. She is surprised, but returns his warmth.)*

Let's go... the rasam will get cold.

## SCENE 10

***The Hive***

*The Young Woman is standing by herself, holding a cup of coffee, waiting. The Leader walks up to her.*

**LEADER**
Waiting for someone?

**YOUNG WOMAN**
Haanji, do minute ke liye...

**LEADER**
Only English in the office!

**YOUNG WOMAN**
Sorry, ma'am.

**LEADER**
This is not the first time you are being told. It is nearly one year since you joined. Your head is still in your village.

**YOUNG WOMAN**
Jabalpur is not a village, ma'am. It has a population of...

**LEADER**
All same.

**YOUNG WOMAN**
There is an airport.

**LEADER**
You are early today.

**YOUNG WOMAN**
To be on time at the desk, ma'am.

**LEADER**
Or to be on time at the coffee counter.

**YOUNG WOMAN**
We don't get coffee at the PG ma'am, only chai.

**LEADER**
You don't get good company at the PG, only at the counter here.

**YOUNG WOMAN**
Matlab? I mean, beg your pardon, ma'am?

**LEADER**
People are talking.

**YOUNG WOMAN**
Talking?

**LEADER**

We are keeping a watch on you.

**YOUNG WOMAN**

Anything wrong in my work, ma'am?

**LEADER**

Anything wrong in my work!

**YOUNG WOMAN**

I am dot on time, ma'am, always. I have 100 per cent attendance, no leave, no breaks.

**LEADER**

And still...

**YOUNG WOMAN**

No customer complaints, ma'am.

**LEADER**

The company you are keeping is not good for you.

**YOUNG WOMAN**

Ma'am, the girls in the PG are very decent. All of them work in this office. You know them, three of us are in your team.

**LEADER**

You think you are smart, eh? Girls in the PG! What about the boys who get into the PG?

**YOUNG WOMAN**

Ma'am?

**LEADER**

We are keeping a watch on you.

**YOUNG WOMAN**

The office, ma'am? The company?

**LEADER**

I told you. We are keeping a watch on you.

**YOUNG WOMAN**

Yes, ma'am.

**LEADER**

One year in the company and people learn to talk back.

**YOUNG WOMAN**

Ma'am, HR had a session with us last month. All the girls. Ramji-sir met us in small batches, twenty–twenty-five at a time. All the girls. He explained.

**LEADER**

HR had a meeting?

**YOUNG WOMAN**

Yes, ma'am. It was after that Sheila Agarwal dhamaal. There was total confusion in the office. Half the girls were on Sheila Agarwal's side, half were completely against her. All e-mails and SMSes were about Sheila, Sheila, Sheila.

**LEADER**

Stupid girl, going and getting pregnant!

**YOUNG WOMAN**

She said...

**LEADER**

I know what she said. She was stupid.

**YOUNG WOMAN**

It was a question of rights. She said that openly, ma'am. Ramji-sir agreed, ma'am. He arranged that Saturday half-day workshop with Dr Mrudula Kulkarni. She showed us how to be... matlab well protected. Very good workshop, ma'am.

**LEADER**

Forget Sheila Agarwal. I am talking about you.

**YOUNG WOMAN**

HR told us clearly, ma'am...

**LEADER**

I am talking about you, chokri.

**YOUNG WOMAN**

HR told us clearly, ma'am. Ramji-sir said that what we do outside office hours is our business. It is of no concern to the company.

**LEADER**

We all know that!

**YOUNG WOMAN**

Nobody in the company can be concerned. Unless...

**LEADER**

Unless!

**YOUNG WOMAN** *(Taking out a slip of paper)*

Unless (a) it happens inside the office, (b) it happens during office hours, (c) it com-pro-mi-ses office security, and (d) it com-pro-mi-ses company in-teg-ri-ty.

**LEADER**

You are getting too close to him.

**YOUNG WOMAN**

Close to whom, ma'am?

**LEADER**
He is getting too close to you.

**YOUNG WOMAN**
Who, ma'am?

**LEADER**
Hari! *(A pause)*
It is not good for you!

**YOUNG WOMAN**
Not good, ma'am?

**LEADER**
Not good for either of you.

**YOUNG WOMAN**
But there is nothing in the office, ma'am.

**LEADER**
What about the com-pro-mi-sing acts outside the office?

**YOUNG WOMAN**
No comment, ma'am.

**LEADER**
What do you mean 'no comment'?

**YOUNG WOMAN**
HR clearly said...

**LEADER**
HR is turning into a bloody trade union or what?

**YOUNG WOMAN**
HR knows about Hari, ma'am.

**LEADER**
Knows what?

**YOUNG WOMAN**
Hari talked to HR six days ago.

**LEADER**
Talked to HR about what?

**YOUNG WOMAN**
Hari has... proposed marriage.

**LEADER**
And you?

**YOUNG WOMAN**
I said yes.

**LEADER**
And that mangetar fellow waiting for you in the village?

**YOUNG WOMAN**
He is not waiting for me. Nobody is waiting for me.

**LEADER**
You were fixed up, no?

**YOUNG WOMAN**
Was... He did not think he was fixed up. Took the deposit my father gave his father and vanished.

**LEADER**
So... this! Are you serious?

**YOUNG WOMAN**
Yes Ma'am.

**LEADER**
What about Hari?

**YOUNG WOMAN**
He has always been serious.

**LEADER**
You silly fool! What do you know about Hari? What do you know about boys who come to work here?

**YOUNG WOMAN**
I know Hari.

**LEADER**
Because he proposed to you?

**YOUNG WOMAN**
He proposed long ago. I agreed only a week ago.

**LEADER**
Listen to me! Oh god, make this girl listen to me! Listen... a young man like Hari does not know the difference between a proposal and a proposition. All he can think is proposals. It comes from all those B-grade Bombay films he sees from the time he is in the cradle. Whatever the lafda, the end has to be shaadi. When he comes to the city and sees a girl – hundreds of girls – like you – his dialogue is all proposal. But you know the juices inside are all about proposition.

**YOUNG WOMAN**
You are telling me this.

**LEADER**
I should know.

**YOUNG WOMAN**
I have told you na, I am very serious about it. What others say and do is absolutely zero. Not important. Only what he does next matters.

**LEADER**

Look, I have nothing against you – or Hari. I... don't want to come between you if you are going ahead with his... proposal. But you should know... you are a woman... you should know...

**YOUNG WOMAN**

I know Ma'am.

*(The Young Woman walks out abruptly. The Leader takes out her cell phone and dials a number.)*

**LEADER**

Please report at my desk as soon as you come in... Yes, before you go to your work station... See you.

*(She walks across to her desk and takes her seat. She types furiously, dashing off a mail. She dials a number on her phone.)*

**LEADER**

Ramji? Good morning... You have seen it already? Good. No, I did not intend to file a case formally – not just yet. It is more like an alert. Also, I wanted to take your advice on how to proceed... Yes, I know about it. He has lodged a complaint against me. It is a joke, isn't it? A harassment complaint against me just when I am going out of my way to... Yes, yes, I know about the Supreme Court directives and all that bullshit... I do not believe this can be called sexual harassment. The fact is, his performance is unsatisfactory, he just has not delivered... Oh, it is so easy for anybody to level a charge of harassment... All right, we can meet this afternoon. Thanks.

*(The Young Man enters and walks up to her.)*

**LEADER**

So... do I say congratulations? *(No response)*

Do you want to make the announcement or will HR make it? *(Pause)*

So, which one of you will quit? Don't look so surprised. You know the company policy. We don't encourage husband and wife working in the same office. One of you will have to go. Either way it will need a clearance from me. *(Pause)*

Why did you do it? Could we not have cleared up things nicely between us? After all you got out of it yourself... You had the gall to call it harassment! It was mean. You will have to withdraw the case... if you know what's good for you.

## INTERLUDE 3

***The Counsellor's clinic***
*The Counsellor is at the desk, studying his notes. The telephone rings.*

**COUNSEL**
Yes? That's right, speaking... Yes, I know him. As a matter of fact he has an appointment this afternoon. I am... What? Are you sure... ? Yes, yes, of course, I will be there as soon as I can... the new emergency block on the left side... Straight away... It should take me about fifteen minutes... When do you think it might have happened... ? I see... I see... Yes, I am starting now.

## SCENE 11

***A park***
*The Young Woman and the Young Man are seated.*

**YOUNG WOMAN**
Don't look so glum. It's not the end of the world.

**YOUNG MAN**
You don't know her.

**YOUNG WOMAN**
It's the start of a new world, after all.

**YOUNG MAN**
You don't know her.

**YOUNG WOMAN**
I can't say I know her as well as you! But I can say I know you better than she knows you.

**YOUNG MAN**
Funny!

**YOUNG WOMAN**
No? *(Pause)* Or is there something she knows that I don't?

**YOUNG MAN**
Look, Have I kept anything from you? The fact is that it has all gone out of control now. The company has set up an Enquiry Committee.

**YOUNG WOMAN**
Company ko maaro goli. Who cares! Let's talk about preparations for the big day.

**YOUNG MAN**
Ohho! Can't you see how serious this is? I can lose my job!

**YOUNG WOMAN**

You were going to put in your papers anyway.

**YOUNG MAN**

That was last week. A lot has changed since then.

**YOUNG WOMAN**

What has changed? We have talked about it twenty times. If the company wants one of us to quit, who should it be? You or me? Pros, cons, trade-offs, costs, benefits, *vagairah, vagairah.*

**YOUNG MAN**

That was one week ago.

**YOUNG WOMAN**

We decided the best would be for both of us to quit. We would show them! Then you said at least one of us should hold on while the other is looking out for a job.

**YOUNG MAN**

Now it is no more a question about you or me leaving the company. It is a question of whose case the company is going to accept. I file a complaint against her, and even before it is properly registered, she files a complaint against me! And then, this...

**YOUNG WOMAN**

This what? You have done no wrong.

**YOUNG MAN**

It is not as simple as that. You will not understand.

**YOUNG WOMAN**

I will not understand... so explain it. Why this private suffering?

**YOUNG MAN**

She has power!

**YOUNG WOMAN**

That does not mean she can threaten you just like that. The company has set up an Enquiry Committee, na? Mujhe toh yeh kuch blackmail jaisa lag raha hai. *(Pause)* Is it... ? Is there something I don't know? This is not the office. There is no camera recording everything. You can talk. Tell me everything. Don't be afraid. I will understand everything.

**YOUNG MAN**

You won't.

**YOUNG WOMAN**

You were her lover, na?

**YOUNG MAN**

Not her lover!

**YOUNG WOMAN**

Something like that... *(Pause)*

**YOUNG MAN**

Something like that. It was a trap.

**YOUNG WOMAN**

You liked being her lover?

**YOUNG MAN**

Matlab?

**YOUNG WOMAN**

How was she?

**YOUNG MAN**

How can you ask such a question? You?!

**YOUNG WOMAN**

I am asking because I want to know. What can I do to make you happy? Happier?

**YOUNG MAN**

She was... oh god, why are we talking about this? Why now?

**YOUNG WOMAN**

Because it is important. We must talk about it.

**YOUNG MAN**

How can I expect you to understand?

**YOUNG WOMAN**

I will try. You can expect me to try. *(Pause)*

Look, you remember our first time? You insisted on wasting all that money on a spa because they had a private room. I knew when we were in that room that it was not your first time. You were experienced.

**YOUNG MAN**

I tried not to show it.

**YOUNG WOMAN**

You were not very successful.

**YOUNG MAN**

You did not mind?

**YOUNG WOMAN**

Very late for you to be asking that. But, no, I did not mind.

**YOUNG MAN**

You were as fresh as a jasmine bud.

**YOUNG WOMAN**

I was not.

**YOUNG MAN**

I would never have guessed.

**YOUNG WOMAN**

I was more successful than you. *(Pause)*

It is much more than that. I knew about the trap you were in. I had my own. I knew what you were struggling with, not just one trap.

**YOUNG MAN**

I am still not free.

**YOUNG WOMAN**

You will be, soon. All of this will be put behind. We will start a new life when we leave this company and set up home.

**YOUNG MAN**

It will not be so easy.

**YOUNG WOMAN**

All right, it will take some more time. This case... although the best way to solve this case is for both of us to quit the company. Both cases closed in one stroke.

**YOUNG MAN**

If only it could be as simple as that.

**YOUNG WOMAN**

It is up to us, na? We don't have to make things more complicated by simply dragging on the cases.

**YOUNG MAN**

We can't get married now.

**YOUNG WOMAN**

I told you I understand. We can wait.

**YOUNG MAN**

We can't get married. It would be better if we end this right here.

**YOUNG WOMAN**

End... ?

**YOUNG MAN**

Right now... before things get more complicated.

## SCENE 12

***Post mortem***
*A tight spot into which the Counsellor steps in. A voice is heard.*

**VOICE**
Were you able to identify the body? *(He nods)* That is all for now. Please be available for any further investigation. The Police Department has taken over the case.

**COUNSEL**
How did he... ?

**VOICE**
The note he left behind is in great detail. He stabbed her twenty-six times, he says. One for each year of her life. He held the blood-soaked knife in his hand when he hanged himself.

**COUNSEL**
Can you say when he... ?

**VOICE**
About three hours after he met you. That is why you were called.

**COUNSEL**
I...

**VOICE**
He mentions you in his note. He thanks you.
*(Fade out. A tight spot again, into which the Leader steps in. A voice is heard.)*

**VOICE**
Were you able to identify the body? (She nods)
That is all for now. The case is outside the responsibility of HR now. The company is only obliged to provide any information sought. Please be available for any further investigation. As and when.

**LEADER**
Her body... How did she... ?

**VOICE**
Eight floors. The terrace food court. She found a way to get on to the parapet at the rear.

**LEADER**
Any idea of a motive?

**VOICE**
Her roommates say she was in great distress for over a week. That is all we know.

**LEADER**
I am shocked.

**VOICE**
So are we all. This is the second case within this half year.

## SCENE 13

***Justice Krishnamurthy's chamber***
*Justice Krishnamurthy and the lawyer are at the small round table.*

**LAWYER**
I will be sorry to see you go.

**MURTHY**
Kicked upstairs, as they say.

**LAWYER**
I am sure I speak for most in the Bar. This Court will certainly miss you.

**MURTHY**
At least that is what they can be expected to say at the farewell tea.

**LAWYER**
No, really, you commanded a great deal of respect...

**MURTHY**
After the samosas and sandwiches have disappeared.

**LAWYER**
For your honest and upright judgments, whatever your personal views in the matter.

**MURTHY**
My personal views...

**LAWYER**
They were always so considered, well thought out. Nobody could question their weight.

**MURTHY**
Not to forget the weight on my head.

**LAWYER**
Oh, I am sure you were under pressure sometimes.

**MURTHY**
Sometimes?

**LAWYER**
But you never showed it, never talked about it.

**MURTHY** *(Laughing)*
Sometimes!

**LAWYER**

It is so nice to see you relaxed like this. Actually laughing. It is another side of you. So relaxed.

**MURTHY**

You know, I own a Maruti 800. Nothing more. I took a loan to send our son for his MBA.

**LAWYER**

The whole Bar Council is aware of all this, sir.

**MURTHY**

Only now, thanks to the Missus, I have decided to invest in a flat, so that we have a place after my retirement.

**LAWYER**

You can't talk about retirement yet, sir.

**MURTHY**

Taking a second loan.

**LAWYER**

Are you looking forward to your new posting?

**MURTHY**

Yes, on the whole, yes. But it means all the hassle of packing, shifting, unpacking. The house is in such a mess.

**LAWYER**

I am sure it will be worth all the trouble, sir.

**MURTHY**

Thank god, our son is coming down for a few days. He can help.

**LAWYER**

How nice of him to come and help you pack.

**MURTHY**

A surprise visit, really. He might as well help in packing while he is here. We haven't seen him for over a year.

**LAWYER**

You will now be much closer to him, I believe.

**MURTHY**

That's right. Just four hours by road. That is an attraction. The Missus is very happy. We can have him and his wife over on week-ends. His wife Ratna.

**LAWYER**

Sir... I have something for you, a small gift. It is a very small token of my respect and gratitude for you. *(She takes out a small gift-wrapped packet.)* I have learned so much from all the appearances in your court – especially in the last few years. I know I am going to miss you.

**MURTHY** *(Moved)*

Thank you. May a judge break his code for just a moment to say that the feeling is mutual? I have learned a lot from you too.

**LAWYER**

Sir, there have been landmark judgments from your courts. I have been privileged...

**MURTHY**

You were right about the divorce case, you know, the incompatibility one. It went uncontested.

**LAWYER**

And it is now quoted widely as a landmark ruling, and included in hundreds of handbooks all over.

**MURTHY**

You must take the credit. It was not without your valuable input.

**LAWYER**

I did my bit, sir.

**MURTHY**

Well, I have to leave now. The packers are coming in at 3. And the Missus insists that I am present when they pack the library books. *(Starts to leave)* I will not say good bye. I know we will meet again. Thanks once again for this gift. I know it will be very special. If my guess is right, it will find a place at my desk in the new office.

*(He leaves. A beat. She quietly wipes a tear. Her phone rings. She takes it out.)*

**LAWYER**

Yes? From his residence? He was here just a moment ago... No, not in his chamber. He said he was going home... He must be near his car right now. Would you like me to go out and call him?

*(She puts the phone away and stares ahead.)*

## SCENE 14

***Justice Krishnamurthy's home***

*The old sofa and coffee table are covered. Sound of a door opening and closing. Murthy enters and sits on the covered sofa.*

**MURTHY**

I am home. *(No response)*

Is it possible to get some coffee? I will attend to the books in the library immediately. I promise.

*(Vimala enters. She has a tumbler of coffee in her hand. She is distraught. She hands it to Murthy and waits.)*

**MURTHY**
Has Cheenu arrived?

**VIMALA**
Yes.

**MURTHY**
Where is he?

**VIMALA**
In his room.

**MURTHY**
In his room? Well, tell him I am home. Call him down.

**VIMALA**
He doesn't want to come down.

**MURTHY**
And Ratna?

**VIMALA**
She is not here.

**MURTHY**
Not here? Has she... ?

**VIMALA**
She has not come. Cheenu is here by himself.

**MURTHY**
What's the matter? Is anything... ?
*(Vimala drops to the floor and buries her head in his lap, sobbing convulsively.)*

*Fade out*
***Close of play***

# Second Shift Muster

*Conversations with moving parts*

***Vijay Padaki***

FOR
**JENNY HARRIS**

## CHARACTERS IN THE PLAY

SARDAR .................................. *A blue collar who also works from home*
RANEE .................................................................. *Wife of Sardar*
BICHHU ............................................................. *A distant nephew*
RAMJI ....................................................................... *His father*

## INTRODUCTION

*Second Shift Muster* was written in the mid 'nineties. It was the time when the first effects of the liberalisation of the Indian economy were beginning to show. There were the obvious beneficial effects. There were also some unforeseen effects. There were scores of people like Sardar, who worked with their hands all their lives, were proud of their skills, but were finding themselves out of place in the changing economic context. It was also the time when we saw the growth of the builder-developer business in urban locations, with old buildings being knocked down to create high-rise apartment and commercial complexes.

1997 was the year of the Golden Anniversary of Indian independence. The Royal National Theatre (RNT) in London had decided to celebrate the milestone event suitably. An exchange project was taken up with Bangalore Little Theatre called Project Nadya. A group of young women from England would work with a group of young women from Bangalore and nearby places. The combined group would work on a chosen theme together through workshop exercises. The Bangalore group included two young women from NINASAM in Heggodu. In the first phase of the project, the combined group from London spent time in Bangalore and Heggodu. The workshop theme was 'Growing up as a Girl Child', seeking a gender identity around universal values. The outcome of the workshops was presented to an open audience in Bangalore. In the second phase of the project, the team from Bangalore went to London and was placed in a select number of theatre companies as interns to on-going theatre productions.

The play *Second Shift Muster* was performed by the National Theatre in London as part of the Golden Jubilee celebrations. It was also to showcase the BLT-RNT collaboration. Jenny Harris, Director-Education at the National Theatre was introduced to BLT by Michael Norton, the Founder-Director of Centre for Innovation and Voluntary Action. Michael was an old India hand, familiar with my professional work. He had arranged research funding for me that led to two important book publications. He took additional interest in Bangalore Little Theatre. Jenny took the lead in the collaborative project and steered it all along. She remained a friend of BLT till her untimely passing away. She was responsible in some measure for Robi's Garden being performed in London with the support of the Bangladesh High Commission. She tried till the end to have *The Prophet and the Poet* performed in the UK, either by the BLT team or a local team of artists. It was not to be.

The collaboration with RNT was also the beginning of BLT's serious involvement in Theatre Education.

## Language Notes

*Mala:* Garland, usually of flowers.
*Maistry:* Skilled worker, usually foreman.
*Pumpkin and chillies:* Used in an inaugural ceremony to ward off evil.
*Janta/Janata:* People, common folk.
*Shankar Jaikishan:* Composer-lyricist, musical duo in Hindi film industry.
*Sangam:* Hit film of the sixties.
*Dabba:* Tin, container.
*Bol Radha Bol:* Popular refrain of song from the film 'Sangam'.
*Mohalla:* Colony, quarter of town.
*Ramji ka bachcha:* Son of Ramji.
*Mela:* Country fair.
*Phirang:* Foreigner – usually derogative.
*Mama:* Maternal uncle.
*Musth:* Crazy, literally intoxicated.
*Bhajiyas:* Fried snack.
*Jalebi:* Fried sweet dish.
*Lagataar:* Continuous onslaught.
*Bhabiji:* Brother's wife, addressed with respect.
*Pahad (Kalipahad):* Hill (named after Kali).
*Modha:* Low seat/hassock made of reeds.
*Bhoosa:* Hay, useless stuffing.
*IAS:* Indian Administrative Service, civil service.
*Pukka:* Okay, done.
*Atta:* Flour.
*Crore:* Ten million, a hundred lakhs.
*Lakh:* A hundred thousand.
*Pooja/Puja, Pujapaat:* Worship, worship ritual.
*Katori:* Small bowl, usually steel or bronze.
*Mooli:* Radish.
*Toran:* Buntings.
*Khari biscuit:* Puff pastry biscuit.

## FIRST PERFORMED

At the Royal National Theatre, London, June 1997. Celebrating 50 years of independence in India. Showcasing a collaborative project with Bangalore Little Theatre

*In association with* .............................. WATERLOO CONNECTIONS
*Directed by* ........................................................ ARTI PRASHER

*The entire play takes place in the basement room of Sardar and Ranee. The play has a duration of between 35 to 40 minutes.*

## SCENE 1

***In the basement***

*A basement room put to many uses day and night. A work table that has seen much service. Two vises of different sizes, tools, boxes and cans of parts for repairs, and work on different projects in different stages of progress. An old model table fan is on.*

*A working stool. On the stool is Sardar, bent over the table, and fast asleep. Street noises outside and a reluctant beam of light through a skylight window placed high suggest that morning has broken. Presently the sounds give way to the slam of a door offstage. No effect on Sardar. Ranee enters, descending a short flight of rickety wooden steps. She goes about a morning routine, moving in and out of a room within the room, partitioned imaginatively with hessian. She barely looks at Sardar as she talks. She begins by replacing the previous day's garland of flowers on a framed photo with a fresh string of flowers.*

**RANEE**

He was there again this morning. Looked as if he hadn't gone home at all – if he has one that is. Looked as if he had been stuck on that unfinished compound wall by the maistry to shoo the prowlers away. Or to keep off people peeing there – at least till he'd handed it over to the landlord. Or maybe the shops were closed and he couldn't get the pumpkin and chillies to hang up, and decided on a substitute... When did you finish? I don't think I heard you wind up. But then last night you wouldn't have heard a pack of asses braying in the room with that wedding procession outside... It was the same hideous stoop, one leg up on the wall, the other dangling, the same idiotic grin – you know, like a – like a – oh well, like an idiot – a drooling idiot. I thought I'd get there early today – before the queue starts – but he was there... You could at least put your own bedding away. Look at them – like two bloody graves. You could put an inscription on the floor. Here they lie, side by side, united till the end of time.

*(Rolls up beddings, puts them away)*

United – huh! You know, it could have been the same with all those emperors. Shah Jahan, for instance. You think he really and truly doted on that Mumtaz female like we are told? He was a bloody schemer for all we know. An operator, like any other ruler type. All he wanted was something to be remembered by. And who cares who paid for it! Then that woman must have insisted on joining him on his tours and travels – and on being seen by his side. And a lot of her being seen. A great embarrassment that must have been – what with at least a dozen other begums screaming their heads off in protest, and threatening to leak out stories of the great Emperor's midnight pranks... You think the landlord gives us free electricity – running that fan all night? Or do I have to include that too in my list for the morning? *(Switches off)*

Here – done... When they finally knock down the building and put up a fancy apartment house, I hope they leave the basement as it is. Not just for us. I mean forever. A mausoleum concealed by a fancy apartment house. We'll ask for two simple stone slabs right here. And the inscription. Just simple stone slabs. It will remain a mystery. What faith were they? Were they buried here, or is it their ashes? Who knows, people might queue up to peep into this monument of eternal – of eternal... What a sight it will be outside!

Three queues running – one for the municipal water, one for the shithouse, and the longest, grandest one for the mausoleum of Sardar and his Ranee. No, Ranee and her Sardar. It sounds more cultured that way. Don't forget my brother paid the rent for seven long years here. And my father before that for – god knows – at least three years... I don't think that compound wall will be completed though. The landlord will be dead and gone. The maistry will be rotting in his grave. We'll have just that unfinished brickwork – separating the janta from the apartment-wallahs. And whatever happens, that wretch will be there – seated in the same spot, with the same stoop. The same idiotic grin... You better get your tea yourself. I have more than enough on my hands today. Late by half an hour too...

*(Withdrawing into partitioned area)*

Do you think he's really ogling us? As they all keep saying. They are even thinking of having him roughed up. I don't know. It's sickening all right. But I don't know, I think he's just an idiot.

*(Sardar stirs, adjusts his position, but remains at the table. There is a polite knock. Sardar does not respond. Shadow at the window. More knocking. Sardar wakes up, goes out to the door, taking his time about it.)*

**SARDAR**

Closed. Come later. Sorry, no exceptions. Later – come tomorrow.

*(Entering)* Thinks he owns the place. Just because he's paid an advance... Who put the fan off? Ranee!

**RANEE** *(From inside)*

You have to make your own tea.

**SARDAR** *(Disoriented awhile)*

This fan must be kept running for another hour at least. *(Switches it on)* And then I must reset the bearing assembly... Where's my bedding?

**RANEE**

Where it should be. On top of mine. That's about as close to...

**SARDAR**

God, it's seven already! You think the line might have cleared by now? Maybe I could lie down for half an hour or so... The trouble with Ramji's band is they are all over sixty. Buried in Shankar-Jaikishan. They haven't learned a thing after Sangam. The same bloody tumtumtumtumtaaraara, wedding after wedding. Worn-out bloody bandwallahs playing worn-out tunes on worn-out instruments. Deadly! I couldn't concentrate. I had to redo the soldering four times. Got it done anyhow... Ramji's son – when did he say he's coming?

**RANEE**

Any day now. Today, tomorrow, any day.

**SARDAR**

He's coming back loaded, no? Five years in Muscat – must have made a packet.

**RANEE**

Nice boy – very smart – a good boy. I knew he would do well.

**SARDAR**

The one clever thing he did was to run away when he got the chance. Another month of idling and Ramji would have put a collar on his neck and hung a dabba drum from it, 'Go on, bang it – earn your bloody meals in this house... ' Tumtumtumtumtarrarrarra – bol Radha bol...

**RANEE** *(Emerging, in a fresh sari, bag in hand)*

I wonder if he's bringing anything for us. Ramji, I know, is hoping he'll get the new trumpet he asked for. Poor man, the one he got from the army disposal must be at least two hundred years old.

**SARDAR**

I'll tell you what that Ramji ka bachcha will get for Ramji – one number 2-in-1, one number demonstration cassette with it, and two numbers cassettes of latest hoohah music. As for you and me, be thankful if he remembers to visit you on his return to this street.

**RANEE**

Come on – he's your nephew after all.

**SARDAR**

Huh! Everyone in this mohalla is related to everyone else. We are all uncles and nephews. *(Pause. Sardar goes about his work of tidying up at the table.)*

**RANEE**

What have you thought about Ramji's request?

**SARDAR**

What request?

**RANEE**

You know what I'm talking about. He asked...

**SARDAR**

He asked you. He has said nothing to me.

**RANEE**

I told you about it as soon as...

**SARDAR**

Did you tell me? Or did you ask me? *(Goes into the partitioned room)*

**RANEE** *(Trying again)*

He asked over a month ago. We talked about it the same day. You said 'Huh... we'll see.' And you haven't had the time or the right frame of mind since then to say yes or no clearly.

**SARDAR** *(Off)*

He's my nephew after all.

**RANEE**

Does that mean yes? *(No reply)* Should I tell Ramji when I see him this morning? *(No reply)* If you don't hurry up, there will be no water in the municipal tap.

Sardar emerges wearing a lungi and vest, a large aluminium mug in hand, and goes to the door without speaking.

One more thing – Babu asked if you could fix the petromax in his shop sometime today. *(She moves to the workbench)*

**SARDAR** *(At the door)*

One more thing. Don't try any tidying up at the workbench. Leave it as it is. *(Exits)*

**RANEE** *(After a pause, to the table fan)*

One more thing. If you don't wipe that silly grin off your silly moon face, I'll dump you on that wall outside. Next to that drooling idiot.

*(Checks her bag, keys, moves towards the exit. Stops at the steps, returns to the workbench. Pauses. Picks up near empty teacup and saucer to clear up. Pauses. A mischievous idea. She tosses the leftover tea into the fan, which promptly spits it back on her. She is startled.)*

## SCENE 2

*Sardar at the workbench. He is still in his lungi and vest, a thin towel tied on his head. He is tidying up, a weekly routine. There is discipline, method, loving care in his work. He attends to the table fan, talking to it and his tools even as he works.*

**SARDAR**

No oil bath this Sunday. Too bad. Let's see if we can manage it before lunch. No matter if we can't, what? There's always next Sunday. And a Sunday after next Sunday. Fourteen Sundays more before the year of Sundays ends... There, you sit there now, in your place, nice and well behaved. Nice and clean. As all good boys should be. At least on Sundays... You'll be off today, won't you? Don't be in a hurry to get back here.

They need you there, you know. Poor Pittu, her fever hasn't subsided yet – this is no time for you to be packing off on a holiday... Poor Pittu. Lovely little girl. All of sixteen, and ready to become the next prime minister of the country. Where did she learn to jabber like that? Jabber, jabber, jabber. Chatter, chatter. She's going to make it up there one day. Just you wait and see... So – you mind your running nose now, and go and sit by her side, and give her the comfort and cheer she needs. And tell that lazy father of hers to at least dust your backside – at least once a week. Here – shine your shoes a bit. That's better. You look really smart now... Like those boy scouts who came here last week. Wonder what they did with all the names and addresses they collected. Wonder what boy scouts become when they grow up. Doctors? Engineers? Building bridges, factories. Ships, airplanes. Tall, sky-scraping buildings. These new apartment buildings – I wonder if any of them was a boy scout...

Huh – funny people these building-wallahs. Like barbers at the January mela. Seat you down, start you off, and rush off to start on the next customer. And you're stuck there till he gets back to you. These people who take the apartments – how can they be such fools? So blind? Why do they waste so much money on a – what can you call it – a house? Dabba upon dabba upon dabba – they want to put all their belongings in there and live there? But then, who understands these people anyway? What they do, why they do it, where they get their money from, where it goes. How it changes colour... Not for you, my friend, thank your stars. No, there's nothing to regret. You may be old, a bit wrinkled, but you are a warrior. A warrior, you know that? And we are all proud of you, every one of us at this workbench. Aren't we, boys? I bet you didn't know this yourself. I just found out myself last night, just before I screwed on the backplate. Hmm? Oh, you knew already? You kept it a secret? Yes, yes, I understand – yes, of course. If that phirang social worker found out, it would be disastrous. He'd snap you up, and crate you, and ship you off. And before you could say Jai Shreekrishna, you'd be erected obscenely on a stand in some cold and gloomy room, in some icy godforsaken land. Never to be switched on, only to be peered at now and then through a plastic case... Mr Ring Spanner 1112, what are you doing here under the emery, huh? I know, I know, you worked overtime all through the last shift – you were so good, so reliable – but come on, now, off you go, into your own quarters. In with your brothers, 9 to 20, all six of you. All ring spanners together, next to the box set here. Wait a minute – here, let's take that muck out from behind your ear – that's it. All right, you can sleep it off now. Get some good rest now, my friend. You've earned a day off...

*(Through the following passage, there is a slow fade out to complete blackout.)*

You know, there used to be a saying my mother was fond of repeating. About a fish in a cooking pot, celebrating his good fortune because he was in water – and laughing at the chicken being undressed for a roasting. *(Pause)* Do you think I can come and look you up some time? I will be going that way at least once a week. I could stop to enquire about Pittu. Her mother's people and my own uncle were... *(Pause)*

Come on now, look up. Chest out – that's it. Yes, yes, of course – no, I won't forget to mention it to him. You are not to be kept near the window. The draft and the rain spray are definitely not good for you.

## SCENE 3

*The room is empty. Everything in place as at the end of the last scene. The fan is gone. A figure at the skylight.*

**BICHHU**

May I come in? Hello! May I come in? Is anybody home? Hello... Is this the home of Shambhuji? The one they call Sardar? *(He tries the door. It is open. He lets himself in, climbs down the steps cautiously. Stops.)*

**BICHHU**

Shambhumama?

*(He moves slowly, explores the room, the inner room too, briefly, examines the workbench. He picks up a half-assembled calling buzzer, finds it fascinating, sits at the stool, and begins to examine it. Ranee appears, talking as she enters.)*

**RANEE**

They are coming. I just met Ramji on the way up. He said Bichhu had gone ahead and he'd come along soon. You'd better get moving or they'll... Who are you? Where's Sardar? What are you... wait, wait a minute – oh, ho ho, why you're...

*(Rushes to greet him)* Bichhu! Bichhu, you rascal! Why didn't you say you were – when did you – how long have you been sitting there? All by yourself? Where's Sardar? Your Mama?

**BICHHU**

Just now. I came in just a minute ago.

**RANEE**

And Sardar?

**BICHHU**

There was nobody. I just came in and sat down.

**RANEE**

Just like your Mama – to leave the house open and disappear.

**BICHHU**

He must have gone somewhere close by.

**RANEE**

At this time? No, wait – I know, he must have gone... it doesn't matter. He'll be back. Now – let me look at you properly! You are... you're just the same! The same naughty face, the same mischief in your eyes. The moochhie – how long have you had that?

**BICHHU**

Oh, ever since I...

**RANEE**

It looks good. You look good with a moochhie. Have you grown taller? No, it's your shoes, I think. Ay, look at your pants – musth! But you have put on some weight. At last! You were a bamboo stick when you left. Food good there, haan?

**BICHHU**

No complaints. I ate well. *(Pause)* I'm glad I could come a little earlier.

**RANEE**

Just like those days! You would stop on your way back from school, and I'd make hot bhajiyas for you. I bet you missed my bhajiyas.

**BICHHU**

No, it was not...

**RANEE**

And hot jalebis on special occasions – when your gang won the cricket match.

**BICHHU**

The tennis ball cricket matches!

**RANEE**

Do they play cricket there?

**BICHHU**

They're crazy about cricket. They don't play much themselves, but they're crazy about watching cricket.

**RANEE**

What a funny country! Why did you go anyway?

**BICHHU**

I told you before I left...

**RANEE**

You ran away.

**BICHHU**

I did not... run away.

**RANEE**

I didn't even give you a decent going-away meal. You dropped in one day, and you were gone the next day.

**BICHHU**

I couldn't see you. I wanted to, but I couldn't. There were seven of us in the group. We were told to stay together all the time.

**RANEE**

Did you think of me sometimes? *(Pause)* Did you think of any of your two hundred relatives in this corner of the world?

**BICHHU**

No, I did not.

**RANEE**

Well, you get marks for telling the truth at least.

**BICHHU**

There was no time. No time for thinking, daydreaming – it was just work, work, work. From the first day to the last. Lagataar work – three hundred days a year.

**RANEE**

Sundays? Holidays?

**BICHHU**

We went to sleep on Saturdays and got up on Monday to get back to work. Hardly any holiday. Oh yes, they let us off when Indira Gandhi died.

**RANEE**

There must have been so many of you from this country. They couldn't possibly ignore you.

**BICHHU**

We slept through the morning, and did some shopping in the evening. There was a whole crowd of Indians out in the streets that evening.

**RANEE**

Oh, how stupid of me. Let me put the tea kettle on.

**BICHHU**

No hurry. Let Shambhumama come.

**RANEE**

Is your father coming or no?

**BICHHU**

He said he'd be along. Ah, that might be him at the door.

*(Ramji and Sardar are at the entrance.)*

**RAMJI** *(Off)*

The first thing he wants to do is to open a business. No more working for a boss, he says. *(Entering)* Bhabiji, it's me. And see who I picked up at the tea shop. If you don't keep an eye on the man, he'll burn up all your money from teashop to teashop.

**SARDAR**
Oh, go on, Ramji. It's Sunday.

**RANEE**
I was about to get the tea started, Ramji. You'll have a cup, no?

**RAMJI**
Of course, of course. No saying no to Bhabiji's tea.

**RANEE** *(To Sardar)*
And you, Sahibji?

**SARDAR**
Hmm – yes.

**RANEE**
Look at Bichhu here. Hasn't he grown? He's a man! *(Bichhu goes to Sardar to touch his feet. Sardar raises him, embraces him.)*

**SARDAR**
How are you, boy? *(Bichhu mumbles pleasantries. Sardar holds him at arm's length.)* You have grown. Good solid arms, working man's hands. They fed you well there?

**BICHHU**
No complaints.

**SARDAR**
When did you come?

**RANEE**
When you were idling away at the tea shop!

**SARDAR**
I only stopped for five minutes – on my way back, after delivering the fan. *(He moves away to the workbench.)*

**RAMJI**
I can vouch for that. He was all by himself. And he paid for only one cup.

**RANEE**
So – did you get the new trumpet you wanted?

**RAMJI**
Oh, no! There was no time, he said. But – ho ho – he got me such a big 2 in1. And some cassettes.

**SARDAR** *(Looking at the buzzer)*
Ranee – I told you not to touch anything on the bench.

**RANEE**
What are you talking about? I just got in a minute ago. *(Goes into the other room)*

**SARDAR**
Then who... ?

**BICHHU**
I'm sorry Shambhumama. That buzzer – I was looking at it when I came in. It looked really dead and gone. *(Sardar drops to his knees looking for a fallen part under the bench.)*

**RAMJI**
I was telling you, Sardar, the first thing Bichhu wants to do is to start a business...

**SARDAR**
It is neither dead nor gone. It has another thirty years to it at least.

**RAMJI**
I had spoken to Ranee some time ago...

**BICHHU**
Who uses a buzzer like that now? Is it worth the repair?

**SARDAR** *(Rising)*
Here it is. The fibre washer. I knew somebody had fiddled with the assembly in my absence.

**RAMJI**
So... I thought if we all met together, we could see how it might work. *(Pause)*

**SARDAR**
As long as God keeps making fibre washers, these buzzers will keep working.

**BICHHU**
Nobody buys these anymore. It's only musical doorbells now. There is a model that plays ten different tunes one after the other.

**SARDAR**
How much does it cost?

**BICHHU**
Here? Oh, about eleven hundred rupees.

**SARDAR**
Eleven hundred? You know what I'm charging to repair this buzzer? Nine rupees. For old Udham, I might even do it free.

**BICHHU**
I know a way by which we can get them in kits. It will cost us about four fifty a piece. If we price it at seven hundred, will make two fifty per piece. Easily one fifty nett. Maybe more – two hundred.

**RAMJI**
That's a good example. There are other ideas. *(Pause)*

**SARDAR**

Who will buy?

**BICHHU**

In this city alone – without any special cost in advertising – my guess is, say, easily six thousand pieces in the first year.

**SARDAR**

Six thousand new homes?

**BICHHU**

Not all new. Some in new homes, some replacements. About half and half.

**SARDAR**

So, about three thousand replacements. What happens to the old ones – bells, buzzers, bing-bong chimes? *(Pause)*

They will be homeless. Cast out like used matchboxes.

**RAMJI**

That is only with a humble start. In about a year we can afford an office, a peon. Some people can be hired to go about and sell more pieces. We can even think of fifty thousand pieces per year.

**SARDAR**

Fifty thousand, a lakh, ten lakhs. Put all the cities and towns together – Oh God, what will that number be? A great big mountain of discarded, destitute, doorbells. As high as Kalipahad in my mother's hometown.

**BICHHU**

For any such business there must be sales, of course, plus good service. A good service section.

**RAMJI**

That is what Bichhu has been saying. The first thing in a business is a good service section.

**SARDAR**

Just think what it means Ramji. A great big mountain of doorbells like that – how much it will have in it. How many tons of steel, how many tons of copper. And do you know there will be silver and platinum in the contact points.

**RAMJI**

Sardar, leave this childish talk. We are talking business now.

**SARDAR**

Do you know the quality of the steel that goes into making those bells? Why do you call it childish? Didn't you once tell me how perfect the metal must be to make your trumpet? And how it all goes into the cost of the trumpet?

**BICHHU**

I think Shambhumama is actually thinking of another kind of business. Aren't you Mamaji? *(Pause)*

**SARDAR**

Hmm? No, sorry, I was thinking of – sorry, my mind was somewhere else.

**RAMJI**

Some good idea for using the scrap after fitting the new units?

**SARDAR**

No, nothing like that. I was just thinking – why must opening a door be so costly?

## SCENE 4

*A discussion in progress. Ramji, Ranee, and Bichhu on modhas, odd chairs. Sardar on his stool, also drawn into the group, but not quite in it. There has been a lull.*

**SARDAR**

I have to think about it.

**RAMJI**

Of course, of course. We don't want to push you into anything without your...

**BICHHU**

Take your time. We have till tomorrow evening to decide.

**SARDAR**

Tomorrow? But from tomorrow I'm on second shift. I go at three, and come back only after midnight.

**BICHHU**

We have the morning then. And the rest of today.

*(Pause. Sardar rises, changes his mind, sits again.)*

**RAMJI**

I was telling you. It is very, very important to start soon – or we get left behind.

**RANEE** *(Cautiously)*

Sardar will be a full partner?

**RAMJI**

Of course. But the first thing to do is to start the business. That is what Bichhu has been saying.

**BICHHU**

The first thing to do... is to have a place to run the business. That's the very first thing. Shambhumama doesn't realize what he is sitting on.

**SARDAR**

I know, I know. They came and offered me a huge sum. One full lakh, they said, if I moved out.

**RANEE**

They sent messages that if Sardar was dissatisfied, they wouldn't mind...

**BICHHU**

One and a half? Two lakhs? Bhoosa! You won't get a tin shed for that – after you've passed through the racketeers to get there.

**SARDAR**

Let's go through those steps once again. *(Pause)*

First, we register this place as a workshop?

**BICHHU**

Yes, and very important – we put up a board outside. Intercontinental Appliances and Service. Or something, like that. IAS! Sounds good, doesn't it? IAS!

**RANEE**

The board must say, 'Established 1980.'

**SARDAR**

And that is all right, you say – to write 1980.

**BICHHU**

It is the truth. You have had a workbench here since 1980. I only have to convince the fellow at the Corporation office when I am filling in the form. That can be done. Leave that to me.

**RAMJI**

Next, we arrange a meeting with the builders.

**BICHHU**

No, that comes later. They will seek a meeting with us. We don't ask for a meeting. What you have to do is simply file a case in the police station. They have built a wall on this compound.

**SARDAR**

It is only half built.

**BICHHU**

All the better for our case. They have started building a wall. They have dumped building material. These are encroachments – illegal occupation of the compound space. We object.

**RANEE**

Bichhu, they told us clearly that the sale of the property is all pukka. Otherwise, how could they start work?

**BICHHU**

That is what they will say. What do you know about their methods? Why no work for four months? Because it takes a lot to get the papers in order. A lot of patience. A lot of money.

**RAMJI**

Meanwhile they collect advances from all those who want to book their flats. Cash down. No guarantee they'll get the flats. Cash down straight.

**BICHHU**

That is why we must act fast – before the property is legally in their name. Once they have the money, things will move in their favour.

**RANEE**

Whatever happens, they'll at least get rid of that grinning idiot on the wall.

**RAMJI**

That boy there from the workers' camp? He'll be thrown out.

**SARDAR**

Come on, Ramji. He is harmless.

**RANEE**

I don't know. I'm always scared passing that way.

**SARDAR**

There's one in every family, Ranee. He's no different from that fourth child of Jamuna – they call her Gogi, no?

**RANEE**

Gogi? Poor, sweet, Gogu? How can you compare the two? This one is hideous. He may be small, like Gogi, but he looks forty or fifty.

**SARDAR**

Gogi is about thirty-five, if you'd care to count the years. They are like that. They stop growing up, but they live on and on.

**RANEE**

God! I'd never put Gogu on a wall like that.

**SARDAR**

You haven't been inside Jamuna's house, have you? She will tell you, quite proudly, that Gogi is trained to do all the kitchen work before the actual cooking – washing, peeling, slicing, cleaning the rice, kneading the atta – trained! And she is far more reliable than her two educated sisters.

**BICHHU**

Are we talking business or are we opening a home for the headless?

**SARDAR**

There must be a purpose. There must be a reason why god above produces so few brilliant people, and a few Gogis, along with a whole herd of ordinary folk like us.

**RANEE**

I am sorry, Sardar. I was just scared.

**SARDAR**

We haven't understood the purpose. We don't even try. *(Pause)*

**BICHHU**

Shall we continue?

**SARDAR**

Tell me, Bichhu, how old is this earth of ours?

**BICHHU**

What?

**SARDAR**

How old is this earth?

**BICHHU**

How old? I don't know. Thousands of years old.

**SARDAR**

Thousands? How many thousands?

**BICHHU**

I don't know. You tell me.

**SARDAR**

I didn't say I knew the exact answer. I thought you would know.

**BICHHU**

This is 1995. So, I suppose... about eight or ten thousand years.

**SARDAR**

Eight or ten thousand! That's what you learned by going to the Middle East. Addam and Avva, and the prophets, and the holy wars. Then came the steam engine. Then the aeroplanes, then the bombs. Two plus two plus two, and ten thousand years. Do you know what a crore is like? Not in Rupees. In years? On Monday how many crore years would this earth be?

**BICHHU**

I don't know about all that. It's a lot of nonsense anyway. What I know is that Man arrived on this earth with a bang. His job is to make the most of it while he is here – to rule the earth. Each man must do that in his life time, and go out with a bang too! *(Pause)* And we must act fast.

**SARDAR**

My mother used to say – you'll remember Ramji – she used to say, how funny, you could see the peak of Kalipahad from her kitchen window, but it wasn't visible when you started to climb the hill.

**RAMJI**

Shambhu, Sardar, times have changed. If Ammaji was alive, she'd find a saying for that too – we must move on with time.

**SARDAR**

There is something wrong, Ramji. I can't accept it, it's not natural. How can we go on spending more and more on things that give us less and less in return?

**BICHHU**

A couple of lakhs a year is no small return.

**SARDAR**

The income – that's part of the problem. It has to be spent, it is not only what you get out of it.

**RAMJI**

You don't want to make more money?

**RANEE**

Sardar...

**BICHHU**

All I know is that Shambhumama, Sardarmama, is the best mechanic in this part of the city. Maybe the best in the whole city. He may not know it himself, but we all know it. If he chooses to put his talent to proper use, the world around him will be willing to pay. *(Pause)*

**RANEE**

Bichhu, Ramji, look... You see the workbench there? When Sardar sits down to work there, it's the only world he knows, the only world he cares to be in.

**SARDAR**

It's more than that Ranee. It's different.

**RAMJI**

You have had a hard life Sardar. You have struggled. Everybody in the mohalla knows how you have struggled. Don't you think you have earned a jack up in life, at least now?

**BICHHU**

Are you going to be repairing buzzers and stoves till you die?

**SARDAR**

No two stoves are the same. No two irons, no two table fans. Each of them is an independent soul.

**RAMJI**

You work with them, you know them best. All we are saying is...

**SARDAR**

Only a family doctor knows how to reach the soul. Not your two-hundred rupee injection-wallahs.

**BICHHU** *(Moving away)*

Mamaji, I don't understand this. We are talking business, you are talking pooja-paat or cabbage gardening or some such thing. We are talking in lakhs, you are talking in soiled notes of tens and fives. We are talking about a service station. You are... sorry, mamaji, you are chained to this workbench. *(Pause)*

**RANEE** *(Anxious, but in control)*

You don't know the Sardar, Bichhu. Even you, Ramji, you don't know him, his work. Let me tell you about a job he took last year. He sat down after dinner – it was about eight o'clock. He kept all the spares, in all their katories on his left. He laid out all the tools on his right. The fan was in front of him. Then he called me. He wanted me to blindfold him. Cover his eyes with two hankies as pads, and his towel wrapped around them. I did it. He asked only for some silence after that. I moved away, spread our two beds, sat down, and watched him. He sat still for about two minutes, as if in a trance, with his hands resting lightly at the edge of the table. Then he began... What can I tell you? The fan seemed to know his every move, his every silent instruction. It moved with him, it was one with him. When he finished, at about one o'clock, the table was as orderly as at the start. All the tools on his right, the spares in their katories on the left, the scrap and the muck, in the plastic bowl below – and a beaming, grateful, fully-recovered patient before him, as he undid his blindfold.

*(A long awkward pause. Ranee moves to Sardar.)*

His fingers, his hands, his arms – they are the most gentle, the most tender, but rock steady in their mission.

**SARDAR**

God took I don't know how many crores of years to make them what they are, Ranee.

**RAMJI**

Bichhu, son, Sardar is trying to tell us that he has some...

**BICHHU**

If he wants so badly to remain where he is, that is his business. But why must we be held back because of... *(He stops. Ramji and Bichhu look at Sardar, who is moving to the workbench.)*

**SARDAR**

People are growing too fast. It's not good for them. It's not good for the plants and crops either. I heard it makes them weak. Why do they grow a mooli two feet long? It tastes foul. There will be a disaster sooner or later. People too – they want things, more things. Before they ride bicycles, they want cars. They can't fix leaky taps, they want washing machines. What sort of a zoo are they putting themselves in?

**BICHHU**

It is simple, mamaji. There is more money in the world. People can have more, because there is more.

**SARDAR**

Is there? They can't look at themselves in a mirror, they want TV. *(Takes out a gleaming torque wrench)*

Here, look at this. Original Stanley. It's at least thirty-five years old. My foreman presented it to me when he retired and went away. He had got it from his boss. Read what is written on the inside of the lid.

**BICHHU** *(Reading)*

'If it is good, it will carry. If it carries, it must be good.'

**SARDAR**

Who will receive it from me?

**RAMJI**

Bichhu, are you sure you want to take this any further? *(Pause)*

**BICHHU**

Okay, Shambhumama. We will stop here. We will stop for the day. I will return in the morning, early, and we can take another look at the plan.

**RAMJI**

There is nothing to fear. Bichhu is quite capable. He will take care of everything.

**SARDAR**

You are very keen... on continuing tomorrow?

**BICHHU**

We must. For your own good.

**RAMJI**

Bichhu, son...

**BICHHU**

No, there is no need for pretence. They should know.

**RANEE**

Bichhu... Ramji...

**BICHHU**

I can still use my part of the investment any way I wish to, right? I can also book a flat here, right? They need my money. They will accept it, it's good money, in cash. If they ask me – just suppose they ask me – what I know about a certain Sardar who lives in the basement of the old building... what shall I tell them?

**RANEE**

Ramji, is this your son talking, is this Bichhu?

**BICHHU**

If they can't take a statement from a nephew, who can they take from?

**RAMJI**

Let's go, son. Poor Sardar is tired. You are coming in the morning anyway. *(He moves to the exit and waits, Bichhu moves to Sardar.)*

**BICHHU**

We can't turn back now, Sardar... Shambhu mamaji. You can take till tomorrow morning, but you must come along. Here, I brought a gift for you when I came. *(Presses an envelope into Sardar's hand)*

It is what you think. Money. Treat it as an advance. There's fifty thousand there. It will be useful for immediate expenses. It is a gesture of our sincerity – an earnest deposit.

## SCENE 5

*Early next morning. The beddings are still on the floor. Sardar is alone in the room. He has fashioned a toran with the hundred rupee notes on a long length of jute string. He tacks a length of the toran on three sides of the workbench, then tacks several rows of it on the front side. The toran is unending. He ties a length along the partition, then criss-crosses two lengths over the room. There is lots more. He places the rest on the workbench, changes his mind, drops them on the beddings. He returns to the workbench, sits facing it as if starting work, very slowly buries his head in his arms on the table as at the start of the play. Moments later he straightens and turns in his stool to face the room. Ranee enters. She pauses briefly to notice the decoration and moves into the partitioned room.*

**RANEE** *(From within)*

I'll be out in a minute. The tea is on. *(Pause)* Did you sleep all right? You were lying on your back the whole night. At least till I fell asleep. I couldn't make out if you were awake or asleep. When I got up you were in the very same position. *(Pause)* On your back, straight as a beam. Did you hear me getting up? *(Pause)* I really wanted to lie down a little longer – with you – next to you. But you know what the morning rush is like out there. Once the sun is up. *(She steps out. She has a long roll of tinsel in her hands. She looks brighter too.)*

I had to change my blouse. *(She moves to the workbench)*

I must tell you. There were two boys tossing pebbles at the... little fellow... on the wall. He whined and covered his face. It only made the boys laugh and want to throw some more pebbles. I shooed them away. Aren't you happy?

*(She picks up scissors from the workbench. Through the following, she moves about the room clipping bits of the tinsel and adding them to the lengths of toran, beginning with the workbench.)*

I was. And when I moved away, I saw the shy smile of gratitude on the little fellow's face. I was really happy then... I was happy for you, too. Happy for us. I have the most wonderful Sardar in the world as my man, and he has me, Ranee. The best mechanic in this part of the city, they said. What do they know! The best jalebis on this street, they said. What do they know of the Ranee and her emperor... ? Bichhu is a good boy. Just a bit wild. He always was, do you remember? But he always meant well. He wants to leave a mark, I think, in everything he does... How silly he looked when he dropped in here on his way back from school, offering to run errands, or asking for help in his lessons. How silly and awkward. Of course there was a crush. He knew that I knew. And I knew what a tonic it was for him – to find his heart fluttering at a maddening pace at least once a day... He'll do well. I am sure he will. He must watch that temper of his, though. He was cocky as a lad. It suited him. But he's a bit impatient now. His temper and his impatience – if he can keep a check on that, he'll do very well indeed... He could learn so much from you.

It's too bad he decided to push off like that. He could have worked with you – as an apprentice. He would have learned a lot. Then, if he went out and saw the world, and worked with new machines, and made money – who knows, who knows how these things turn out... How would it have been if we had our own son? He'd go to school and college. He'd go abroad too. Pick up many new things like Bichhu – so many wonderful new things happening every day. He would have your bedrock and his knowledge of the world. His eyes and ears, and your heart...

We will have tea.

*(She finishes and withdraws into the other room. Sardar rises slowly, moves his stool to above the beddings on the floor. He then places two modhas above on either side of the stool, and waits above his mudda. Ranee enters with two cups of tea and a saucer of khari biscuits. She places them on the stool and goes back to the other room. She returns with a stainless steel saucer with a green-and-gold plastic decorative garland on it. She replaces the previous day's flowers on the photo frame with the garland and joins Sardar for tea. They sit. They sip their teas quietly, slowly. Presently, Ranee keeps her cup down, looks at Sardar, and places her hand on his knee. Sardar responds. He keeps his cup down, rises, and takes Ranee's hand. They move below to the beddings, pause, and look at each other, warm and close. Sardar turns slowly, picks up the*

*remaining toran, and steadily wraps it around both of them. When he finishes he embraces Ranee gently and speaks.)*

**SARDAR**

You are not in a hurry to go to work? Stay home today.

*Fade out*

***Close of play***

# BANGALORE LITTLE THEATRE

## Six Decades of Wholesome Community Theatre

In 1960, a small group of committed persons in Bangalore sought a theatre experience that could be a genuine alternative to the order of the day that was called BBC Theatre – British Bedroom Comedy. The group included the talented couple, Scott and Margaret Tod, and at least four other expats, along with a handful of Bangaloreans. They had a vision of a Community Theatre best described by the slogan invented 25 years later: *Think Globally, Act Locally.* Bangalore Little Theatre came into existence with a play reading in the last week of September that year. The first production on boards in December 1960 was Moliere's *The Prodigious Snob*, more commonly known as *The Would-be Gentleman.*

In 1962, within a year of inception, BLT arrived at a character and identity for itself: to maintain pride in its strictly amateur status, but to conduct its affairs in a thoroughly professional manner. The group gave itself a constitution and, through that, a participatory style of functioning. The group was seen as belonging to a membership, and therefore to be managed transparently by an elected management committee. The founding members were the first to give way to younger members to take the group forward.

Way back in 1963, BLT produced its first Indian play in English, an original adaptation of *Mrichhakatika* (The Toy Cart of Clay) by a founder-member, Prof B Chandrasekhara. Since then, the group has maintained the conscious policy of producing Indian plays periodically – translations, adaptations, original scripts, by its own members and others. Not surprisingly, two of the six awards for contemporary playscripts instituted for the first time by *The Hindu* in 1993 landed in BLT. The first prize was for the play by Vijay Padaki, *Credit Titles,* a political satire on intellectual property rights for patenting life forms. A Special Prize was awarded to another member, Ambika (Poile) Sengupta.

Old-timers of BLT have often been asked the secret of the group's long life when, in contrast, we see hundreds of cases of groups starting with a bang and dropping by the wayside in a couple of years. The difference, it seems, is in the simple fact that BLT is a community-based organisation and, therefore, a membership-driven group. From this fact has followed a number of guiding principles that appear to have served BLT well over the years. For instance:

- The participatory and transparency principles in management (with all financial transactions completely open and made available to the entire membership)
- The highly open leadership structure around an elected Managing Committee (rather than being founder-centric or personality-driven)
- The constant development of new talent, including new directors (rather than being dependent on the same old hands or breeding star complexes)
- The pursuit of the higher purpose, the constitutionally-enshrined objective of promoting the theatre and related arts in Bangalore (rather than the attitude of 'let's do another play')

All of this actually makes it far more difficult to 'manage' the organisation. It is so much easier to let a charismatic leader take charge and 'run' the group as he (or she) wishes.

The significance of these principles is understood better when we see that a sizeable majority of the theatre talent in Bangalore, including the more recognised names, has been in BLT productions, workshops and training programmes earlier. They continue their affiliation with BLT even if they perform under other banners.

Related to this point is one other indisputably important feature of BLT. It is the only English-language theatre group in Bangalore (perhaps anywhere in India) with strong links to the local-regional theatre, building bridges across language divides. Many of the stalwarts on the Kannada stage and screen have been either life members of BLT or have been prominently involved in some capacity or the other. After all, among the founders were personalities like Prof B Chandrasekhara, Nani, Shivaram, Seetharam, V Ramamurthy and S Ramaswamy. Then there were CR Simha, Vimala Rangachar, SG Ramachandra, KC Sekhar, Suresh Heblikar, Paddu, Shankar and Arundhati Nag, Ashok Rao.... And many many more – including some who went on to become Presidents of Karnataka Nataka Academy! Indeed, BLT has been a substantial support to Kannada theatre groups in their start-up stages.

BLT has invested heavily in training and outreach activity. In the late 1970s, BLT introduced for the first time in Bangalore a comprehensive introductory programme for newcomers to the theatre, based on the Stella Adler system. Since the mid '80, the group has made its Summer Project on Theatre (SPOT) a regular training event. It has come to be recognised as the most prestigious training event in the city, because of the quality of inputs provided. And it continues to be a part of BLT's social commitment. Other groups and productions snap up the talent from these training projects.

In 1993, the group initiated an annual Festival of Short Plays (SHORTS), aimed at promoting theatre activity among the college and youth population. With the audience response as enthusiastic as seen, the scale of the Festival may well be enhanced considerably in the coming years.

As a socially-responsible theatre society, BLT has readily taken on many a fundraising production for worthy causes. In 1970-71, BLT's production of the new play by Badal Sircar, *Evam Indrajit*, was the first fundraising event to contribute to the Prime Minister's Fund for the Bangladeshi (then East Bengal) refugee crisis. An original script, *Head Start*, by Vijay Padaki, was produced for CRY in January 1996. Since then BLT has made a constitutional commitment to dedicate one production for a charity every year. The group also provides various kinds of help to theatre projects in colleges, schools, clubs and other institutions.

With the high repute in training and outreach activity, it was only logical for BLT to set up an Academy of Theatre Arts in 2008. The stated mission of the Academy is to enrich the theatre institutional system through the thrust programme of *Theatre Education,* thus building the societal base for the true appreciation of the theatre and, indeed, all of the performing arts.

# THE SERIES EDITOR

**Vijay Padaki** is a Theatre Educator based in Bangalore. He has worn two caps for most of his life with equal facility. He has been active in the theatre for sixty years. He has been a management professional for over forty-five years.

Vijay is a psychologist and behavioural scientist by training, and founder-director of The P&P Group, a management resource centre that has programmes of research, consulting and training in the areas of Organisation and Institutional Development. A good part of the work of The P&P Group is devoted to the effectiveness of large development programmes. Among his earlier assignments, he headed the Human Resources Division of India's oldest cooperative R&D institution, Ahmedabad Textile Industry's Research Association (ATIRA), which also helped set up the first Indian Institute of Management in Ahmedabad. Later, he was a member of the founding faculty at Indian Institute of Management, Bangalore, the founder of a Centre for Management for the textile industry in Ahmedabad, and a Visiting Professor at Indian Institute of Science, Bangalore to initiate a programme in R&D Management. He was a Senior Associate at the National Institute of Advanced Studies in its early years.

Vijay joined Bangalore Little Theatre in 1960, the year of its inception, and later served the company in many capacities – as actor, director, trainer, writer, designer and administrator, including two stints each as Secretary and President. In 2008, the institutional set-up was restructured. Bangalore Little Theatre Foundation was created as a Public Charitable Trust. It was done with the purpose of reinforcing the organisation's strengths in outreach activity, and thus *rededicating the commitment to social development goals beyond performance.* The Trust requested Vijay to provide the leadership to a newly-created Academy of Theatre Arts in its formative years. The Academy is developing a long-term programme thrusts to strengthen the institution of theatre education and practice in India.

Vijay has been responsible for institutionalising several activities of BLT, such as the annual summer workshop for newcomers to the theatre (SPOT), from which has emerged a large number of the theatre personalities in Bangalore, the History of Ideas programme of biographical plays, the Courtyard Theatre programme, and the Children's Theatre programme, which includes the annual flagship children's play as a partnership production to support a charity. Vijay conceived and initiated the highly successful Trainer-Training programme and the Directors Training programme in Bangalore.

He has forged several international partnerships with BLT over the years. The John F Kennedy Centre for Performing Arts in Washington invited him to serve as an advisor to the India Festival in 2011. The same year, he gave the Harold Clurman lecture at the Stella Adler Studio in New York. More recently, the Ministry of Culture invited Vijay to initiate a programme of Arts and Heritage Management in India.

Vijay has written over 50 original plays. He has also adapted or translated several play scripts. Seagull Books has published a volume of two Gujarati plays translated by him. In 1993, Vijay won the award for the best contemporary play script instituted by *The Hindu* for the play *Credit Titles*.

## PUBLICATIONS IN THE SERIES

### Volume 1: FOUR CLASSICS on the Indian Stage

Contains original English language adaptations of Indian classics. These include ***The Toy Cart of Clay,*** an adaptation of the Sanskrit Classic ***Mrichhakatika*** by Sudraka; ***The Anklet,*** an adaptation from Ilango Adigal's Tamil Classic ***Silappadikaram***; ***Kurukshetra Burning!*** based on ***Smashana Kurukshetra*** in Kannada by Kuvempu; ***The Echo,*** an adaptation of ***Chomana Dudi*** in Kannada by Shivarama Karanth.

### Volume 2: THE HISTORY OF IDEAS Programme of new plays

From BLT's highly acclaimed History of Ideas programme, plays include ***The Prophet and the Poet,*** based on the Gandhi-Tagore exchanges; ***Finding Ananda***, rediscovering the life and work of Swami Vivekananda, with the Bengal Renaissance as the backdrop; ***Tiger! Tiger!*** revealing the humanistic side of Tipu Sultan; ***Monsters in the Dark,*** an original adaptation of the Pulitzer award book ***The Emperor of All Maladies*** by Siddhartha Mukherjee, sub-titled A Biography of Cancer; ***Einstein's Dreams,*** an original dance theatre adaptation of the novel by the same title by Alan Lightman.

### Volume 3: CHILDREN'S THEATRE Programme of new plays

Containing plays from BLT's hugely successful Children's Theatre programme, this volume includes ***The Ungrateful Man,*** a tale from the Panchatantra; ***The Magic Drum,*** a collection of stories from the book by the same title by Sudha Murty; ***Ali Oh Baba,*** a retelling of the tale from the 1001 Arabian Nights; and ***The Court Jester,*** the tales of Tenali Rama.

## Volume 4:
## FOOTPRINTS and other plays

These plays were written by ***Vijay Padaki*** in the period 1986 to 2002 and represent explorations in combining form with content. There is a humanistic undercurrent in the plays, an affirmation of the human spirit, the innate ability to question the given, so often remaining suppressed, and the ability to find alternatives. It is known that a lot of his writing has been influenced by field experiences in his professional engagements. The content of the play has often (not always) begun as a case study, intriguing in itself, but demanding an alternative perspective. The alternative perspectives have provided the raw material for the play scripts. The play scripts should explain themselves. Footprints is presented as 'fictional science', raising the serious question of the human species being Nature's mistake, the price to be paid by the rest of the earth.

## Volume 6:
## SALT LICKS and other plays

The plays in Volume 6 reflect on the continued Western orientation of Indian communities till today. As a character in ***Salt Licks*** says: 'Go West, young man, to rediscover the East. And don't be in a hurry to get back'. The first play in the publication series refers to a peculiarly Bangalore society of elders fixated in the Raj, calling themselves the Empire Loyalists. If it was 'Great Britain' at one time, it was the American Dream later. In the pre-liberalised economy, young people went to extremes to get admission in American colleges and universities. Any university, any course, any location, it was only important to get there first. And yet... there was something so human in their dreams. The collection in this Volume can be called ***Vijay Padaki's early plays.*** The stories are set in the period early 'seventies to early 'nineties. The ubiquitous 2-in-1 music system in the plays creates a special place for itself. Two plays in the set need further explanation. ***Gold and Silver*** was written at the time of an exchange project with the Royal National Theatre celebrating India's Golden Anniversary of Independence. ***Evening Shadows*** is an original English language adaptation of *Sandhya Chhaya* by the Marathi playwright Jaywant Dalvi. The loneliness of an elderly couple is compounded by the son not returning from America.